SIGN CRIMES/ROAD KILL

Other books by Joyce Nelson

Sultans of Sleaze: Public Relations and the Media
The Colonized Eye: Rethinking the Grierson Legend
The Perfect Machine: TV in the Nuclear Age

JOYCE NELSON

Sign Crimes/Road Kill
FROM MEDIASCAPE TO LANDSCAPE

between the lines

Published by Between The Lines
           394 Euclid Avenue, #203
           Toronto, Ontario M6G 2S9
           Canada

Cover photomontage by Richard Slye
Cover design by Goodness Graphics
Typesetting by Adams & Hamilton
Printed in Canada

Between The Lines receives financial assistance from the Canada
Council, the Ontario Arts Council, and the Ontario Ministry of
Culture and Communications through the Ontario Publishing
Centre.

Portions of this work first appeared in *Borderlines, Broadside,
Canadian Forum, Cinema Canada, Compass, Fuse, Graffiti, In
Search, La Parole Métèque,* and *This Magazine.*

CANADIAN CATALOGUING IN PUBLICATION DATA

Nelson, Joyce, 1945—
   Sign crimes/Road kill

ISBN 0-921284-53-5 (bound). – ISBN 0-921284-54-3 (pbk.)

1. Mass media. 2. Environmental protection. 3. Television –
Psychological aspects. 4. Business and politics. I. Title.

P90.N45 1992   302.23   C92-093718-7

Within an imprisoned society, writing can exist
only as denunciation or as hope.
– Eduardo Galeano

I am grateful to the Between The Lines collective for their untiring
support of my work and for making this publication possible. I'm
also thrilled to work again with editor Robert Clarke and to have
another fine cover illustration by Richard Slye. As well, I want to
thank the people of Ontario, without whose financial assistance
through the Ontario Arts Council the text would have been
far more difficult to complete.
– J.N., December 1991

Contents

☐ A Brief Introduction

It can be a beautiful thing to dance all night in an evil time.

– Michael Ventura

When the going gets weird, the weird turn pro.

– Hunter S. Thompson

SIGN CRIMES/ROAD KILL is what the critics might call an "uneven" collection. But I wanted it to be uneven. Life is uneven. It's also quirky and idiosyncratic (the book, life), but I wonder, is it (the book) weird enough? We're living in highly weird times – times when the only meaningful and adequate response seems to be to follow the hints of Thompson and Ventura. The pieces collected here are part of my own continuing path of "turning pro," my own limping dance in an evil time.

I've been investigating and writing about sign crimes for fifteen years, but only relatively recently has roadkill caught my attention. Now it seems inevitable to me that the environmental degradation all around us would – of course! – be the likely outcome of a mass-media monoculture bent on destroying diversity worldwide. You reap what you sow, and this millennial century has sown devastation as our legacy. Perhaps, in our collective denunciation and hope, we can save something worthwhile for the future.

In selecting from more than seventy magazine articles and essays published so far in My Brilliant Career, I've tried to keep repetition to a minimum. Nevertheless, some personal obsessions are revealed here: obsessions like Walt Disney, Pierre Juneau, Marvin Minsky, and others you'll easily notice. While I still have many of those obsessions, I've added new ones to my life: trees, water, and Allan E. Gotlieb – but especially trees.

I've also tried to avoid overlap with material in my other books, with one obvious exception. "Packaging the Populace" rides again. The original *Fuse* piece got reprinted in *Sultans of Sleaze* as part of a longer chapter, but I think it deserves to stand on its own here, especially because it was selected by Doug Fetherling for the 1990 edition of *Best Canadian Essays* (Saskatoon: Fifth House Publishers). I'm happy to say that a similar fate has been dealt to "The Saga of Space Dorks," included in the 1991 collection, *The Thinking Heart* (Kingston: Quarry Press), edited by George Galt. Susan Crean is also including that one in her forthcoming collection of feminist writing from *This Magazine* called *Twist & Shout*. It's great to see Space Dorks get such wide exposure.

Personally, this text marks the end of an era. As the subtitle says, there is a journey in these pages, a movement from mediascape to landscape – reflecting my growing recognition of the severity of environmental crises under way. I'll probably never stop writing about sign crimes because they're fundamental to our culture. But I've been adding to my repertoire, opening up my knowledge-base, educating myself about other areas. As the poet said, she not busy being born is busy dying. So I'm following my weird muse, and it's taking me in new directions: different genres, other obsessions and topics, perhaps more challenging dance-steps. As the Gnostic gospels (another obsession here) put it, "Those who dance not, know not what cometh to pass. Amen!"

I
Mediascape

☐ Mickey Goes to China

I like the dreams of the future better than the history of the past.
— Thomas Jefferson

History? I don't have the faintest notion of it.
— Donald Duck

THERE IS SOMETHING in the American psyche that abhors the past, flees from it as its own immigrant population fled the Old Country to begin again in the New World. This fear and loathing of the past, of history itself, fuels an obsession with the new. No other culture is more obviously predicated on the constant and unceasing replacement of things, goods, ways, and means. An almost completely anti-traditional society, the United States prides itself on the built-in obsolescence that underlies its economy, its social philosophy, its national *Zeitgeist*. Nothing is built to last. The traditional, the old, the past – history itself – must be obliterated and buried by the great bulldozer of "dreams of the future." Perhaps it is this American trait that prompted Sigmund Freud to remark: "America is a mistake, a giant mistake." As we shall see, this flight from the past and an obsession with dreams of the future play a major part in the nation's political decisions.

By contrast, much of the rest of the world has deep cultural ties to the past – an abiding rootedness in, and respect for, the reality of histories reaching back through thousands of years and countless generations. To Asians and Europeans especially, the American loathing of the past and fascination with dreams of the future must seem somewhat incomprehensible – at the same time that it has its charming sides.

I am looking at an Associated Press photo that appeared in *The Toronto Star* on October 24, 1986. As an AP photo, it undoubtedly received widespread exposure throughout the world, given the wire service's domination of news coverage globally. In any case, the photo would have captured the attention of editors everywhere because of its "news value." "Mickey Goes to China" shows a human-sized Mickey Mouse extending his hand towards a group of Chinese youngsters. Two of the children are similarly reaching towards Mickey. In the background the Great Wall of China is faintly visible, extending along the rolling hills of the countryside. The caption for this photo reads:

> Mickey Mouse, the world's most famous rodent, entertains a group of young fans at the Great Wall of China, one of the world's most famous landmarks. Mickey and his cartoon chum, Donald Duck, were visiting China yesterday to promote their new weekly television series, *Mickey and Donald.* The half-hour show premieres Sunday (October 26) on the China Central Television Network.

With this wording, the caption writer has correctly identified the central opposition working in both the photo and the situation: "the world's most famous rodent" posed in front of "one of the world's most famous landmarks." In the photo, all the eyes of the spectators meet at a single point: the figure of Mickey. No gaze seems to be directed towards the Great Wall. The viewer of the photo itself, however, can see both and can therefore perceive the fully ironic message of the photograph.

Mickey is clearly privileged both by composition and framing and by the characteristics of the camera. Because he looms in the foreground, the largest object in the photo, he commands the attention of spectators within and outside the frame. He is further privileged because the camera lens does not make the background, the Great Wall, as crisply focused as the foreground. Thus, "one of the world's most famous landmarks" is here dim and vaguely represented – visually no competition for "the world's most famous rodent," whose sharp focus and stark photographic tones further contribute to his privileging. The Great Wall is eclipsed.

Let's again return to the wording of the caption, whose anonymous writer seems increasingly brilliant the more one studies this photograph. Because captions must always summarize the action in the fewest words possible, it is significant that this one makes a point of including the word "cartoon" in the phrase "Mickey and his cartoon chum, Donald Duck...." In a sense, the word is unnecessary. It is a given, universally understood, that Mickey and Donald are cartoon characters. We do not need to be told this. And yet by including this unnecessary word, the caption writer has underscored a subtle aspect of the central opposition at work: that between "landmark" and "cartoon."

The Great Wall marks the land. It is unique to China, even the *sign* of China, but a sign that has its own substance in the millions of rocks that form its pattern. It is no more transportable or exportable than the land itself, of which it is an outgrowth. By contrast, Mickey is also a sign – perhaps even *the* sign of the United States, but a sign that is completely insubstantial, a mere cartoon, a floating image, nothing more than a representation, and as such *fully* transportable and exportable. The Mickey Mouse standing at the Great Wall is a representation of a representation (and so this photo is giving us a representation of a representation of a representation ...). The point, though, is that the landmark is tied and rooted in place. The cartoon is free-floating, able to alight anywhere – even on the China Central Television Network.

Here we begin to perceive the full irony of this photo, which captures the dynamic opposition between substance and insubstantiality, landmark and representation, Wall and Cartoon. In showing these competing signs of China and of the U.S.A., the photo reveals that no wall can keep out Mickey, whose very insubstantiality is his passport behind all walls. In the age of the exportable, mass-produced image, the very notion of walls has forever changed.

Having alighted behind the Great Wall, Mickey is here seen raising his hand in a kind of ambassadorial salute. He has, of course, performed this function in other places and other times – most notably at the opening ceremonies for Japan's Disneyland – and he will undoubtedly appear at the groundbreaking ceremonies for the new Euro-Disneyland being built just outside Paris. Indeed, since 1935, when the League of Nations recognized Mickey Mouse as an "international symbol of good will," Mickey has been travelling as an ambassador throughout the world. But, we must ask, just who or what does Mickey represent?

It is obvious, of course, that Mickey and Donald represent not just the Disney Corporation but also the U.S.A. and, beyond that, the imperialist ideology so well delineated in that wonderful book *How to Read Donald Duck*, by Chilean authors Ariel Dorfman and Armand Mattelart. But let's go a bit further.

China is one of the world's most ancient civilizations, thousands of years old, steeped in tradition, fully grounded in history. The Great Wall represents this history, not just in the sheer age of its gradually crumbling rocks, but in the very length and scope of its reach, stretching across the landscape for hundreds of miles. We might say that in the AP photo the Great Wall is the sign of human history itself, which has always served as a kind of container from within which the present and the future grow. Like a containing wall, the human past surrounds and nurtures us; the past provides meaning for the present and understanding for the causes and shape of events and for the possibilities that may emerge from its roots.

Perhaps at its deepest level, then, this photo is about time. The Great Wall is the sign of the human past, of human history. The land on which it stands is the eternal present: the continuing here and now of the earth. The children in the photograph are the sign of the future, the hope of the future emerging out of earth and human history and reaching like young shoots towards the possible. But then of what is Mickey the sign?

In their analysis of the Disney cartoon-world, Dorfman and Mattelart reveal a place that is strangely antibiological. Though based on animal characters, this world is by no means "earthy" or instinctual. Rather, it is without biological roots, without reproduction (none of the characters have, or are, parents), without aging, without change. These characteristics are also features of the Disney parks, which, in their seemingly "lifelike" animatronics and plasticity, beneath the surface convey an eerie celebration of lifelessness in the perfection of simulacra. In contrast to the real world of human imperfection, change, biological roots, and the foment of history, the Disney world is fixed and unchanging, bloodless, and ahistorical. It is not so much that time has stopped there but rather that time has never entered. The cartoons and simulacra, endlessly reproducible and endlessly repeated around the globe, are outside of time.

We begin to sense why this Disney world could arise out of the American context. In a society caught between the flight from history and dreams of the future, the Disney ideology neatly eliminates time itself. Fleeing the past and its containment function – which, after all, places limits on human endeavour – the American psyche nevertheless needs some form of container for stability. It finds this container in its technologies and technological systems, which embrace the individual within a kind of matrix. The technological universe holds all the appeal of the new and the dreams of the future while it appears to be outside time: inorganic, non-biological. The Disney world is the best expression of this technological containment, replacing the living world (so subject to change and time) with cartoons and creation outside of time. Unlike the cultural-historical matrices of the real world, the Disney matrix is a replica, a land of the undead. Mickey is the ambassador. In the AP photo he may be said to be the sign of the end of time. A walking death-mask, he alights behind the Great Wall and reaches a hand towards the children.

At the 1986 Iceland summit the U.S. government clearly scuttled an opportunity to reach an agreement on the dismantling of nuclear weapons. This possibility would have meant a coming-to-terms with the sins of the past, a mature grappling with the results of former errors, mistakes, goals, and mistrusts that had brought the real world to the brink of annihilation. It would also have meant, in some sense, a deep recognition and acceptance of our biological nature, our vulnerability within the real world of life and death. In preference to this opportunity for undoing the mistakes of the past and therefore making a step towards maintaining this imperfect, messy, biological and historical world, Reagan's America chose to pursue Star Wars. The allure of technological, lifeless perfection surpassed the appeal of simple biological safety. Like a cartoon of the new, the theoretical prospects of Star Wars seemed to dance before Reaganite eyes. In a culture nurtured on a world of the undead, the choice of another death-technology is not that surprising.

(1987)

❐ In Search of Context

"WE'RE LIVING IN the age of an information explosion." Usually when a writer trots out that phrase, it's to get us feeling all warm and smug inside – like, how *lucky* we are, and how *did* those poor suckers in the past manage?! Actually, the information explosion has done little but muddle our minds and turn information into trivia. That's what happens when information is reported devoid of context, which is how most news items are reported these days. An individual news story connects with nothing else and becomes just another curious item in a series of newsy non sequiturs.

A classic example of this is the 1983 story of the National Film Board vs. the U.S. Justice Department. My file on this topic contains a couple of dozen newspaper clippings and a few magazine columns. As a news item, it got lots of media coverage. But it got almost no context at all, even though plenty was available.

The story involves three Canadian documentaries labelled "propaganda" by the U.S. Justice Department: *If You Love This Planet* (directed by Terri Nash), *Acid From Heaven* (directed by George Mully), and *Acid Rain: Requiem or Recovery* (directed by Jim Turpie) – all produced by or for the NFB. By mid-February 1983, U.S. Justice had ruled that the films had to be registered under the Foreign Agents Registration Act, a law passed in 1938 to, in Chief Justice Stone's words, "identify agents of foreign principals who might engage in subversive acts or in spreading foreign propaganda." The Act defines "political propaganda" in part as any communication intended to "prevail upon, indoctrinate, convert, induce or in any other way influence ... any section of the public within the United States with reference to the political or public interests, policies or relations of a government of a foreign country." Under this registration the three films, when circulated in the United States, must carry an opening section clearly stating that they are not approved by the U.S. government. In addition, a list of viewers' names must be kept for inspection by the U.S. Justice Department.

The story hit the front page of *The Globe and Mail* on February 24. On that same day, the Canadian embassy in Washington alerted *Washington Post* staff writer Cass Peterson, whose write-up got front-page coverage in the *Post*'s February 25 edition. Although *The New York Times* did not run a news item on the issue, it devoted an editorial to the subject on February 26. Given such prestigious print coverage, TV networks on both sides of the border picked up the story, usually showing clips from *If You Love This Planet*, at the time an Oscar nominee (eventually a winner) dealing with nuclear war.

In the Canadian media the story remained "news" for weeks, with subsequent coverage devoted to such things as Ted Kennedy's hosting of the films at a showing on Capitol Hill, the mounting publicity and attendance for the films on both sides of the border, reactions from various Canadian politicians, interviews with the films' directors and various NFB representatives, and background information on the Foreign Agents Registration Act.

In other words, the incident gathered steam and, in the process, became its own context. Follow-up reporting took us deeper into the story – more details, more reactions. But few connections were made between the story and anything else happening at the time. The result is that the incident tended to be treated as an interesting fluke of Justice behaviour, rather than as a revealing part of a larger pattern. For example, any number of contexts might have been chosen for this particular story, rather than have it provide its own. I'll mention three:

One. On February 22, two days before the NFB / Justice story broke, federal environment minister John Roberts released a three-volume, thousand-page report on acid rain – the results of a two-and-a-half-year study conducted jointly by Canadian and U.S. scientists. The report was supposed to lead to a Canada-U.S. clean-air pact, long delayed. But the two teams of scientists were sharply divided over the evidence and did not agree on mutual recommendations. The Canadian team of scientists urged immediate cuts in pollution. The U.S. team recommended further study before any action be taken. It was a highly controversial news item on its own, but for our purposes the most interesting part of *The Globe and Mail* coverage was one sentence, as reported by Michael Keating: "A spokesman for the State Department said the joint reports will be released today *without comment or press conference.*"

In the age of an information explosion, this is how to bury or kill a news story. I combed through *The New York Times* for February 22 through March 3 and found no mention at all of this major acid rain study and confrontation, though it was front-page news in Canadian papers. Cass Peterson of *The Washington Post* covered it well for the February 22 edition, but told me that the only way she knew of the study was because the Canadian embassy alerted her to it in advance and gave her copies. She said the librarian for the U.S. Environmental Protection Agency actually called *her* to find out how to get ahold of the joint reports.

Not surprisingly, then, the U.S. media did not use this major and controversial joint study on acid rain as a context for understanding the U.S. Justice Department's ruling on the films – two of which are documentaries about acid rain. In the Canadian media, where acid rain is a familiar story, the overt connection was perhaps less necessary to make. Both stories were front-page items in *The Globe and Mail* just two days apart. Nevertheless, reporter Michael Keating reminded readers: "The demand for registration of the films under the Foreign Agents Registration Act ... comes in the middle of discussions between the two countries on acid rain pollution and the testing of the cruise missile." U.S. readers, for whom this connection would have to be made more overtly, were left in the dark. The U.S. Justice Department's ruling on the three films remained unconnected to the State Department's position on acid rain.

Two. On February 24, the same day that the NFB / Justice story appeared in *The Globe and Mail*, U.S. Secretary of State George Shultz (also a key figure in the acid rain discussions) announced the Reagan administration's plan for "Project Democracy" – an $85 million campaign to promote democracy around the world during the coming year. *The New York Times* called it "a major program in an ideological competition with the communists" and quoted one congressman who considered Project Democracy to be "multi-million-dollar propaganda." The program was to be administered by the U.S. Information Agency.

The ironies of the State Department's action were evident to at least some U.S. media reporting on the NFB / Justice ruling. *The*

Washington Post stated: "The brouhaha hit the State Department at a particularly sensitive time, two days after Secretary of State George P. Shultz announced an $85 million overseas propaganda effort with the words: 'Don't be nervous about democracy, about holding the torch up there.'" A February 26 editorial on NFB / Justice in *The New York Times* stated:

> Secretary Shultz sounded like Tom Paine as he pleaded with Congress for $85 million to promote freedom.... But that very day his colleagues at Justice shamed America's democracy by ruling that three Canadian documentaries be branded as propaganda before they could be shown in the land of the free.... What Mr. Shultz grandly calls "Project democracy" has work to do, all right. At home.

I combed through *The Globe and Mail* for several days and found no mention of the Project Democracy news item at all. Not surprisingly, then, the Canadian media (at least to my knowledge) did not use Project Democracy as a context for understanding or illuminating the NFB / Justice ruling, although the ironies are inescapable.

So Canadian readers were left in the dark. The U.S. Justice ruling on the three NFB films remained unconnected to the U.S. State Department's action regarding Project Democracy – its own propaganda effort.

Stranger still, *The Toronto Star* of February 27 carried a Canadian Press item stating: "*The New York Times*, in an editorial yesterday, remarked that the treatment of the Canadian films was ridiculous. The National Film Board of Canada, the newspaper said, 'has won international acclaim for the quality of its independent productions.'" No mention of Project Democracy – the main ironic point of the *Times* editorial. I guess I always thought that Canadian newspaper editors read the major U.S. papers, and vice versa. But maybe they only read the wire services.

Three. By mid-February, Ronald Reagan's "Sewergate" had hit the fan, with major allegations that the Environmental Protection Agency was in collusion with big business regarding the environment. President Reagan ordered the Justice Department to investigate the serious allegations raised by six Congressional subcommittees. Since this was the same Justice Department that considered acid rain films to be subversive propaganda, one would think that this connection might have deserved comment in the media. To my knowledge, it was ignored on both sides of the border.

The Information Explosion tends to obscure connections rather than illuminate them. Individual news items may flare up momentarily, standing out against the overall din, but unless these items are linked to larger patterns they become cinders of trivia floating about the transient spectacle of news. What is needed in these times is more in-breadth reporting that provides meaningful contexts.

(1983)

☐ A Catch-22 in Canadian Broadcasting: The Myth of the "Single System"

ANOTHER GREAT FLURRY of debate, white papers, policy studies, commissions, and god-knows-what-other official grappling is once again under way in an attempt to deal with Canadian broadcasting. In the midst of all the verbiage, it's useful to take a look at a structural problem that, to my way of thinking, is absolutely central to the whole broadcasting morass in this country. Not surprisingly, that problem is embedded in, and masked by, language itself.

In this case, the crucial phrase, enshrined in the 1968 Broadcasting Act, is the notion that Canada has a "single system" of broadcasting. Those two words have done more to screw up Canadian airwaves and broadcasting sovereignty than any other two words in the English language. It's worthwhile to consider their origins.

In the mid-1920s Canadian broadcasting was initially chaotic: three or four radio stations in any one city shared time, all using the same frequency, and there was bitter infighting for the few available frequencies that the U.S. had left to Canada as the result of its greedy grab for most of the spectrum. Moreover, most Canadian radio stations had only 500 watts of power, or less, while many U.S. stations boasted 50 kilowatts and were beginning to gain network affiliates in Canada. It was in this context that the first Royal Commission on Broadcasting, the Aird Commission, was appointed in 1927.

The Aird Commission took a strong pro-Canada stance. When its report was released in 1929, the Commission expressed concern that Canadian private commercial broadcasters were not interested in serving underpopulated sections of the country and were broadcasting mainly U.S. programs. The Commission declared that broadcasting should serve the national interest by reflecting Canadian ideals and culture, by promoting national unity, and by educating in the broadest sense of the word. Finally, the Aird Commission recommended that, to meet these goals, all broadcasting in Canada should be nationalized as a publicly owned corporation independent of the government.

Despite widespread support for this recommendation, two lobbies argued against nationalization: the Canadian Association of Broadcasters (CAB) and the Canadian Radio League (CRL). The CAB, a group of private station owners, supported the status quo and especially their "right" to affiliate with U.S. networks. The CRL, a group of Canadian businessmen, offered its own proposal which envisaged a network of high-power, publicly owned stations and affiliated privately owned community stations. The private stations, as the CRL saw it, were to be subsidized by receiving the public stations' programming free of charge.

In the midst of the varied proposals and interests, in May 1932, Parliament passed the first Broadcasting Act. It established the publicly owned Canadian Radio Broadcasting Commission (CRBC, which eventually became the CBC) and gave it two major functions: to regulate all broadcasting in Canada, and to itself engage in broadcasting. The CRBC was to be funded entirely by Parliamentary appropriations, and it could purchase existing private stations as well as construct new public ones.

Superficially, the broadcasting system established in 1932 seems like the "mixed system" called for by the Canadian Radio League. But in fact, by giving the CBC the powers to both broadcast and regulate all broadcasting in Canada, Parliament made the public network the controlling frame for the whole system. According to the Act, the CBC, with its public-service goals, was to set the boundaries within which the private-sector broadcasters would operate. The private stations were permitted to exist only as very small, circumscribed adjuncts within the national system, and their purely financial incentives were to be well-boundaried and structurally overridden by the powers and goals of the public-sector CBC.

To picture the 1932 broadcasting structure created by the Act, think of a big circle (the CBC) containing within itself a smaller circle (the private-sector broadcasters). The CBC, as both regulator and broadcaster, would ensure that any broadcasting element contained within its boundaries contributed to the national goals outlined in the Broadcasting Act. By granting the CBC these dual powers – or, to use a phrase from biologist / philosopher Gregory Bateson, by making the CBC "the higher logical type" in the structure – the Act created what was quite clearly a "single system" for broadcasting in that the structure was non-contradictory to public-service goals. The purely financial incentives of the private-sector broadcasters would be curtailed and contained by the more broadly empowered CBC. Both theoretically and practically, this single system was comprised of a structure and goals that explicitly coincided.

In practice, however, Parliament did not honour what it had created in the Act. From its inception the CRBC was not adequately funded to exercise the structural powers it had been granted. For example, when the CRBC set up its nation-wide radio network in June 1933, there were 6 publicly owned and operated stations and 32 private stations in the network. By 1936, when the CRBC became the Canadian Broadcasting Corporation, only 2 more publicly owned stations had been added, while the private sector had grown to 75 stations. Had Parliament been serious about the structure it had created, funding would have ensured that public-station expansion at least kept pace with the private sector. According to the spirit of the Act, funding should have allowed the CBC to buy up private stations as it expanded.

Instead, Parliament did not follow either the spirit of the Act or its stated terms. Rather, the private-sector stations were allowed to blossom across the country – ostensibly as the means for distributing CBC's network programming. At the time this was apparently not deemed problematic. Indeed, this form of distribution was argued to be the most practical and effective way of expanding the single system at the least expense to the government. Moreover, as the regulator of the whole system, the CBC would be able to see to it that the private stations continued to operate only as circumscribed adjuncts.

But here we may see an initial double bind at work, springing out of this compromise to Aird's recommended nationalization. While it empowered the CBC to manage, control, and regulate the entire national broadcasting system, Parliament also refused to grant enough funding so that the CBC could exercise those powers. This may explain why the CBC itself, almost from its inception, struck a self-destructive note in its relationship with the private-sector stations.

For example, the CBC's nation-wide distribution system consisted of a basic network and a supplementary network. In the 1930s the basic network was composed of 6 publicly owned and 12 privately owned stations. The supplementary network consisted of 20 private stations. All of these 38 stations received, free of charge, three hours of CBC-produced non-commercial programming each evening. This was clearly a boon to the private stations because, at no cost to themselves, they were assured of filling a substantial portion of their airtime. Although only the stations in the basic network were required to air the programming, most of the private broadcasters in the supplementary network did too. By all accounts the CBC's programming was consistently good and popular.

Nevertheless, it was decided that the CBC would not only give this free programming to the 12 private stations in its basic network, but also that it would *pay* them to broadcast it: an absurd decision in any case, but especially so given the broadcasting structure. As the regulator in the single system designed to meet national goals, the CBC could quite simply have required that all stations in its basic network (and in its supplementary network, for that matter) broadcast the provided programming. Instead, by paying the private stations to do so, the CBC implied that it didn't have the power to regulate them and that the private stations were somehow outside the system. In retrospect this decision was a disastrous one, both politically and psychologically. It also ensured that the CBC, already underfunded by Parliament, would continue to be further financially bled by this ridiculous payment to the private stations – an expensive practice that continues to this day.

But despite these serious erosions of the CBC's powers, the structure and goals of the single system as constituted in the Act were non-contradictory. They did not remain that way for long.

In 1942 another Parliamentary committee reiterated that the CBC was empowered, if necessary, to take over private stations in order to extend national coverage. It also opposed private-sector plans to expand group ownership of private stations. But by the mid-1940s private broadcasters were calling for "co-equal status with the CBC." They proposed to establish their own networks, compete with the CBC, and have the "right" to become affiliates of U.S. networks. To accomplish this the CAB began lobbying for a separate regulatory body, independent of the CBC. It was thus arguing for a fundamental change in the broadcasting structure.

The response came from the Royal Commission on National Development in the Arts, Letters and Sciences – the Massey Commission – which was appointed in 1949. The commission defended the single system constituted in the Broadcasting Act of 1932, especially its goals and the circumscribed role of the private sector. In no uncertain terms, the Massey Commission stated:

> Broadcasting in Canada, in our view, is a public service directed and controlled in the public interest by a body responsible to Parliament. Private citizens are permitted to engage their capital and energies in this service, subject to the regulation of this body. That these citizens should enjoy adequate security or compensation for the actual monetary investment they are permitted to make, is apparent.... But that they enjoy any vested right to engage in broadcasting as an industry, or that they have any status except as part of the national broadcasting system, is inadmissible.... The only status of private broadcasters is as part of the national broadcasting system. They have no civil right to broadcast or any property rights in broadcasting.

Shortly thereafter, however, the lucrative prospects for the new medium of television gave fresh impetus to the desires of the private-sector lobby, which conveniently ignored the pronouncements of the 1949 Massey Commission. Reappointed to consider the role for television in Canada, the Massey Commission of 1951 continued to urge that the CBC retain all regulatory and broadcasting power, that private stations be licensed only after the CBC had established a national TV service, and that all private stations be required to serve as outlets for CBC programming.

But the government of the day seemed to feel a special urgency about television. In December 1952, after only two CBC stations had been opened (in Montreal and Toronto), the government announced: "Now that television has started, it should be extended as widely and quickly as possible to other areas." This urgency, whatever its specific political roots at the time, can be partially accounted for by the technological bandwagon mentality characteristic of modernity. In particular, colonized countries seem to feel that by amassing the latest hardware promoted by the United States, they will thereby gain entry to new status. The tragic flaw, however, is that there is always a significant lag between hardware implementation and indigenous software production. The rush to get the technology in place creates a vacuum: the technology is there, but there is nothing to put on it. This is the situation that the U.S. entertainment industry depends on, with its glut of software, programming, movies that almost immediately flow into any available foreign space. A country has to protect that interval, that lag between hardware and indigenous software production, to keep its screens for itself. Quite literally, a country has to keep the technology (in this case, TV) turned off until its own software production has geared up fully and can fill the available air-time – and the air-time must also be managed according to the availability of indigenous product.

These factors are crucial during the start-up period for a new technology, but the overriding impulse is to simply get the technology in place as quickly as possible. This is what happened in the early 1950s as the Canadian government rushed to expand television "as widely and quickly as possible to other areas" after putting in place only two public CBC stations. The technology-fetish overshadowed all other concerns.

Parliament provided funding for only four more publicly owned TV stations, and the government announced that the private sector could apply for TV licences in all other areas of the country. This was essentially a repetition of the radio situation of the mid-1930s. By ignoring its own broadcasting history, the country was doomed to repeat it. Was the CBC to control the broadcasting structure as created by the Broadcasting Act of 1932? The government seemed to be saying: yes and no. Were the private stations permitted to exist only as circumscribed adjuncts to the CBC's national TV service? Again, the government was entirely ambiguous.

To make matters worse, it was decided in 1953 that TV and radio broadcasting should be financed by advertising revenues and an excise tax of 15 per cent on receiver sets and parts. Given the national public-service goals for broadcasting and the structure of Canada's single system, this form of financing was the least appropriate one that could have been chosen. Moreover, revenues from the excise tax were to quickly dry up once the TV-set buying spree was over.

Similarly, the government and the broadcasters accepted the advice of U.S. experts (sent up by RCA, parent company for NBC-TV) to adopt the same television technology being used in the U.S., rather than opt for the (at the time) incompatible and superior TV systems being developed in Britain and Europe. To have chosen a different TV technology for broadcast and reception in Canada – in effect, an "electronic curtain" serving as a technological border for the country – would at the time have clearly been consistent with the stated goals in the Broadcasting Act – that broadcasting serve specifically Canadian needs and goals.

With the government acting in such contradictory ways and ignoring the implications of its own decisions, the CAB lobby began to push more forcefully. Pressures for a separate regulatory body – a change in structure that would benefit the private sector – came to a head with the appointment in 1955 of the Royal Commission on Broadcasting under the chairmanship of Robert M. Fowler. Once again a Royal Commission, reporting in 1957, reiterated the position that all Canadian broadcasters constitute a single system in which "the private broadcasters are a complementary but necessary part and over which the Corporation (the CBC) through the Board of Governors has full jurisdiction and control." The Commission concluded succinctly that "free enterprise has failed to do as much as it could in original program production and the development of Canadian talent, not because of a lack of freedom, but because of a lack of enterprise."

Nonetheless, the Fowler Commission recommended one important change: the creation of a second public agency responsible to Parliament. This agency would regulate all broadcasting, including the direction of policy and the supervision of the CBC's operations. This recommendation was a significant step towards the creation of a fully separate regulatory body. Under the Diefenbaker government it became the full structural shift for which the private sector had been pressing.

Early in the 1958 election campaign, private broadcasters found a sympathetic ear in the person of Progressive Conservative leader John Diefenbaker, who was fully in favour of private-sector gains in every realm. In a campaign speech in Kenora, Ontario, Diefenbaker stated (as reported by The Globe and Mail for March 19, 1958) that "the time was long overdue to assure private stations competing with the public broadcasting system that they would be judged (for their performance) by an independent body as the need arose. They should not be judged by those who are in competition with them." The statements reflect a fundamental misunderstanding of the broadcasting structure as constituted in the Broadcasting Act. Not surprisingly, under Diefenbaker, the new Broadcasting Act of 1958 removed regulatory powers from the CBC and granted them to a separate, independent broadcasting regulatory body – the Board of Broadcast Governors

(BBG), which later became the Canadian Radio-Television and Telecommunications Commission (CRTC).

In his book *The Public Eye: Television and the Politics of Canadian Broadcasting, 1952-1968*, political scientist Frank Peers described the significance of the new Act:

> *Although nowhere clearly stated*, the implications of the new bill in 1958 was that the publicly owned CBC should have considerably reduced stature, and that the private broadcasters would have a status approaching that of the CBC. A new regulatory agency would be set up and, for the purpose of its regulations, the CBC and private stations would be equally subordinate to it.... Since the new bill contained more explicit provisions for the authorization and regulation of networks, it could be assumed that the government expected that a private network would be formed to compete with the CBC. (emphasis added)

What's most important about this 1958 piece of legislation is that it tried to pretend as though nothing significant had happened to the broadcasting structure despite the change. The Broadcasting Act of 1958 refers to "the continued existence and efficient operation of a national broadcasting system" – implying that there was still a "single system" like the one constituted in 1932. But obviously the new structure was much more like two competing systems – one public and one private – with a new referee for both.

Using the image of one big circle (the CBC) containing within itself a small circle (the private broadcasters), we can see that by removing regulatory powers from the CBC, the new Broadcasting Act of 1958 effectively took the small circle out of the confines of the big one, made them about equal in size, and set them both to not only bouncing off each other but a third entity as well – the independent regulatory agency. This radical change in the Canadian broadcasting structure was effected *but not acknowledged* by the Act, which blithely continued to speak of a "single system" upholding the old national, public-service goals, even though the private sector had now been made fully competitive with the CBC and fully able to operate within the financial incentives of the marketplace.

For its part, the CBC had thereby been demoted to the status of competitor with the private sector (competing for ad-dollars, audiences, and imported programs). Nevertheless, it was still obliged to carry the lion's share of public-service responsibilities. Had the

demotion of the CBC been accompanied by full Parliamentary funding for all its operations, CBC carriage of virtually all public-service
responsibilities might have made sense. Instead, by having to rely on
advertising revenues and private affiliates (which it continued to
pay), the CBC was constrained by the same financial incentives that
rule the marketplace shared with the private sector, while having to
perform the overwhelming number of public-service functions
assigned to it.

The Broadcasting Act of 1958 perpetuated the illusion by continuing to refer to a "single system" of broadcasting dedicated "to safe-
guard, enrich and strengthen the cultural, social and economic fabric
of Canada." Such goals have rarely been lived up to by the private-sector broadcasters. Since 1958, private broadcasters (in order to get and
maintain their licences) have always made glittering promises about
how they will contribute to Canadian broadcasting sovereignty. But
because their real goal is financial – and since the revised, but unacknowledged, structure frees them to follow this incentive – they simply import U.S. programs because that is cheaper than producing
their own.

For its part, the broadcasting regulatory agency (CRTC) has seemed
to think since 1958 that by assisting and fostering the private broadcasting sector, somehow – perhaps cumulatively – that sector's con-
tribution to the stated national broadcasting goals might add up to
something significant enough to prove that there is indeed a "single
system" of broadcasting in this country.

In fact, there is no "single system" at all. At one time there was, at
least in structure and in theory – but the 1958 Act effectively abol-
ished it, while pretending that nothing had been changed. It is this
pretence – maintained by valiantly reiterating the old goals (which
actually did fit the old structure) and by continually reiterating the
rhetorical phrase of the "single system" in all CRTC decisions – that
has helped erode and destroy Canada's broadcasting sovereignty.

To use an analogy: the human body *is* a single system. Its various
components co-operate and co-ordinate to maintain life. Though we
may speak of "the nervous system" and "the circulatory system,"
these various bodily functions do not compete with one another. If
they do, the body dies. In terms of the broadcasting marketplace, the
private sector *does* compete with the CBC. Perhaps it always did, but
at least in the old structure that impulse was contained, bounded, and
potentially curtailed so that its energies might contribute to the

health of the whole. But the 1958 Act changed the structure and freed the private sector to be a fully separate entity following entirely financial incentives.

Thus, the relevant questions become: Why has this structural change never been acknowledged? Why has the myth of the "single system" been maintained for some thirty years despite all evidence? Why this rhetorical pretence on the part of the CRTC in decision after decision? Such denial is beyond my comprehension.

Nevertheless, the myth of the "single system" has worked extremely well for the private sector, which has been fostered and pampered over the years by a regulatory agency apparently bent on proving that this "single system" exists, and would work, if only yet another concession were made to private sector desires. Whatever the motivation, there are any number of historical examples – the Greenberg / Bronfman bailout of pay-TV's First Choice, and the creation of private "super-stations" are typical mid-1980s instances – suggesting that the illusory notion of a "single system" has been continually used to justify CRTC decisions that merely cater to private-sector expansion.

In 1980, for instance, the CRTC allowed the merger of Canadian Cablesystems Ltd. of Toronto and Premier Communications Ltd. of Vancouver – creating a corporate cable-TV entity three times larger than any other cable firm in Canada. To those who opposed the creation of such a large conglomerate because of the dangers of concentrated media ownership, the CRTC (according to *The Globe and Mail*, July 13, 1980) "pointed out that the Broadcasting Act spoke of a 'single Canadian broadcasting system.'" On the other hand, when the CBC wished to use that "single system" to distribute its proposed TV-2 network via cable, the CRTC nixed the proposal by protesting that the service would reach only a "limited" audience.

By the mid-1980s the CRTC had agreed to let private TV stations co-operate in producing "Canadian content" shows, with each station getting on-air credit for such productions. Meanwhile, the CBC, clearly committed to producing quality Canadian programming, was continually getting its budget axed. In a speech on February 7, 1985, to the Canadian Club, CBC President Pierre Juneau stated that after the most recent $85 million cut, the CBC had suffered budget cuts totalling more than $420 million since 1978, or "more than $60 million a year."

To me, it's clear that the myth of the "single system" of broadcasting is the mechanism used over the years to simultaneously pamper / expand the private sector and demote / hamstring the CBC. This doesn't explain why such decisions have been made, though the results point to the similar privatizing mind-set at work in mainstream politics despite the rhetoric.

Nevertheless, it looks for all the world as though in practice things have come full circle: back to a (this time implicit) structure similar to that of 1932. Now, however, the labels for the circles in our mental imagery are decidedly different. With the CRTC rather obviously "on-side" with the private sector – and having been on-side for quite a few years – the private broadcasting sector has become the "higher logical type." Today private broadcasting is the larger controlling circle containing within it the smaller circle: a circumscribed, well-bounded, and effectively curtailed and diminished adjunct – the CBC.

(1985)

☐ Adventures in Wonderland

ABOUT TWENTY MILES north of Toronto, in the midst of rolling farm-land, there arises (where Nature neglected to put one) a mountain.

This mountain, being built of structural steel and poured concrete, will, upon completion in 1981, stand a hundred and fifty feet tall. Its painted plaster cliffs and crevices, its sculpted crags and clefts, its chiselled cleavages will glisten mawkishly in the bright Ontario sun. The estimated one hundred thousand people who will visit this mountain each day will for the most part be oblivious to its meaning, like other camera-laden tourists walking unguided through Stonehenge or Easter Island or the temples of the Mayan.

For another few thousand people, especially those who live within the shadow of the monolith, this mountain growing in their midst represents something vast and far-reaching, something bordering on the grotesque, like a magnified pimple on the smiling face of a bureau-crat. For them, the story of this mountain begins, like any story arbi-trarily must, years ago: probably in the early 1950s.

At that time, a rather remarkable man (whose father was a Cana-dian) dreamed up a particular blend of show business and technologi-cal engineering which he called "imagineering." He applied his con-cept first to some acreage he'd purchased in southern California near Anaheim, and he named the result after himself – Disneyland.

So successful was Walt's idea that during the early 1960s he began planning for another "theme park," an even larger one that would perfect his concept of imagineering and represent all he stood for in terms of the American way of life. To this end, he began buying up "worthless" swampland in central Florida – a total of forty-three square miles (2,400 acres) just south of Orlando – before anyone discovered what was happening. Unfortunately, Disney died before his Disney World opened in 1971 – a gargantuan facility that dwarfed the mere 180 acres of Disneyland. But he prepared for his own passing. He left films of himself to speak at subsequent meetings of the board, and rumours persist that his body is being held in suspended animation for later recovery (presumably, the ultimate in imagineering).

In a sense, these North American theme parks are predicated on the fact that many of our cities are atrocious places to live. Disney himself seemed to have felt that, and he designed his parks to be models of supreme organization – blissfully happy workers and complete cleanliness – with vast underground pneumatic trash-collecting systems that whoosh garbage to the central dispose-all at sixty miles per hour. He also left designs for a park that would replicate the world, or more explicitly, the world as he felt it should exist under optimum environmental and political conditions. His plans called for a sanitized, deburglarized, air-conditioned, experimental world replica in which young people from every country would live for a year at a time in a showcase designed to exhibit solutions to future technological, political, and scientific problems. In 1982, this Disney dream will come true ... partially. The Disney corporation will open a new park next to the Magic Kingdom in Florida – a park called the Experimental Prototype City of Tomorrow. It will feature high-tech exhibits in such fields as communications, energy, oceanography, and transportation. These exhibits will be sponsored by major corporations and governments solicited by the Disney organization.

But we're running ahead of our story. Because of the Disney success, theme parks began springing up all over the United States during the 1970s. By 1975 there were twenty-three major U.S. theme parks in operation. Basically, a theme park differs from a tourist attraction like, say, Niagara Falls in that a theme park is almost entirely person-made, like a permanent stage-set incorporating reproductions based in fantasy and fact. The larger theme parks are composed of several "theme areas," often unrelated to one another but combined into a kind of surrealistic whole. For example, at Miniature World (in upper New York state) replicas of the Taj Mahal, Notre Dame Cathedral, and the CN Tower nestle cosily side by side – defying space, geography, history, and, of course, logic, like some hallucinogenic-induced playground. At King's Dominion (a theme park outside Richmond, Virginia) there is a 120-acre safari park to be viewed from a mono-rail, a thirty-three storey replica of the Eiffel Tower, and Yogi Bear's cave in Happyland.

But perhaps the most integrated example of a theme park is the one planned for southern Alabama – to be called "The Holy Land." This will be a 200-acre park with a Sea of Galilee, a Noah's Ark, a Tower of Babel, a walled city of Jerusalem complete with Wailing Wall, a Garden of Eden, and special areas devoted to Ancient Babylon, Ancient Rome, and Ancient Egypt. Rides will include slave-ships, a Jonah's whale, motorized camel and elephant trips through a plastic desert to the Pyramids, and a twelve-thousand-seat Colosseum where imagineered Christians will be thrown daily to the lions. Towering over all these activities will be a one-hundred-foot statue of Jesus, which lights up at night.

Quite possibly such theme parks may be seen to be the culmination of several separate processes or threads, which here knot together in conspicuous interrelationship. One of those threads is the drive towards "corporate diversification," which during the late 1960s and early 1970s became a "buzzword" within U.S. industry. Here, too, Disney was a leader: long ago using his animated feature filmmaking as the ground for spinning off endless merchandise, comic books, TV shows, the California Institute of the Arts, and, of course, the theme parks (now including Tokyo Disneyland – a $300 million park being built in Tokyo Bay, Japan).

In a sense, corporate diversification provides a clue to the deeper meaning of Disney's concept: imagineering. More than the mere application of technological gimmickry to his show-biz generated images, imagineering also means what its root words say – the engineering of our imaginations. What could be more efficient and effective than to first people our imaginations and fantasy life with the figures of his feature film spectacles, and then to build giant stage sets where those fantasy images in our imaginations may come to life. Arguably, this is exactly the function of his theme parks: the reaping of a second financial harvest from the seeds sown by the first (the films and TV programs).

While this seems to be a rather unremarkable point, it takes on more significance when we realize that now virtually all of the major U.S. companies engaged in film and television production have followed the Disney lead – diversifying their operations to include the widest range of leisure time and consumer products. Program suppliers such as Paramount Pictures, Warner Brothers Pictures, MCA-Universal, MGM, Twentieth Century-Fox, Columbia Pictures, and the three parent companies of the commercial U.S. networks have corporate holdings in everything from sugarcane, oil, and titanium, to pinball machines, frozen foods, rent-a-cars, sports teams, records, musical instruments, toys, video-games and discs, perfume, hotels, movie theatres, cable-TV companies, candy, book, and magazine publishing companies, tourist attractions, carpets and furnishings, Coca-Cola bottling franchises, and pantyhose. In other words, not only does the U.S. television industry shape our attitudes about leisure-time and consumption, but it also increasingly owns the means for fulfilling those desires. Like Disney, they are all into imagineering.

Another of the threads that seem to culminate in the knotted configuration called the theme park is the tendency over the past fifteen years for mass tourism to merge with theatre. This is increasingly the case as tour operators expand the scope and reach of the business and as millions more of the middle classes take advantage of relatively inexpensive inclusive tour charters (ITCs). Obviously, the sheer number of tourists able to converge upon any one tourist spot has meant that any such place must be completely readied to withstand and accommodate its guests. (This means that a tour operator like Suntours must have prearranged everything including air flights, guides at the terminal, hotels, dining room staff, sewers and drinking water, roads, boutiques and entertainment, sight-seeing, local nightlife.) Clearly, one logical extension of the packaged deal can be seen in the success of holiday resorts like Club Med, Club Guava, and Negril Beach Village – completely self-contained and isolated "villages" built like stage-sets representing the indigenous culture, but actually quite removed (even geographically) from contact with that culture. The other logical extension is the theme park, which provides everything in one large setting and unabashedly substitutes reproductions for reality. This in itself may be one of the messages of the "codes" currently operating in mass tourism: reproductions are preferable to reality because they are so much more manageable, predictable, safe. *Especially safe.* According to the codes of mass tourism, culture shock must not be allowed to happen. It must be replaced (and a vast industry exists to ensure this) by the quaint, the picturesque, and by the Spectacular: all of which enhance our pleasure and guarantee that this pleasure will be uninterrupted. The embodiment of such Spectacle is the U.S. theme park: Disneyland, Disney World, the Alabama Holy Land, Dogpatch U.S.A. Miniature World, the Land of Oz, Six Flags Over Texas, Opryland U.S.A.

With such attractions luring Canadians south of the border,

Canada's international travel deficit has been climbing annually since 1967 (the year of Expo). This deficit tripled in 1975, doubled again in 1976, and by 1980 was approaching the figure of $2 billion. In other words, in terms of tourism, that much more money annually leaves the country than comes into it. And so, to compete, it seemed necessary to make changes here. One of those changes is occurring within the closest thing to a theme park that Canada had for a long time – Marineland and Game Farm in Niagara Falls, Ontario.

Marineland and Game Farm is the creation of John Holer, a Yugoslavian immigrant who arrived penniless in Canada over two decades ago. A former wine chemist and circus animal trainer, Holer spent his early years in Canada working as a construction labourer and later in the dry docks of St. Catherines, Ontario. Gradually, he taught himself engineering and bought a small parcel of land on which he erected two water tanks with glass portholes. In them he placed three California sea lions and offered an hourly underwater show. In his spare time Holer studied a U.S. submarine which was in dry dock, and with the help of his co-workers he designed an idea of an amusement ride based on pneumatically driven submarines. When he tried to sell his idea he found that most amusement parks were way behind him. Finally he sold his design to a New Jersey company that found a client willing to pay $14,000 for the design. The client (considered to be an "eccentric" in the park business in those days) was Walt Disney. Holer split the money with his dock worker friends and used his share to expand his aquarium show – adding more animals, land, and trees.

As a theme park, Marineland and Game Farm was designed to be much closer to nature than its U.S. counterparts, which usually build a landscape rather than preserve one. Yet now, in the face of increasing competition, Holer seems to be giving way to the high-voltage, Spectacular American design. Current expansion plans include a mono-rail, an artificial waterway with boats, the world's largest steel roller-coaster, and an imposing replica of a European castle.

Another of the changes brought on by the escalating travel deficit and the increased competition from U.S. theme parks is that massive plaster mountain arising north of Toronto near the towns of Vaughn and Maple. It is to be the centrepiece of Canada's first full-fledged theme park, "Canada's Wonderland" – 320 acres of rides, restaurants, Chinese pagodas, a replica of the Crystal Palace, medieval buildings, waterfalls complete with real cliff-divers, live entertainment ... everything. The original plans for Canada's Wonderland called for five specific theme-areas: World Expo 1890 (which is where the Crystal Palace will come in), Medieval Fair (with take-out mead?), International Street, Frontier Canada, and the Happy Land of Hanna-Barbera. The park is due to open in May of 1981.

Back in 1973, when the plans for the park were first made public, residents of Maple and Vaughn began protesting on the grounds that the park would be an environmental nightmare and would irrevocably alter the character of their towns. A year later, Family Leisure Centres of Canada purchased the disputed 320 acres of prime farmland and began efforts to have the land rezoned for recreational use. In 1976, Ontario treasurer Darcy McKeough wrote to the Vaughn Council that representatives from the company had twice been told in meetings with the ministry that the area was unsuitable for a theme park. In 1977, Ontario agricultural minister William Newman released a study reporting that the soil on the site was of uncommonly high quality and that developing the site could lead to land speculation, which would drive farmers out of the area. In 1978, however, the Ontario Municipal Board gave permission for rezoning the land, over the objections of the Maple Ratepayers Association and a group from Vaughn called Sane Approach to Vaughn's Environment. These two groups decided to appeal the decision to the provincial cabinet, asking that the government study the project on the basis of the Environment Assessment Act.

In May 1978, under questioning by NDP Member of the Legislature Marion Bryden, McKeough reversed his stand on the park, saying, "I'm not prepared to forever simply think that this province is going to stand still, as members of the NDP would have it." Premier William Davis added, in response to Bryden, "Are you against children having fun?" Agricultural minister William Newman also appeared to flip-flop on the issue. When Donald MacDonald of the NDP protested that the park would gobble up 320 acres of prime farmland, Newman retorted, "You're against jobs, too, eh?" By the end of May 1978, the Ontario cabinet had given its approval for Family Leisure Centres of Canada to build the park.

The financing for the park is mainly Canadian. Long-term loans have been committed by Sun Life Assurance Company of Canada, Standard Life Assurance Company, The Toronto Dominion Bank, and the Lumberman's Mutual Casualty Company. However, ownership of Canada's Wonderland is 75 per cent U.S. Great West Life Assurance of Winnipeg holds 25 per cent ownership, and the other 75 per cent is held by the parent company of Family Leisure Centres of Canada – Taft Broadcasting.

Like the other U.S. television conglomerates, Taft Broadcasting has been diversifying its holdings these past few years. One of its subsidiaries is Hanna-Barbera Productions, which is why Canada's Wonderland will have people dressed up as lovable cartoon characters (Yogi Bear and Boo Boo, the Flintstones, Huckleberry Hound, Pixie and Dixie, Quick-Draw McGraw, Snooper and Blabber, Augie Doggie and Doggie Daddy, Scoobie Doo) to mingle among the crowds just like they do in U.S. theme parks. Such a feature is a staple of all the other theme parks owned by Taft Broadcasting: King's Dominion near Richmond, Virginia; King's Island near Cincinnati; Carrowinds, near Charlotte, North Carolina; and the Happyland of Hanna-Barbera in Los Angeles – which all together reported a 1979 operating profit of $11.2 million (up 13 per cent from the previous year). Of course, to be a good corporate citizen Taft has commissioned a Montreal animator to design an animal cartoon character with a Canadian slant. At last report, one prototype developed by the Montreal animator is a beaver in a modified Mountie hat.

Another part of Taft Broadcasting's corporate family is Worldvision, one of the largest distributors of U.S. television products in the world. This distribution network, which currently peddles such products as *Little House on the Prairie, Eight is Enough, Love Boat,* and the *Doris Day Show* to underdeveloped Latin American countries especially, was originally built by the ABC network during the 1960s. By the end of the decade the distribution network comprised sixty-eight stations operating in twenty-seven countries. By the early 1970s, the FCC (U.S. regulatory agency) had limited the foreign holdings of the U.S. networks; moreover, it was no longer profitable for them to be involved in distribution since the networks were no longer producing the majority of their programming. Worldvision and Taft Broadcasting joined hands and are currently looking forward to the coming of coloured televison to many key Latin American areas, which will help the market for reissuing reruns and will undoubtedly raise the price for programs.

Taft Broadcasting also owns and operates sixteen television and radio stations in Ohio, New York, Missouri, Pennsylvania, and Alabama. And here's where our story takes a remarkable twist, ultimately juxtaposing in outlandish fashion Yogi Bear and Boo Boo with such U.S. luminaries as Jacob Javits and Patrick Moynihan.

In 1976, two pieces of legislation – one U.S. and one Canadian – were passed within months of one another. It must be emphasized (as will be clear later) that neither piece of legislation had anything to do with the other. The U.S. legislation was an amendment to its Income Tax Reform Act – an amendment known as Section 602. This amendment limited the number of business conventions that Americans could attend outside the country and still qualify for tax exemptions covering their expenses. The limit was two per year. In addition, this amendment placed rather strict limitations on what qualified as legitimate per diem expenses, and it imposed necessary forms to be filled out and verified by the conventioneers, called for the attaching of the schedule for business meetings, seminars, etc., and generally made it far less attractive for conventions to be scheduled outside the United States The result was that Canadian hoteliers began losing business, lots of business: close to $100 million per year in cancelled conventions.

Since that time, Canada's government has been trying to get the U.S. legislators to pass an amendment to Section 602, which would exempt Canada from the legislation. After all, in many of the organizations that formerly convened in Canada, at least 20 per cent of the membership was Canadian. According to Tom Fletcher, executive head of the Canadian Government Office of Tourism, most high-ranking officials within the United States concur with Canada's position. The problem, which has kept negotiations deadlocked for nearly four years, arises from one of the most powerful lobby groups in the United States.

Here we must return to that other piece of legislation, this one passed by the Canadian government in 1976-77. Bill c-58 stated that Canadian companies placing advertising on U.S. border TV stations in order to appeal to a Canadian audience would no longer be able to gain tax exemptions for such an expense. The bill was intended to encourage Canadian companies to advertise on Canadian stations. The resulting repatriated revenue has helped Canadian broadcasters, especially newer stations such as CKVU in Vancouver, CITV in Edmonton, CKND in Winnipeg, CITY-TV in Toronto, and the Global Network. But, of course, the thirteen U.S. border broadcasters felt extemely miffed by this Canadian tax law. Until that time, about $20 million a year in Canadian advertising revenue was flowing into their pockets. (This amount, by the way, was actually a mere pittance in terms of their combined coffers, and since the bill went into effect the

U.S. border broadcasters have made up for the lost revenue by selling more ad time in their own local markets. In terms of Canadian broadcasters, however, the $20 million a year represented ten per cent of total Canadian advertising revenues and more than the net after-tax profits of Canada's entire private television sector.)

So the powerful U.S. broadcasting lobby machine was rolled into place. It seized upon the Canadian effort to negotiate an exemption from Section 602 (regarding convention business) and has tried to link the two separate issues – lobbying for a trade-off. What the U.S. broadcasters are saying, in effect, is: "We won't let our legislators change Section 602 (worth $100 million per year to Canada) until you change Bill C-58 and give us back 'our' $20 million per year."

Two of the thirteen U.S. border stations most affected by Bill C-58, and the strongest (financially and politically), are in Washington state and New York state. The two New York senators, Javits and Moynihan, are in full agreement with the broadcasting lobby, probably because several of the border TV stations are in their state and one of them is owned by (you guessed it) Taft Broadcasting, perhaps the most formidable member of the lobby. According to one Canadian government official, the whole mess would end if Taft Broadcasting convinced the other members of the lobby to back down.

But so far that doesn't seem to have happened. Lately the broadcasting lobby is calling for reprisals against Canada's filmmaking, recording, and other cultural industries – the products of these industries would be restricted from entering the United States under alterations in trade laws. There are many ironies to this whole situation, including the parallels it contains with the ghastly Canadian Co-operation Project of the 1940s and 1950s. But clearly, conglomerates like Taft Broadcasting like to have it both ways: making Canadians into complacently imagineered spectators and financiers of the corporate brand of culture.

Just recently Robert Duffy reported for *The Toronto Star* that Taft has cut the number of theme areas in the park down to four, eliminating Frontier Canada until possibly 1982, "if all goes well." As predicted by the opposition, there is a major scramble for land sites all around the park by hoteliers, moteliers, and fast-food outlets. And the developers of Canada's Wonderland have put in a rezoning application for a twenty-thousand-seat amphitheatre just north of the park on Major Mackenzie Drive. Negotiations are already underway with a U.S. theatrical and concert booking agency for headliner events.

"Once upon a time," says a promotional pamphlet put out by Canada's Wonderland, "in a place not far away, a magic spell was cast. A mountain with a beautiful waterfall appeared in an enchanted land that is everything dreams are made of. A land we call Canada's Wonderland. Come climb the mystical mountain...." For many, that great white mountain, which will soon glisten majestically against the Ontario sky, will undoubtedly come to resemble a massive gift dropped by the great American Eagle.

(1980)

☐ Capitalism, Despair,
and the Media Machine

THE OTHER DAY, while riding on the streetcar, I saw one of the most disturbing ads I have ever seen in my life. It wasn't what you might expect: no blatant, lurid sexism; no lush depiction of female pulchritude tempting passengers to buy some geegaw or another. Rather, it was an ad for a facial moisturizing cream, with the slogan: "Because Beauty *Really Is* Only Skin-Deep ..." The sharp cynicism of those words struck me like a slap on the face.

Somehow, that sort of cynicism seems increasingly to characterize the media messages that so bombard us these days. At times I begin to wonder if all sense of inner values, human ethics, and principles is being steadily eroded by a Media Machine geared entirely to the profit motive. What the media messages seem to say, over and over like a litany or mantra, is that the only thing that matters in life is the glamour of wealth.

That message is clearly present in ads, whose beautiful people look out at me with a kind of pitying disdain for my inept, insufficient being. What their superior gaze seems to say is: "I'm Okay, you're not." I am meant to look into the space of the ad and see its lavishness, its luxury, as the true measure of successful living ... and thus the measure of my own personal failure. The glamorous ads hold up to me the standard by which I should judge my life and my self. I am meant to feel envious, worthless, and motivated – all at the same time: envious of the glamorous people, worthless because of my own obvious shortcomings, and motivated to change all that by buying something.

John Berger, who brilliantly analyzed this function of advertising images in his book *Ways of Seeing* (Penguin, 1972), writes:

Glamour cannot exist without personal social envy being a common and widespread emotion. The industrial society which has moved towards democracy and then stopped half way is the ideal society for generating such an emotion. The pursuit of individual happiness has been acknowledged as a universal right. Yet the existing social conditions make the individual feel powerless. He lives in the contraction between what he is and what he would like to be. Either he then becomes fully conscious of the contradiction and its causes, and so joins the political struggle for a full democracy which entails, amongst other things, the overthrow of capitalism; or else he lives, continually subject to an envy which, compounded with his sense of powerlessness, dissolves into recurrent day-dreams.

While Berger limits his discussion to the realm of advertising, it seems clear that glamour, and the envy it is meant to inspire, are not at all confined to that realm alone. Increasingly, they are evident in much of the non-advertising content of the media as well. This is especially the case as the journalistic raison d'être of the North American media disappears, giving way to life-style coverage of the rich and famous.

Television is especially geared to this glamorous function, or function of glamour: partly because of its roots in the entertainment (movie) industry rather than in journalism, partly because of its strictly commercial business structure on this continent. We easily forget that its real purpose is *not* to deliver shows to us, but to deliver *us* to sponsors. In the North American context of corporate-sponsored broadcasting (which includes PBS and the CBC) any TV show that does not deliver the right demographics in terms of desirable audiences for the sponsors' messages will be cancelled. And "desirable demographics" means purchasing-power.

Essentially, all the mainstream media must be seen in this light: not as delivering content to us, but as delivering us to advertisers. Desirable demographics is the bottom line in the media machine, and virtually every decision about content flows from this bottom line: will this particular article / program / item appeal to the audience our sponsors want? (Any discussion about media censorship / self-censorship must begin with this fact of business: the selling of audiences to sponsors. It is so basic an operating premise that editors / producers are often unconscious of self-censoring according to its dictates.)

The least controversial and most predictably successful media content, as well as the most assured draw for audiences with purchasing-power, is content that enshrines celebrity, glamour, and wealthy life-styles. In the glamorous sets and fashions and possessions that characterize so many TV shows, in the exciting jet-set activities and scintillating gossip and astronomical incomes that are the content of talk shows and the entertainment pages of our newspapers, in the sheer excessiveness of the celebration of wealth that is the primary message of the mainstream media, there emerges a particular definition of "success" by which we are meant to measure our lives.

In other words, the media serve the function of determining our daydreams. They define what is desirable for personal happiness and success, and beyond that they set the limits for the aspirations of society-at-large. These standards and limits posed by the media are now almost entirely superficial: a measuring of existence totally in terms of products, life-styles, and accoutrements.

Of course, ads have always posited this limited view of human existence. Under capitalism, that is their function: to enshrine consumption as the reason for living. But in earlier eras other social institutions – the nuclear family, church, school, community, the arts – were viable structures that held up for us larger human values to give meaning to our lives, greater standards by which to measure personal success, wider dimensions for human aspiration. Now, to a very great degree, the media have taken over the roles of those social institutions. This is especially true of television, which for millions of people is church-school-community-arts all rolled into one.

In many ways, it is to our benefit that the traditional social institutions are crumbling under the impetus of change. For many segments of society, the traditional structures have been straitjackets of oppression. But in that interval between the demise of the old structures and the rise of new alternatives, we face a period of confusion and doubt: a lack of what Toronto Jungian analyst Marion Woodman calls the social "ritual containers" that necessarily encompass our personal lives. Without such structures, our lives are vulnerable and private. The danger I see is that the media have stepped in to fill that breach, to assume the roles and even the power of the various social institutions that once shared among themselves the whole range of socializing functions.

This great post-World War II transformation of society needs to be carefully examined. What are the implications for a society in which communal experience is now largely mediated? (What we tend to have in common are the TV shows we watch, the movies we've seen, the millions of ads we've been exposed to, etc.) What are the implications for a society in which the media have more impact than any other social institution? And since the mainstream media increasingly enshrine glamour and wealth as the measure of existence, we must also ask: What are the implications for a society in which the larger human values and aspirations are subsumed under the rubric of purchasing? Not only are those values and aspirations trivialized – "Beauty *really is* only skin-deep" – they are also strictly confined to serve capitalism's purposes. (If you want to scare the pants off your vulnerable psyche, read James Altas's article "Beyond Demographics" in the October 1984 issue of *The Atlantic:* a detailed update on psychographics research used by advertisers.)

As I see it, one result of this great postwar transformation is a widespread despair throughout the society. People *need* a sense of larger meaning for their lives, hunger for a real sense of human connectedness and face-to-face community, long to feel that their lives make a difference, will have counted for something in the larger scheme of things. But without the "ritual containers" that once made possible the expression and experience of these larger human values and aspirations, the meaning of life becomes ... shopping.

The despair (often unconscious) that results from this state of things is quite useful to capitalism. We attempt to fill the void within, this lack of larger meaning, through a surfeit of consumer products which each promise to fulfil us in some way. And the Media Machine continually reassures us that *this is* the meaning of life. Thus, a vicious circle is perpetuated: the void remains unfilled, consumption does not alleviate the hunger, despair returns to send us out in search of another purchase that may bring meaning to our life.

"Who can doubt the role of the mass media in depoliticizing the public?" states British filmmaker Peter Watkins in his scathing critique of the media in the October 1984 issue of *Cinema Canada.* "The relationship we have at the moment with the mass media is one of total and absolute subservience, generally speaking." It is this subservience that will be altered as we create new social structures, new "ritual containers" that reaffirm humanity and reclaim powers that are meant to reside in real community interaction, not in mediated major markets.

(1985)

◻ CanCon Conundrum

THERE IS SOMETHING horribly ironic about CBC President Pierre Juneau's recent speech to the Canadian Conference of the Arts in Ottawa. As reported by Sid Adilman in *The Toronto Star* (October 18, 1985), Juneau, lamenting the Americanization of Canadian television, revealed some ghastly details from a recent study of 1984 programming practices on English-language Canadian TV stations and networks, both publicly and privately owned. "Only twenty-eight per cent of all English-language television (including pay-TV) in Canada is Canadian," he told the conference. "In prime time (excluding pay-TV) from seven PM to eleven PM, only twenty-six per cent of all programs available on Canadian screens are Canadian."

The worst figures come from the area of television drama, where only one-and-a-half per cent of the 17,500 hours of dramatic programming aired in 1984 was Canadian – leading Juneau to state: "In English, for every hour of Canadian drama on Canadian TV and cable, there are more than forty-five hours of foreign drama (predominantly American). We're outnumbered forty-five to one." Rising to the occasion, Juneau declared: "We have abandoned our national stage to another society. Yet all the principles in our legislation, in our official statements, in the conclusions of royal commissions in the last fifty years emphasize opposite objectives."

The irony here is that if there is any one person responsible for the dismal, Americanized state of Canadian television, it is probably Pierre Juneau himself. As the first chairman of the Canadian Radio-Television Telecommunications Commission from 1968 to mid-1975, he presided over a broadcasting regulatory agency that simply failed to regulate, thereby setting a pattern by which private broadcasters would continue to Americanize their schedules, reap huge profits and further consolidate through mergers, contribute virtually zip to Canadian production, and receive nothing more than a rhetorical slap on the wrist from the CRTC for their cultural irresponsibility.

Certainly that is the view of Herschel Hardin in his book *Closed Circuits: The Sellout of Canadian Television* (Douglas & McIntyre, 1985). Tracing the embroiled politics of Canadian television from the creation of the CRTC in 1968 up through the pay-TV fiasco, Hardin documents one bungled CRTC decision after another, exposing a regulatory agency seemingly in bed with the private sector (though perhaps politically unconscious of its position) and evidently unready to change the cozy relationship. It is a bitter and caustic book, a litany of sellouts and cultural scandals, written by one of Canada's most knowledgeable broadcasting critics. It is also a timely publication, given the current flurry of broadcasting task forces, CBC budget cuts, and an apparently ahistorical milieu in which to consider the Canadian telecommunications future. Finally, though, *Closed Circuits* is most welcome for its usefulness: it is filled with revealing statements from CRTC hearings, documents, correspondence – the kind of material gleaned from years of researching, attending hearings, and actively trying to intervene in the regulatory process. As founding president of the Association for Public Broadcasting in British Columbia and as general manager of Capital Cable Co-operative, Hardin has well over a decade of personal experience to draw upon in his provocative exposé of regulatory betrayal, private broadcasters' hypocrisy, and the general sellout of Canadian television's potential.

For example, if CBC President Juneau wished to understand how it is that Canadian prime-time came to be so deluged by U.S. programming, he need only read Herschel Hardin's second chapter, "The Canadian-Content Regulations of 1970." There he would find that a man named Pierre Juneau, as chairman of the CRTC, was a significant player in the high-rolling game of Americanizing the airwaves.

By the time of the CRTC's creation it was already apparent that Canadian private broadcasters were taking the easiest and cheapest way out of their programming responsibilities by simply filling their schedules with U.S. shows. CTV, the private English-language network, had become a skilled bidder for Hollywood product, while contributing minimally to Canadian production. On private radio stations, Canadian musical talent was similarly unheard of, or from.

Juneau and the CRTC, in the first blush of their regulatory duties, decided to alter this programming imbalance.

On February 12, 1970, the CRTC "proposed that Canadian television fill sixty per cent of its prime-time hours with Canadian programs and that thirty per cent of all music on radio stations would have to be Canadian." Following this preliminary announcement, the private-sector broadcasters immediately hit the fan – going into high gear to lobby against this outrageous suggestion. (Never mind that a 40 per cent quota for foreign programming was incredibly generous in comparison to Britain's 14 per cent restriction on TV imports, or the United States' estimated 2 per cent *de facto* quota on foreign programming.) The Canadian private sector screamed like a cat caught in the blender: raising spectres of bankruptcy, of an "electronic curtain," or of their hallowed schedules being reduced to wrestling shows featuring Yukon Eric and musical numbers like "Squaws Along the Yukon."

By the time of the official announcement on Canadian content scarcely three months later (May 22, 1970), Juneau's CRTC was demonstrating "a willingness of the commission to meet the commercial broadcasters halfway."

Though the CRTC stood firm on the 30 per cent Canadian music rule for radio stations (which, by the way, is why the Canadian music Juno Awards are so called), it allowed AM stations to count their 30 per cent Canadian content over the whole broadcast day rather than in strict four-hour periods: a practice that must have led to a lot of late-night Canadian scheduling at first. In television the CRTC upheld (for a time, as we shall see) its allowance of 40 per cent non-Canadian programming for prime-time – defined as 6:30 PM to 11:30 PM. Of the allowed two hours of foreign material each night, only three-quarters, or ninety minutes, could be from the United States. But in the same breath Juneau's CRTC ruled that TV stations could calculate their content averages for each calendar quarter rather than every four weeks. Even worse, the CRTC gave the private CTV network (which originally was to meet the 60 per cent Canadian prime-time requirement by September 1, 1971) a thirteen-month extension to October 1, 1972 – more than two years away.

And that concession was quite probably the one that broke the ruling's back. The private sector continued over the next two years to fight tooth and nail against such limitations on their licences. Hardin writes: "By April 1972, the commission had drawn back so far in forced retreat on Canadian content in television as to make the 1970 'landmark' hearings almost meaningless, except for the image they projected."

By 1972 the CRTC had reduced the scheduled prime-time Canadian content requirement from 60 per cent to 50 per cent, at the same time generously extending its definition of prime-time by an hour – from six PM to twelve AM – which would allow suppertime and late-night news to make up the bulk of Canadian programming. Further, as Hardin says:

> The requirement that only three-quarters of imported programming could be American (in prime-time as well as generally) was eliminated. Under the new formula, all of the peak viewing hours of 7 p.m. to 10 p.m. could then be filled with American imports, rather than just 90 minutes ... a wholesale change backwards. Moreover, the basis on which content averages were to be calculated, already adjusted from every four weeks to each calendar quarter, had been further broadened to a whole year. This would allow stations to lever more of the Canadian content requirement into the slack summer months.

Any regulatory agency and / or country that allows 50 per cent of its televised schedule to be foreign must be not only crazy but also prepared to withstand the shock of figures like these: in 1984, of 5,500 hours of news specials on Canadian TV, 54 per cent were foreign-originated; of 10,400 hours of all variety, music, and quiz / game programs, 25 per cent were Canadian; 47 per cent of programs in all categories were from U.S. sources; and (to repeat) of 17,500 hours of dramatic programming, 370 hours (or 1.5 per cent) were Canadian.

"The solution is not to erect electronic curtains," Juneau declared to his Canadian Conference of the Arts audience. "No serious person advocates closing down American signals already pouring into our system. The solution is production." After reading Herschel Hardin's book, one realizes that we've heard it all before, especially from that other Pierre Juneau who, fifteen years earlier, could have changed everything.

(1985)

☐ Roland Barthes and
   The NFB Connection

Since myth robs language of something, why not rob myth? All that is
needed is to use it as the departure point for a third semiological chain,
to take its signification as the first term of a second myth.
                                        – Roland Barthes, *Mythologies* (1957)

IF THERE ARE TIMES when structuralism and semiology seem like
foreign imports, critical methodologies to which we must adjust and
adapt ourselves but which emanate from distant cultures, it comes as
a rather pleasant surprise to learn that early on in his illustrious
career, Roland Barthes –a major figure in French structuralism and
author of *Mythologies, Writing Degree Zero, S/Z, Pleasure of the Text*
– made a film for the National Film Board.

Of Sport and Men, an hour-long black-and-white production, was
made in 1961 in Montreal. I heard about the film only recently,
through a teacher of cultural studies at the University of Toronto,
who invited me to view it with his class. He, in turn, had learned of it
through colleagues exploring the sociology of sport. I mention these
contacts only to illustrate that the film has had a reputation and a
viewership among sociological circles, but appears to have escaped
notice from film studies practitioners.

The film is fascinating on several levels, and it certainly deserves
to be rescued from the impending oblivion which may be in store for
it, since, according to executive producer Guy Glover, *Of Sport and
Men* has been withdrawn from the NFB catalogue for 1977-78. There
is always the hope that a deluge of requests for booking might avert
the archival abyss.

The credits on the film itself call *Of Sport and Men* a film "by

Roland Barthes." The late Hubert Aquin is named as producer, Guy Glover as executive producer, but no director, writer, or editor credits appear on the film. Robert Russell is given a translator credit, and Al Bachulus is listed for music. (A librarian at the NFB Reference Library checked the files and found Barthes is listed as writer for the film, but director and editor remained unnamed. To find out the extent of Barthes's involvement in the production and the story behind its making, it seemed worthwhile to contact Guy Glover, who kindly sorted out some of the confusions, shared his recollections about the people involved, and explained the larger context within which *Of Sport and Men* was made.

During the late 1950s, a series called "Comparisons" was initiated at the Board. Made for television viewing, the series, in its first phase, was "an attempt to popularize certain sociological themes" through what were called prestige productions: high-budget hour-long films involving well-known experts as commentators. Between 1959 and 1961, four such films were made: *Four Families* (1959), *Four Religions* (1960), *Four Teachers* (1961), and *Courtship* (1961). Each production involved on-location shooting in four different countries; a famous expert in the appropriate field scripted the commentary and appeared on-camera for studio sequences bridging the location footage. For each film there was a team of at least five directors and crews, with Ian MacNeill responsible for all the studio shooting and a different director sent to each of the four countries being compared. Thus, for example, *Four Families* explored the daily living habits of one family in Japan, another in India, one in France, and one in Canada, with Margaret Mead providing the commentary in the studio.

Each of these four films was first released for television as an English production, and only a year or so later was there a French version made. Hubert Aquin was involved in the preparation of the French versions. After 1961 the "Comparisons" series went into its second phase, during which the hour-long format was abandoned and fifteen half-hour films were produced, also for television. In between these two phases came *Of Sport and Men*. It was given the "Comparisons" logo, but it is quite unlike its predecessors in the series in conception, production, and style.

According to Glover, after the four "prestige productions" had been completed, Hubert Aquin proposed his idea for *Of Sport and Men*: an hour-long film comparing a national sport in each of several countries. There was no more money for another high-budget film of this length, but it was not Aquin's intention to do any of the expensive location-shooting that had characterized the other films. Instead, he argued that the film he envisioned could be made quite inexpensively by purchasing stock library footage from a variety of sources like the BBC and U.S. newsreel companies and by using material from the NFB's own library. Glover recalls him saying, "You could shoot for a year and not have a better selection of material." As well, Aquin's conception of the film did not necessitate studio sequences, but he did most definitely want the expert he had in mind, Roland Barthes, involved in the production.

Glover remembers that Aquin, former film critic for *L'Authorité* and a producer for Radio-Canada, was "a devoted follower of the work of Roland Barthes," whose essays on culture were being discussed enthusiastically in Quebec's intellectual circles at the time. Once the idea for *Of Sport and Men* was approved, library footage of famous sporting events was purchased from several countries and a special editor, Robert Russell, was brought in to work with Aquin. Glover says, "They were very excited about the film, and so saturated with Roland Barthes's approach to analyzing culture and sport that they may have constructed the film according to it."

Barthes was brought over from Paris for a week to write the commentary. He was presented with a cutting copy of the film, a shot list with timings for each sequence, and given space at the Board for multiple viewings at an editing bench. Aquin, Russell, and Barthes worked closely together for the week, preparing two versions of the commentary so that an English and a French version could be released for television simultaneously, a departure from the usual procedure in the series. Robert Russell translated from Barthes's French, a task that Glover recognized as being "almost impossible because of his richly nuanced style." Accordingly, "The two commentaries are really quite different," although *Le sport et les hommes* and *Of Sport and Men* apparently coincide visually in every detail.

When asked whether Barthes involved himself in other productions being made at the Board during his stay, Glover explained that Barthes was quite interested in the Quebec filmmakers and probably spent most of his off-hours in their company. Many of them were familiar with and interested in Barthes's critical work (*Le Degré Zéro de l'Ecriture* was published in 1953, and *Mythologies* in 1957). "Certainly [Claude] Jutra knew Barthes's writings, and Barthes knew of Jutra who had made a film (*Anna la bonne*, 1959) in Paris with Truffaut."

Within the credits for *La lutte*, made in 1961 by Jutra, Michel Brault, Claude Fournier, and Marcel Carrière, there is a printed *hommage* to Roland Barthes. This, plus the coincidence of the similar production date for *Of Sport and Men* and *La lutte*, warranted a phone call to Jutra, who confirmed that "Barthes happened to be passing through Montreal during the time *La lutte* was being discussed, and since wrestling very much interested him as a sport, he was invited to come along during the filming." *La lutte* was shot "without a script or anything" in one evening, with "ten cameras and eight Nagras" – a kind of spontaneous mad-cap event in which "Barthes was just there, hanging around." The film "was a hit in France among the intellectual circles," and the *hommage* was included in the credits "because he and all of us so enjoyed the evening." Although Jutra did not imply that Barthes was any more than a guest on the shooting of *La lutte*, it would certainly be interesting to think about the film in light of Barthes's well-known analysis, "The World of Wrestling," published in *Mythologies*.

The commentary for *Of Sport and Men* is a continuation of the kind of semiological investigation into cultural conventions evident in *Mythologies*. Within the "Comparisons" series the film is an anomaly, indeed, a return to a past tradition of filmmaking at the Board – the compilation film. While ostensibly a vehicle for Barthes's perceptive analysis of five different national sports – bullfighting, Formula car-racing, the Tour de France bicycling event, hockey, and soccer (or "English football" as it is called in the film) – there is also a underlying suggestion of the kind of interrogation of the image itself for which semiology in its couplings with film theory has proved so useful.

Each of the five sections is strikingly different in editing pace, selection of consistent camera style to characterize and shape the material of a section, music, extent and use of cutaways to develop involvement between spectator and sport, the amount of commentary in proportion to use of wild-track sound, and length. If, as Guy Glover claims, Barthes was presented with a *fait accompli* and was not at liberty to alter or make suggestions about the order of edited shots or their lengths, then seemingly the structure of the edited images would impose its own limitations and propose its own conventions for Barthes's analysis. A careful exploration of *Of Sport and Men* as an editing exercise, "a film made totally in the cutting-room," might reveal the visual structure Barthes had to work with – the filmic complications that placed him at one remove from sport as spectacle as the subject of analysis, and confronted him with sport as filmed spectacle instead.

Glover describes *Of Sport and Men* as "a labour of love" for its small team of filmmakers. If rather unlike any of the other "Comparisons" films in the series, at least in its budget and production style, it distinguishes itself by its grounding in a theoretical base by which such comparisons can be made. It is to be hoped that there will be an increasing audience for *Le sport et les hommes* and *Of Sport and Men* in Canada, the source of Roland Barthes's NFB connection.

(1977)

☐ Voices of Authority

SOMETIMES IT'S THE small "filler" items in the newspaper that mentally assume banner-headline proportions in one's consciousness. I came across one the other day that has been bothering me ever since. This is what it said: "According to the Directors' Guild of America, of the 7,332 films produced in the United States between 1949 and 1979, only fourteen were directed by women." That's 0.2 per cent of the total. That's one film every two years or so. To put it even more graphically, you could actually sit down for a twenty-four-hour viewing session, see every one of those films, and still have time for a three-hour lunchbreak.

Of course, you don't have to belong to the Directors' Guild of America to direct a film, and women have made hundreds of films outside the mainstream represented by the D.G. of A. Nevertheless, when it comes to gaining access to the corridors of power in the U.S. film industry (which also means having your film shown in neighbourhood movie theatres), women have pretty much been kept out on the sidewalk.

The situation hasn't been much better for female scriptwriters in the United States even during a time of "heightened consciousness." During the period of April 1982 through March 1983, the combined feature-length production output of all three commercial TV networks, the ten most important independent film studios, and the seven Hollywood major studios included less than 15 per cent scripted by women. Not surprisingly, the women's division of the Writers' Guild of America has called for a federal investigation into industry hiring practices.

Canada is hardly any better. Between 1968 and 1980, of the total of

260 features made with the backing of the Canadian Film Development Corporation (a government agency now called Telefilm Canada), 11 were directed by women. That's 4.2 per cent. And of the forty-
six feature films financially assisted by the CFDC between 1980 and
1982, only one was written solely by women. The most recent available figures on Canada Council grants to filmmakers indicate that
women received a mere 16 per cent of the total allotment.

Given statistics like this, it's hard to stay cognizant of the fact that
women actually constitute the majority of the population in the
world – in Canada, 51 per cent. Indeed, that basic fact is defied just
about everywhere you turn in the media world. Whether it's the number of acting roles in prime-time TV drama (63 per cent male on
CBC-TV, 66 per cent male on U.S. TV networks as recently as 1981), or
the number of on-camera reporters for TV news organizations
(roughly 90 per cent are men), or the number of TV drama writers' contracts issued (for CBC in 1984, 21 per cent went to women writers), or
the number of managing editors for daily newspapers (in Canada, only
one is a woman), there's no getting around the fact that the media are
male-dominated, and markedly so. Further documentation on this
issue is available from ACTRA's National Committee on Women's
Issues, based in Toronto. The committee has been gathering such
information since it was formed in 1980. I mention these statistics
now, in mid-1985, because they provide a useful context for two specific historical events.

The year 1985 marks the end of the International Decade For
Women (1976-85) established by the United Nations. In its "World
Plan of Action" drawn up for the ten years, the UN wisely noted the
importance of the mass media in potentially changing prejudices and
stereotypes about women. In particular, the plan recognized that
these stereotypes would not be changed in, or through, the media
until women themselves were working in significant numbers in all
aspects of the media industry. The plan stated: "Women should be
appointed in greater numbers in media management, decision-making and other capacities as editors, columnists, reporters, producers
and the like, and should encourage the critical review, within the
media, of the image of women projected."

The "World Plan of Action for the Decade for Women" was unani-
mously accepted by more than a hundred governments, including
Canada's. As that decade draws to a close, we need updated statistics
in every area of the mass media – from grant-giving agencies to print

publishing, radio, TV, and filmmaking – in order to see what, if anything, has changed.

One set of recent statistics seems particularly suggestive that, in general, women in the media have made no great leap forward. The figures come from the Canadian advertising industry, and, in mass media terms, you can't get much more mainstream than that. Virtually every TV ad ever made depends, in part, on a specific production technique picked up from documentary filmmaking. An unseen narrator talks over the visuals. In documentary, this tradition is tellingly referred to as "voice-of-God" narration – a term that reveals the assumed credibility and unquestionable authority of the speaker. In advertising, the use of an unseen narrator is (less pompously) referred to as "voice-of-authority." But you won't often hear a woman's voice in that role. In fact, according to a recent joint study by ACTRA and the Canadian Advertising Advisory Board, for the period of September 1982 to August 1983 women were used as the "voice-of-authority" in only 12 per cent of Canadian TV commercials and 28 per cent of radio commercials. The "explanation" for this practice (or should I say, lack of practice) is that women's voices do not convey authority.

The implications of this mind-set extend far beyond the issue of advertising, hiring practices, or even voice-overs. We are confronted here with the basic notion of "authority" itself – how it is perceived, defined, and used – as well as the central question of who speaks, and who does not, in our society. Since the mass media, in the larger sense, "give voice to" individual expression, we are then dealing with the politics of imposed silence: a politics brilliantly analyzed in Adrienne Rich's *On Lies, Secrets, and Silence* (W.W. Norton, 1972) and Tillie Olsen's *Silences* (Dell, 1978). While I am tempted to fill several pages with passages from both works, as well as from Frantz Fanon's *The Wretched of the Earth* (Grove Press, 1968), which deals with the same issue, but from a Third World perspective, I will include only one passage from Rich: "If we have learned anything in our coming to language out of silence, it is that what has been kept unspoken, therefore unspeakable, in us is what is most threatening to the patriarchal order in which men control, first women, then all who can be defined and exploited as 'other.'"

Which brings me to the second historical event being celebrated in 1985. This years marks the beginning of the second decade of operation for the National Film Board's Studio D – the women's filmmaking unit founded by Kathleen Shannon. After ten years of work and an estimated seventy completed films, Studio D has become the most exciting and relevant department in the NFB. In terms of bookings, director Bonnie Sherr Klein's *Not a Love Story* was the most popular film in the whole NFB catalogue for 1981-1982. Terri Nash's *If You Love This Planet* earned that distinction for 1982-1983.

In part, Studio D's films are successful and popular because they are in tune with grassroots concerns. "Too many people have no idea who they are making films for," executive producer Shannon told *Ms* magazine in 1984. "We know our audience." Studio D has established vital contacts with women's groups around the country, and many of its chosen film topics arise from this two-way communication.

Studio D is the only group of women filmmakers in the world with continuous funding to make films. That funding may be minimal by Hollywood (or even Hollywood-North) standards, but important work has been done despite the limitations. As Kathleen Shannon told *Chatelaine*: "The money that the Canadian Film Development Corporation spent on the making of the commercial film *Meatballs* – $1,800,000 – is more than our yearly budget. For the same cost, we produced eight films, including *Not a Love Story, If You Love This Planet, The Way It Is* (the story of a child adapting to divorce), *Dream of A Free Country: A Message From Nicaraguan Women*, and *Attention – Women At Work* (about career options for adolescent girls)."

The films made by Studio D rely on traditional documentary techniques rather than on innovative or experimental film forms. In this sense, they are solidly within the mainstream of conventional filmmaking practice instead of challenging the ideology implicit in those conventions. But Shannon's view on this makes good sense. "I think men tend to put form before content. Women have been putting content before form because there's so damn much that we haven't had a chance to say."

Taking that chance, Studio D's filmmakers (both staff and freelance) have dealt with some of the most controversial issues of our time: abortion (Gail Singer's *Abortion: Stories from North and South*), pornography (Klein's *Not A Love Story*), nuclear war (Nash's *If You Love This Planet*), revolution (Shannon and Ginny Stikeman's *Dream Of A Free Country: A Message From Nicaraguan Women*). Even more important, they have dared to speak from an identifiable point of view, rather than hide behind documentary's traditional stance of "objectivity." According to Shannon, "To present the truth as you passionately perceive it is the only way to make good films."

And it's precisely here that the work of Studio D distinguishes itself. By consciously and overtly taking positions on issues, by turning to women for their views, by training and using female film crews, and by consistently using female voice-overs for script narration, Studio D effectively challenges not only the notion that women have no "authority," but also what Adrienne Rich has identified as the "culture of passivity" assigned to women.

"We're not trying to catch up to men in film," Kathleen Shannon has said. "We're trying to create something new, a different order." As Bonnie Sherr Klein told *The Toronto Star*: "Women really do see things differently from men. It's as if women wear glasses that expose the fact that the emperor has no clothes. Perhaps it's because women have been outside the framework of power for so long, they are able to view the world differently."

This belief in the authority of women's perspective, and this commitment to creating a "different order" are evident in Studio D's latest production – *Speaking Our Peace*. Combining the directorial talents of Bonnie Sherr Klein and Terri Nash, with the scriptwriting skills of Gloria Demers (*Behind the Veil*), the film examines the far-reaching network of militarism as it destructively manifests itself in economic, environmental, political, and even philosophical terms. Simultaneously, *Speaking Our Peace* weaves an alternative order by highlighting the peace work of Canadian women activists such as Margaret Laurence, Dr. Ursula Franklin, Muriel Duckworth, Kathleen Wallace-Deering, Dr. Rosalie Bertell, and Solanges Vincent.

Through films like this, Studio D directly challenges women to own their authority and emerge out of silence and passivity. The work of these filmmakers can be seen as completely oppositional to mainstream pornography (from the Latin: "the writing of prostitutes") in all its forms – whether it's the images of women bound and gagged in the more vicious media, or dutifully mute and manipulated in commercials: obediently following the voice-of-authority / voice-of-God.

(1985)

❒ Metaphorically Speaking: The Great White Screen

THE CONCEPTION behind a project is always central to that project's unfolding. That is the power of metaphor. To give an example, if you conceive of your coming summer canoe trip as an attempt to get into a Guinness book of records for distance covered by canoe in two weeks, that is undoubtedly how your vacation will unfold, with or without the Guinness award at the end. A competing metaphor for the trip would, of course, structure it entirely differently: as an indulgence in lethargy, for instance, or a quiet, meditative meandering. Thus, any project has behind it a central structuring metaphor. This is true even of a nation.

In 1972 Margaret Atwood published a book that attempted to articulate the central metaphor behind the project of Canadian nationhood. It is worth quoting this passage from *Survival: A Thematic Guide to Canadian Literature* (Anansi):

> I'd like to begin with a sweeping generalization and argue that every country or culture has a single unifying and informing symbol at its core.... The symbol, then – be it a word, phrase, idea, image, or all of these – functions like a system of beliefs (it *is* a system of beliefs, though not always a formal one) which holds the country together and helps the people in it to co-operate for common ends. Possibly the symbol for America is The Frontier.... The corresponding symbol for England is perhaps The Island ... The central symbol for Canada ... is undoubtedly Survival, *la Survivance*.

From there, Atwood brilliantly reasoned that "a preoccupation with one's survival is necessarily also a preoccupation with the obstacles to that survival," leading to a view of Canada as a "collective victim" that could choose among four Basic Victim Positions, with the last two as dynamic positions that refuse the victim role itself.

But poets are not the only ones who offer metaphors of nationhood, and in a bureaucratized and technological world their vision is often eclipsed, metaphorically speaking. A year before Atwood's *Survival* appeared in print, someone else was articulating a very different metaphor for Canadian nationhood, a metaphor that (as Atwood tells us) encompasses a specific system of beliefs.

On March 9, 1971, Pierre Juneau (then chairman of the CRTC, later president of the CBC) delivered a speech to the Canadian Club, an august body of corporate movers and shakers. He told them:

> It seems that in order to truly grasp and occupy one's own national space, it is necessary to effect some kind of graphic apprehension, even to imagine a geometric form, which can be readily conjured to mind and is meaningful. To this end, Great Britain saw itself as an island, and France as a hexagon. Should we be thinking of Canada as a Cinerama screen, perhaps the largest on the planet?

In the context of the entire speech, there is little reason to doubt that the metaphor was intended as ironic. Juneau was speaking on the theme of culture and the necessity for producing Canadian content. And yet, there is a little *frisson* in the metaphor as well, as if it were on the edge of being a serious proposal, a rhetorical turn of phrase that follows upon those other metaphors of nationhood for Great Britain and France.

It is even harder to deny this little buzz of excitement in the metaphor when we consider that between 1968 and 1971, the first three years of Juneau's chairmanship, the CRTC had licensed three hundred cable-TV outlets across Canada, setting in place the giant screen envisioned in the metaphor. Might his corporate listeners, many of them involved in television, not have detected both an irony and a seriousness in the metaphor, given such factors? After all, the construction of this giant screen was giving them an excellent rate of return on investment.

Visually, Juneau's metaphor conjures up the vast, snowy landscape that is the North. Thus one might think that the metaphor, like that for Great Britain or for France, has something to do with the land, or the shape of the land that is Canada. But Juneau has specifically, and purposely, chosen a technological device, a movie screen, as his metaphor for nationhood. And it is not just any movie screen that he is suggesting, but a Cinerama screen stretching its white expanse widely across our imaginations. Juneau even hints that we think of it as "the largest on the planet," outdistancing every other possible screen in its dimensions. Since Canada does not claim to have the greatest land mass on the planet, it becomes even more obvious that Juneau's metaphor for the nation is not rooted in the boundaries of the land, but in something else. That something else becomes more clear as we study the implications of the metaphor.

The technological function of any viewing screen is to be a blank, a surface of nothingness, upon which can be projected images that originate from a distance source, the projector. Notice that Juneau does not include this latter device in his metaphor, but only the receptive screen. To equate the country with a Cinerama screen, and the largest on the planet, is to recognize that it plays the role not of originating any images, for after all, a screen cannot do that, but only of receiving the projected images that originate elsewhere. This screen metaphor is thus a metaphor of a nothingness, a blank, waiting to be filled. It is, for a nation, the complete void of identity. A good screen, to function properly, must be kept clean, for any telltale marks on its surface, any stains or streaks that mark the pristine blank, interfere with the clarity of the images projected onto it. A good screen is merely the technological "ground" on which images from elsewhere can play.

We can assume that Juneau was fully aware of these dimensions of his metaphor when he ironically / seriously posited it in 1971. But he also often spoke of the marvels of technology and occasionally posed another metaphor for Canada, this time in full seriousness, as "the most interesting mass-communication laboratory in the world." Should we be surprised, then, that his ironic / serious metaphor has been translated into reality? With its massive, technically sophisticated TV delivery system composed of tiered cable, communications satellites, pay-TV, and superstations, the country *is* that giant screen, the largest on the planet. Metaphors have a way of coming true.

Film critic Kirwan Cox has written: "We create ever-proliferating lines of communication running north and south, and wonder why our identity fails to run east and west." Here we see the full projection apparatus at work: the giant screen does in fact run from east to west, but the projecting line runs north-south, with images originating south of the border and playing across the national screen. Canadian filmmakers and TV producers have difficulty getting their images onto that giant screen. In fact, some of them have to take their work to the giant projector in the south in order to have their images play on the screen in the north.

What Juneau, and (to be fair) almost everyone, failed to see is a situation that is so obvious that it is usually overlooked. There is always a significant lag between hardware implementation and software production. The decision to put hardware in place – in this context, television delivery systems – erects the blank screen upon which imagery or software will play. But once that hardware is in place, there is often nothing immediately available to put on it until indigenous software production gets into gear. This lag between hardware and software creates a temporary vacuum: which is precisely what U.S. corporate endeavour depends on. Indeed, U.S. corporations usually peddle the hardware around the world specifically to create the vacuum, because they have a floodtide of available product that almost immediately flows into every available space. A country has literally to protect that interval, that space between hardware implementation and indigenous software production, or it is flooded by software from outside. But usually the impulse is to get that new technology operating, "on," as fast as possible. And therein is the tragic flaw for nations seduced by the signifiers of "progress," which, under patriarchal capitalism, are always global systems of hardware. In the rush to get the technology in place, nations erect the "screen" but fail to simply let it sit unused until they have their own images, their own indigenous software ready to put on it. By not protecting this interval, by instead being fully seduced by the technology itself, nations are thereby enfolded into the global market that the U.S. projector can reach.

Remembering Atwood's four Basic Victim Positions of Survival, we might see this tragic flaw as possibly a strange combination of Position One: *To deny the fact that you are a victim,* and Position Two: *To acknowledge the fact that you are a victim, but to explain this as an act of Fate, the Will of God, the dictates of Biology ... the necessity decreed by History, or Economics, or the Unconscious, or any other large general powerful idea.* Under the compelling fascination of technological hardware, there is a denial of victimization through the splendid Fate of participating in American Spectacle.

Juneau's ironic / serious metaphor for nationhood signals a process that is occurring worldwide. Culture is something organic. It emerges from the body of the people and their experiences of a particular locale in human time and geographical space. The screen metaphor, which could increasingly apply to all nations, is a fully technological one that rips culture from its moorings in the land and transplants it to the prickly astroturf of international business and global markets. On that plane, there are no countries or cultures, only "superculture" – to use sociologist Kenneth Boulding's term for the fast-food chains, shopping malls, automats, hotel chains, TV formulas, mass fashions, shopping malls, theme parks, internationally advertised products (and shopping malls) that are standardized for the mass market.

But, staying closer to home, Juneau's metaphor serves for other areas besides the viewing screen. The Expo 86 ads proudly announce, "See The World On Our Stage," echoing the situation that has characterized Canada's movie screens since 1896; and the West Edmonton Mall (judging by Ian Pearson's fine piece in the May 1986 issue of *Saturday Night*) presents itself as "a contrived paradise that jumbles together intriguing bits of the world," with its Parisian boulevard, its Bourbon Street, its palm trees, its fountain pulsing to the theme songs from *Chariots Of Fire* and *The Pink Panther*. As Canada disappears into its screens, it's hard to know where we are.

Let's take this metaphor of screens and projections a bit further, into the realm of psychology it hints at. If you have no real identity of your own, you are merely a surface receiving the projections of how others see you, if they see you at all. So, for example, from the United States, Canada receives the projection of itself as a friendly and dutiful ally, or as the empty North with resources for the taking, or as the perfect dumping ground for U.S. product, or as the terrain that most closely resembles Siberia and is thus ideal for testing the Cruise, etc., etc. Once you accept somebody's projection onto you, it's difficult to throw it off. Indeed, it's difficult to know who you really are beneath the images projected. Even worse, you may begin to believe those projections of who you are and act accordingly. You may even begin to think that dumping is fair trade – and that superculture is culture.

(1986)

McMASTER
UNIVERSITY
BOOKSTORE
15:08:45 01 SEP 1992
TRANS NO: 1.A24.13178
CLERK: SD

1 LEWIS MUMFORD	20.35 GX
1922714	
2 FLASHBACKS FROM MEDIASCAP	16.95 GX
1762150	

PRICE SUBTOTAL	37.30
FEDL GST	2.61
TOTAL	39.91
CASH -----------	40.00
YOUR CHANGE	0.09

◻ The Laughing-Heads-of-State Photograph

YOU MAY HAVE NOTICED the September 25, 1984, Associated Press wirephoto of Brian Mulroney and Ronald Reagan that appeared on the front pages of most of our newspapers. Then again, you may very well have scanned right past it. As a news photograph, it is so like the thousands of other meeting-of-heads-of-state photographs that we have seen over the years that its totally predictable content is what is remarkable about it.

The photograph shows the two heads of state seated in chairs in front of a fireplace. Both men are dressed in white shirts, dark suits, and ties, and have assumed the posture that signifies relaxed (but formal) affability: legs crossed at the knee, hands in lap. The chairs are slightly turned towards one another and are placed at the culturally correct distance that indicates polite, but friendly, reserve. This space also allows for the fireplace behind them to be seen, both hearth and mantel. The bottom edge of a gilt-framed painting is visible above the mantel, though slightly obscured by a flowering plant, while on either side rest two identical vases (the type correctly pronounced: "vahsz"). Although the bodies of both men are, like the chairs, slightly turned towards each other, their heads are not. Instead, both men look out, to the left of the camera, at someone or something unseen. Their faces register the squinty eyes and wide-open, top-teeth-displayed mouth that means a hearty laugh is being enjoyed by both men.

As a news photograph, this one is thoroughly typical of a genre that has become an unquestioned staple of news imagery. It is the result of the so-called "photo-opportunity" that is built into every meeting of foreign heads of state. To provide a variety of visual background –

after all, the recurring fireplace gets tedious – the photo-opportunity may take place out of doors: in the tended gardens or the manicured lawns of official state grounds. Or it may, for the benefit of the TV cameras, include some shaking of hands and walking about: *moving* pictures. But in any case, the photo-opportunity now always included in the meetings of heads of state inevitably yields news imagery that seems to signify nothing more than: they met.

While the laughing-heads-of-state photograph is now a staple of print media news imagery, the "scrum" has become the meat 'n potatoes of TV news coverage. *Globe and Mail* reporter John Gray provides this vivid description of scrumming:

> Microphones and tape recorders jabbed forward, cameras brandished, cables stretched, elbows extended, notepads waving and pens prepared to jab – a scrum is not the kind of thing they talk about in journalism schools. Like crazed hornets, the scrummers rush forward and surround any politicians who may or may not have anything to say.... As a means of getting information, the scrum is, of course, next to useless. Almost nobody can hear, almost nobody can get to ask questions, and everyone runs the risk of bodily harm.... Students of language will be delighted to know that Quebec journalists and politicians have also adopted the word "scrum" as a noun. The verb in French has become "scrummer."

As news imagery, the scrum is virtually the structural opposite of the "photo-opportunity." Here the setting is never the tasteful room with fireplace, or the tended state garden, but rather the drab, institutional corridors of power, or even the mundane, gritty street itself. Moreover, all sense of decorum has clearly disappeared. In the frenzy of pursuit, the scrummers hustle unceremoniously to surround their prey: insisting, clamouring for some response. The scrumee, on the other hand, either successfully eludes these pursuers (an event which then becomes news content) or submits to the scrum to say essentially nothing (an event which then becomes news content). In either case, the resulting scrum footage is inherently useful for TV: *moving* pictures.

Like the photo-opportunity, what is remarkable about the scrum is that the imagery it yields signifies almost nothing. As Philip Hilts has noted: "Television news annually spends thousands of man-hours chasing officials from cars to courtrooms, from committee rooms to cars. The pictures mean nothing at all; a still photograph could serve as well. But TV news likes to have 'same-day pictures' of newsmakers." We have come, then, to a point where much of our news imagery – the photo-opportunity, the scrum, the "same-day pictures" of newsmakers – is, at one level, remarkably meaningless. Derived from what Daniel J. Boorstin called "pseudo-events," these images do not inform. Rather, they serve a different function.

A passage from Robert Warshow's *The Immediate Experience* helps to identify that function. Writing in 1946, long before television and the whole media-machine came together, Warshow was nevertheless aware of things to come:

> Nobody seriously questions the principle that it is the function of mass culture to maintain public morale, and certainly nobody in the mass audience objects to having his morale maintained. At a time when the normal condition of the citizen is a state of anxiety, euphoria spreads over our culture like the broad smile of an idiot.

Let us return to the laughing-heads-of-state photograph that is so common in our print media. While generically such photographs tend to signify nothing more than "They met," in an age of anxiety and global disharmony this signification is clearly reassuring. Depending on who's meeting whom, and the level of hostility between them, the photograph can signify, "They met ... and did not tear each other's throats out." Not that this was even a remote possibility in the case of Reagan and Mulroney. Indeed, the hearty, tooth-displaying laugh registered on their faces, as they look to the left of the camera, is historically familiar: it appears again and again, in wirephotos of meetings between presidents and prime ministers, throughout the century.

Several things are noteworthy about this generic, uproarious laugh that has recurred over the decades as a photographic signifier on our front pages and in our newsmagazines. The first thing is that we are never let in on the joke. The second thing is that the laughing heads of state (usually rather unfunny men incapable of sending anyone, much less each other, into gales of glee) are most often depicted – as in the Reagan / Mulroney photo – laughing at someone or something out of range of the camera. This leads me to believe that within the state bureaucracies of North America there is a guild of "photo-opportunity-jesters" – or else one very busy person – whose job it is to ensure that the heads of state, seated at the correct distance before the obligatory fireplace, break into a hearty laugh for the assembled cameras. (I will not speculate on either the training for this position or its job description. I *will* note, however, that the jester seemed to have been significantly absent from the Reagan / Gromyko "photo-opportunities." Or else it was someone just learning the trade.)

More importantly, however, the laughing-heads-of-state photograph seals the participants off in a slightly "other" realm: a realm of not only gilt-framed paintings, porcelain vases, tended state lawns, and inside jokes, but inside information, discussion, and deals to which we are not, and never will be, privy. Indeed, so removed is this realm from our world that it must be mediated for us in safe, carefully orchestrated glimpses: glimpses that inform us of nothing at the same time as they convey a strange, intended euphoria. We are meant to be reassured that this other realm, so removed from our daily lives, is functioning so smoothly in its own mysterious way that it registers elation on the faces of its participants. The hearty laugh enjoyed by Reagan and Mulroney is the visible trace of the euphoria our media spread over the culture like the broad smile of an idiot.

Over the past few months, a veritable orgy of mediated euphoria has oozed through the airwaves in a series of spectacular waves: culminating in the arrival of both the Pope and the Queen (okay, Michael Jackson too) in quick succession. In the midst of all the hoopla, pageantry, parades, the comings and goings, the meetings of remarkable men, the photo-opportunity extended itself to giant proportions: displaying the vast reach of its inherently empty signifiers across the land. As Warshow noted almost forty years ago: "Whatever its effectiveness as a source of consolation and a means of pressure for maintaining 'positive' social attitudes, [the media's] optimism is fundamentally satisfying to no one, not even to those who would be most disoriented without its support."

(1984)

☐ Losing It in the Lobby: Entertainment and Free Trade

WHEN WE HEAR the words "industry" or "manufacturing" or "products," we tend to think of utilitarian items produced on an assembly line: automobiles, canned goods, widgets, shakes and shingles. We tend not to associate the words with anything that might actually touch our souls – as music or images or the printed word can. Thus we have an inner bias against perceiving things like movies, TV programs, books and magazines, records and tapes as in any way "industrial." They seem too pleasurable or ephemeral to be thought of as "products" manufactured by an industry, too intimate to be seen as actually significant to international trade.

This inner bias prevents us from recognizing a hard, economic reality, a reality that is actually crucial to the Canada-U.S. free-trade talks. The whole mass-media / entertainment arena is indeed an industry, and one that has become increasingly central to the American multinational economy. As David Crane noted in a four-part series on free trade for *The Toronto Star*, "For the United States, shell-shocked by Japanese, Korean and other foreign gains in steel, autos, and other major manufacturing industries, entertainment is seen as a growth industry where the United States can continue to dominate."

The huge U.S. entertainment conglomerates are one of the healthiest components of the American economy. Over the past twenty years, as mergers, acquisitions, and take-overs have crystallized media / entertainment ownership in the hands of fewer than fifty corporations, their numerical presence on the "Fortune 500" list has tripled. That list itself – the 500 largest U.S. corporations – comprises fewer than 1 per cent of the 360,000 U.S. incorporated businesses. But the Fortune 500 account for 80 per cent of all sales.

"They are the aristocrats of the American industrial economy," writes media critic Ben Bagdikian, while the other 359,500 corporations are "the peasantry." The largest media conglomerates "are now part of this American economic aristocracy." Not only do they dominate the U.S. domestic market, they earn more than 50 per cent of worldwide film profits, account for over 75 per cent of all TV programs imported around the world, and supply more than 50 per cent of all records and tapes sold on the planet.

Unquestionably, Canada is the top foreign market for the products of the U.S. entertainment business. But that market for U.S. movies, video-cassettes, TV shows, albums and tapes, magazines and books would be even bigger if certain "restrictive practices" adopted by the Canadian government were removed. As a major growth industry in a somewhat "shell-shocked" U.S. economy, the entertainment business is far more central to the trading relations between the two countries than we have been led to believe.

For Canadians, this fact must resonate beneath the public remarks of the trade negotiators on both sides. For instance, U.S. negotiator Peter Murphy has stated: "I'm not sure I fully understand [cultural sovereignty] and I'm not sure what it actually means ... in many ways it appears to be guises for protectionism." More worrying, however, is the position of Simon Reisman, Canada's top free-trade negotiator, who said in April 1986: "Canada's culture – in all its manifestations – has rarely thrived so strongly as it does now." The ignorance in that perspective, coupled with the fact that Reisman's negotiating team includes *no* top-level cultural advisors, spells doom for Canada's cultural industries, which are already hampered by an annual $1.5 billion trade imbalance with the United States through the obvious domination of the U.S. entertainment business in Canada.

Reisman's lack of an informed cultural perspective (not necessarily a nationalist one – a realistic one would do) or advisors to provide one for him suggests that the entertainment business is not central to the free-trade talks. Such a misperception plays directly into American hands for, as we shall see, there is every reason to believe that the actual idea for free trade was instigated, in part, to ensure that the position of the U.S. entertainment conglomerate in Canada would be not only maintained but also strengthened. Free trade with Canada was an American idea – an idea that emerged out of a context in which U.S. entertainment interests were being significantly threatened. To protect those crucial interests, the Americans got the free-trade ball rolling.

To untangle this intricate web of manoeuvrings, consider a front-page news article that appeared in *The Toronto Star* and received far less attention than it deserved. Entitled "Twists of Fate Put Canada on Free Trade Path" (October 26, 1985), the article was less about fate than about U.S. manipulation – which can often seem like fate to those enmeshed in its webs.

In the piece, national affairs reporter Carol Goar revealed that the original idea and initiative for the free-trade talks arose not from any Canadian minds, but from the frontal lobes of the American ambassador to Canada, who planted the seed in fertile Canadian soil. In 1983, Ambassador Paul Robinson invited Sam Hughes, president of the Canadian Chamber of Commerce, to a private lunch in his Rockcliffe home. Over the meal, Robinson talked free trade. As Goar reconstructs the events:

> Robinson explains his position: the United States, with its massive trade deficit, desperately wants to launch a new round of world trade talks, but its major trading partners are balking, retreating behind protective walls. As an interim measure, he says, it has decided to enter free-trade agreements with selected partners, the idea being to show that if the world's 100 or so trading nations aren't prepared to negotiate as a group, the Americans will pick them off one by one. The first free-trade deal is to be with Israel. Why not Canada next?

Hughes was intrigued by the prospect, and more lunches followed, including one to which Robinson invited Thomas d'Aquino, president of the Business Council on National Issues – a lobby group representing 150 blue-chip corporations. Then Roy Phillips, executive director of the Canadian Manufacturers' Association, was brought in on the private discussions. Both d'Aquino and Phillips liked Robinson's free-trade idea, so the U.S. ambassador phoned home. According to Goar: "Robinson gets in touch with U.S. special trade representative Bill Brock. Somewhat taken by surprise by the ambassador's initiative, Brock nevertheless agrees that the idea has possibilities. He cautions, however, that the approach will have to come from the Canadians." Having planted the free-trade idea, Robinson discreetly backed into the wings, leaving Hughes to sound out senior businessmen throughout 1983 and begin mobilizing for closer trade links with the United States.

Not surprisingly, corporate solidarity around free trade transcended subsequent federal electoral shuffling and became the determining voice for later events. (No one, however, seemed to have taken note of Israel's fate as the first free-trade selectee. By early 1985, Israel's communication minister Amnon Rubinstein was saying that the Israeli economy was now totally dependent on U.S. goodwill, that "we have very little manoeuvring room nor the power to say no to specific requests from the United States.")

Let's pause, though, and consider Ambassador Robinson's timing. What was going on in Canada, in and around 1983, which may have spurred Robinson to take an initiative that surprised even U.S. special trade representative Bill Brock? Undoubtedly knowing that a possible free-trade deal would be seen as a luscious liaison by Canada's private businessmen, why would Robinson choose 1983 as the moment to seductively drop this handkerchief at their feet?

If we take the position that the entertainment business is central to the U.S. multinational economy and interests abroad, then certain events of the time suggest possible answers – answers that fully entangle us in the sordid arena of cultural politics and high-powered American lobbying: because one of the more significant things going on in Canada during the months before Robinson served his free-trade lunch to Sam Hughes was that the Canadian natives were restless again about cultural sovereignty, and in ways that could have big repercussions on that annual one-and-a-half-billion-dollar entertainment bonanza pouring south. In particular, Quebec was leading the way with a bill that sounded the alarm in the offices of what many consider to be the most powerful U.S. lobby in existence – the Motion Picture Association of America (MPAA). When it comes to free trade with the United States, no analysis would be complete without a consideration of the MPAA – the most powerful agent for American entertainment conglomerate interests in Canada or anywhere on the planet.

If you were one of the world's one billion TV viewers who, in 1986, dutifully tuned in to the annual rites of spring known as the Academy Awards ceremony, you may recall Jack "Boom Boom" Valenti (which is how host Robin Williams introduced him) presenting the award for best foreign film. The irony of that particular conjunction between award-presenter and award-category was undoubtedly missed by most viewers, but outside the United States – and especially in Canada and Quebec – it should have been seen as the most blatant sign of American arrogance possible. For if there is any single person who has, for the past twenty years, done his utmost to actually *prevent* other countries from making their own feature films or even having their own indigenous film and TV industries, it is Jack Valenti himself, former top advisor to President Lyndon Johnson and long-reigning president of the Motion Picture Association of America.

The sixty-four-year history of the MPAA, and the shorter but more lethal twenty-six-year history of its foreign division – the Motion Picture Export Association of America (MPEAA) – make for a ruthless tale of strong-arm tactics and behind-the-scenes intervention in the domestic politics of most nations around the globe to prevent other countries from in any way interfering with U.S. domination over the movie and TV screens of the planet.

The MPAA and MPEAA represent the domestic and global interests of the top U.S. entertainment conglomerates: Columbia Pictures (owned by Coca-Cola), MGM / United Artists, Paramount Pictures (owned by Gulf and Western), Twentieth Century-Fox, Universal (owned by the Music Corporation of America – MCA), Warner Brothers (owned by Warner Communications), Buena Vista International (distribution arm for Walt Disney), Embassy Pictures, Tri Star Pictures, and Orion Pictures Corporation. These companies, through their subsidiaries, account for the lion's share of all filmmaking and distribution, TV production, magazine and book publishing, music recording and record / tape distribution in the United States and, increasingly, throughout the world. Simply in theatrical film rentals alone, the worldwide domination by these corporations (collectively known as the Hollywood majors) annually generates a foreign box-office bonanza of more than $2 billion, with Canada contributing up to $400 million a year (the largest percentage from any one country) just from its movie theatres. When we add video-cassette sales and rentals ($135 million annually from Canada) and TV program export revenues ($150 million annually from Canada) on top of that, we're talking about an annual global bonanza of over $3 billion (excluding record sales) pouring into the coffers of Hollywood entertainment conglomerates. Unfortunately, Canada's annual tithe to the Hollywood god comprises the heftiest portion of that figure, but as the United States sees it, that portion could and would be larger, if "market forces" were left unimpeded by Canadian government policies.

Obviously, the export of U.S. films and TV programs does more than merely generate 40 per cent of Hollywood's overall profit. The films and TV shows serve to pave the way for American attitudes, consumer life-styles and products around the globe. With the majors' huge parent companies – especially Coca-Cola, Gulf and Western, MCA, Warner Communications, and Disney – fully diversified into every aspect of leisure and entertainment, the companies depend on exported movies and TV programs to popularize the American Way from Burnaby to Bangladesh.

These giant conglomerates must ensure that foreign markets for U.S. screen entertainment remain as open and accessible to the majors as possible, without any "unfair" trade restrictions to hamper that accessibility. Their key lobby – the MPAA/MPEAA – is committed Rambo-style to ensuring that accessibility. Jack Valenti, president for the past twenty years, is the MPAA/MPEAA enforcer: skilfully working behind the scenes to effectively scuttle any foreign legislation that might get in the way of the majors' interests.

Analyzing the "Americanization" of Europe's mass media through films, television, popular music, advertising, and news, a writer for the Paris newsmagazine Le Point observed: "U.S. domination of certain cultural sectors is less a deliberate decision to colonize others than it is the supremacy of a new industry, highly developed in the U.S. but still embryonic in Europe: the culture industry." At the forefront of this mass culture are the screens of the world: film and television. Not surprisingly, the most powerful U.S. lobby in existence concentrates its efforts there.

For any country to have a film industry, it must have local control over three aspects vital to successful operation: production, distribution, and exhibition. It does no good for a country to pour millions of dollars into film production if distribution and exhibition are controlled by alien interests. But that is precisely the role of the MPAA/MPEAA worldwide: to ensure that the distribution / exhibition aspects of the industry benefit only the movies and TV programs of its members.

In 1960, with TV operations expanding around the globe (through the help of U.S. corporations, the military, and the State Department, but that's another story), the MPAA cloned itself to create the MPEAA and vested it with the authority to represent its members in negotiations with foreign governments and entrepreneurs for American movies and TV programs. While the MPAA looks after U.S. domestic matters, the MPEAA operates as a single bargaining unit with foreign customers. This activity is prohibited in the United States itself on anti-trust grounds, but it flourishes abroad under the protection of the Webb-Pomerene Act of 1918, which permits U.S. businesses overseas to function as monopolies with a single sales agent empowered to set prices and arrange contracts for all its members' products. In its foreign activities, the MPEAA is not unlike the U.S. State Department, with which it has ties, and one of its quasi-government functions is to lobby against foreign legislation that would restrict "free trade" for the majors. Through the U.S. State Department, the MPEAA can threaten boycotts and trade reprisals for countries that do not co-operate.

Despite such practices, several countries over the years have enacted legislation to gain some control over their own movie and TV screens. Often such legislation involves setting quotas that dictate a certain percentage of screen time for indigenous productions in order to foster that country's film and TV industries. So, for instance, in Australia 20 per cent of screen time is devoted to Australian productions; in France the figure is 48 per cent, while in Italy 44 per cent of screen time must be devoted to Italian films. Screen quotas and other legislated measures give industries (and cultures) abroad a chance of surviving the massive onslaught of U.S. screen material. Canada, however, has for over sixty years been extremely reluctant to take any such legislated steps and thereby bring down the wrath of the MPAA. Indeed, the history of cinema in Canada since 1922 is not much more than a continuous saga of MPAA intervention and lobbying at the highest political levels to keep the majors fully in control of the Canadian market.

In 1983, for instance, of ninety-seven film distribution companies operating in Canada, ten foreign companies (the majors) controlled 67 per cent of all distribution turnover and raked in 97 per cent of movie box-office profit. That annual $400 million goes directly across the border to finance U.S. production. Meanwhile, Canadian movie theatres have for six decades remained virtually closed to Canadian films: with less than 3 per cent of screen time annually given over (by default) to indigenous films. In part this situation is the result of the largest theatre chains here being owned and controlled by the majors – Gulf and Western's Paramount owns Famous Players, MCA's Universal owns 50 per cent of Odeon: an exhibition tie-in that is completely illegal in the United States itself.

But it's also because the majors fully control distribution in Canada and have no interest in supporting or promoting Canadian screen products, which after all are their competition. In film Canada has had free trade with the United States for sixty years, with the result that the Canadian industry lurches from one crisis to the next. Indeed, the film industry is the perfect example of the "level playing field" the United States wants vis-à-vis Canada.

But in the last months of 1982 and the first few months of 1983, some things seemed to be changing.

As the former head of the Canadian Film Development Corporation, Michael Spencer, has recently noted, in the twenty years that Jack Valenti has been president of the MPAA, Canada has gone through eight federal ministers of communication – giving each an average tenure of two and a half years, against two decades of lobbying expertise for Valenti and sixty years of MPAA/MPEAA business on the Canadian front. Some of those federal ministers have caught on to the dynamics of cultural occupation more quickly than others, and in 1982 Francis Fox appeared to be on the verge of seeing the light. He asked the Foreign Investment Review Agency (FIRA) to investigate the Coca-Cola takeover of Columbia Pictures in the United States, for the purpose of deciding whether Columbia should be allowed to continue distributing movies in Canada under alien ownership. Then Orion Pictures staged a takeover of the U.S. distributor Filmways, whose product had been handled in Canada by the independent Canadian distributor, Ambassador. Orion took Filmways' movies away from Ambassador and arrogantly opened its own distribution office in Toronto. So Fox put FIRA onto Orion as well. Such moves by a Canadian federal minister of culture were indications of a country possibly awakening from the big sleep.

But even bolder moves were being taken in Quebec.

In September 1982 the Fournier Commission had released its report on cinema in the province, recommending major changes that would make the MPAA's blood boil. It had long been obvious in Quebec that something drastic had to be done about film distribution. In sixty years of U.S. domination over that sector, the majors had only *once* bothered to invest in and/or distribute a Quebec-made feature film – *Les Plouffes*. Meanwhile, they had boldly ripped off most of Quebec's $40 million annual box-office without leaving a penny for indigenous production. As well they were taking steps to completely eliminate the province's independent distributors – the only source of support for Quebec filmmakers.

An independent Canadian film/TV distributor can survive only by distributing foreign films along with whatever Canadian product it handles. In recent years, the majors have been squeezing out the

Canadian "indies" through two specific tactics: (1) they buy up "North American rights" to independently produced features like *Return of the Jedi* – ignoring Canada as a separate country whose local distributors should be able to get Canadian rights on such pictures; and (2) they buy up entire film libraries from other distributors outside Canada, keeping those films from being distributed on a picture-by-picture basis by Canadian independents.

By 1982 in Quebec, this second tactic was reaching alarming proportions. Columbia, Paramount, and Twentieth Century-Fox were each making deals with the three largest film companies in France to handle all their films in Canada, thereby taking away the largest source of revenue from Quebec companies. Something had to be done or the entire Quebec film industry would go under.

The Fournier Commission boldly addressed the crisis, inspiring the PQ minister of cultural affairs, Clément Richard, to endorse the commission's report and promise that the long-awaited Cinema Law based on it – Quebec's Bill 109 – would be tabled in the National Assembly by December of 1982. "To consider only the laws of the market," said Richard, "and, in addition, to promote that option, would mean to turn over Quebec's cinema industry to the American majors, bound hand and foot. This would be tantamount to assassinating Quebec's entire cinema industry." Since that description adequately characterizes the English-Canadian film industry – "bound hand and foot" to the majors – it was clear that Quebec was embarking on a radical path of its own. If the damned anglos wanted to keep kissing Valenti's association, fine. But La Belle Province was taking its stand. Clément Richard tabled Bill 109 by December, as promised. Immediately, la merde started hitting le fan.

In its original form, Bill 109 stated that (1) any film distribution company operating in Quebec would have to be 80 per cent Canadian-owned; (2) any non-French-language feature film shown in the province would be limited to a sixty-day run until a dubbed French version (and dubbed in Quebec) was made available; and (3) all film distributors operating in Quebec would be required to contribute up to 10 per cent of their gross annual revenues to a Quebec film-production fund. In one stroke, Bill 109 was effectively forcing the majors to distribute through Quebec "indies," protecting Quebec's language rights, and fostering indigenous film production.

It was a breathtaking bill, one that made the hearts of all nationalists beat faster. After all, Quebec was boldly joining the ranks of those foreign countries who had dared to impose "restrictive practices" on the majors. Ever since 1966, Valenti had been meeting with government officials in Washington to outline the "top ten threats" to MPAA/MPEAA members' foreign box-office bonanza: the "unfair trade practices" adopted by other countries to foster their own film and TV industries. They are:

1. Import quotas
2. Screen-time quotas
3. Discriminatory admission taxes
4. Film rental controls
5. Currency remittance restrictions
6. Requirements that prints be struck in the country of origin
7. Dubbing requirements
8. Foreign prohibition against alien distributors
9. High income taxes
10. Production subsidies / incentives

Whenever any country has attempted to legislate such measures, the MPAA/MPEAA has moved into high gear, with the help of the U.S. State Department. In 1971, for instance, Valenti boasted that his lobbying efforts since 1966 (the year he got the job) had preserved some seventy-five million foreign box-office dollars that otherwise would have been lost to tighter screen controls by other countries. But here, in 1983, we have uppity little Quebec imposing *three* such measures on the majors. "Only Mozambique," protested the MPAA, "imposes stiffer controls on foreign films!" In the Valenti mind, it's enough to turn a saint to sodomy.

But the issue wasn't necessarily that $40 million per year Quebec box-office. After all, that would just about cover a year's supply of Maalox and Preparation H for MPAA members. Nor was the issue necessarily an upstart province like Quebec. Valenti was used to playing hard ball with England, France, Spain, *Mozambique*, for chrissake. No, the big worry was something else. Something nicely summarized by Jack Valenti's friend in the White House.

We [Canada and the United States] are each other's largest trading partner.... We have everything in common, including our heritage and background and language and all. We're very unique.

– Ronald Reagan

The U.S. perception of Canadian "otherness" had long been astoundingly lacking: a mental malignancy which obviously plays itself out on both sides with Canadians adopting the branch-plant mentality and the Americans arrogantly including Canada as simply part of their own domestic market. In this sense, the relationship *is* "unique," for no other country daily endures the humiliation of blithely being denied separate status as a foreign country. This is nowhere more apparent than in the entertainment business and in the operations of the MPAA/MPEAA. Because Canada is considered part of the U.S. domestic market, it falls under the domestic umbrella of MPAA matters, not the foreign dealings of the MPEAA division. In other words, in relation to the Hollywood majors, Canada is not even accorded the dignity of being perceived as a foreign country.

That might seem like a small, academic point, but in the events surrounding Quebec's Bill 109 from 1982 to 1986, it has clearly been the heart of the matter, with PQ minister Clément Richard saying things like "We want Americans to have the same attitudes toward Quebec as they do toward other Western countries" and "What we want is to see Quebec stop being considered part of the U.S. market and become part of the foreign market." In 1983, federal communications minister Fox was known to be fully in favour of Bill 109. He was making his own rumblings about changes on the cultural front and was even toying with the heretical idea that *Canada* should be considered a foreign country and not simply part of the U.S. domestic market. And *that's* what got Valenti's teeth on edge.

With Quebec acting like Mozambique, and the Canadian feds starting to think the same way, a terrible spectre began to rise up in front of horrified American eyes. The terrible spectre of … the Domino Theory. First Quebec, then Canada, then every raggedy-ass little country in the world would be insisting on its own Cinema Law reeking with restrictions of the majors. But even worse, if you're thinking from the head space of U.S. entertainment conglomerates' interests: first the Quebec film industry, then the Canadian film industry, and then the Canadian feds might start thinking of imposing "unfair trade restrictions" on every aspect of that one-and-a-half-billion-dollar annual entertainment bonanza pouring across the border. Not just movies and TV programs, but video-cassettes, books, magazines, records, tapes! Why, if they wanted to, the Canadian feds could start taking *big* protectionist bites, like a ravenous Ms Pac-Man on the loose, out of the entire leisure and entertainment industry. And once nationalizing gets started, who knows where it will end?! The whole cozy set-up with Canada could go right down the tubes.

The Americans are nothing if not crafty, and one of the things they're most crafty about is finding locals to represent their interests. This saves a lot of plane fares, and it also helps them to look as though what they're doing actually has the support of the people within the country they're exploiting. In Canada, the "contras" for the MPAA take the form of an organization called (don't let the name fool you) the Canadian Motion Picture Distributors Association (CMPDA), headed by Millard Roth.

As the hearings on Bill 109 got under way in February 1983, Roth submitted a brief representing the majors and categorically opposed to virtually everthing in the bill. "We do not believe that the Québécois wish to follow the Mozambican model," stated the brief. The legislation, if enacted, "will result in awakening the hostility of persons and organizations involved in the cinema industry, and will isolate Quebec, creating no new employment." (Translation: If Bill 109 is passed, Valenti's MPAA will withhold every @@#$$%*& Hollywood film from Quebec's @@#$$%*& screens!) The majors, continued the brief, "will not accept to be so treated. They are good corporate citizens who pay their taxes regularly, employ Québécois and have done business in the province since the beginnings of cinema."

Well, precisely. Maudits anglais. Salut, salauds.

As murmurs of spring began to spread across the frozen North, the Canadian feds added another wrinkle to the situation. Not only was Quebec not relenting on the bill, but *La Presse* leaked a version of the federal Department of Communications' Distribution Task Force Report, headed by Montreal lawyer Ronald Cohen. Right there in bald print the report advocated "a National Cinema Act" – giving the federal government regulatory jurisdiction over the interprovincial distribution / exhibition of films in Canada and restricting the majors to distributing in Canada only those films for which they possess world rights. Not only that, rumour had it that the feds were about to legislate 50 per cent ownership for all distribution companies operating in Canada. "What it means," Ronald Cohen told *Cinema Canada*, "is that they [the majors] can't have everything."

Clearly, Valenti wasn't used to this kind of thinking or talk from The Friendly Ally, The Good Neighbour to the North, *dammit – from part of the American domestic market!* It was time to turn a few screws.

As Bill 109 got rolling towards becoming law in June of 1983 – clearing first reading, second reading, then article-by-article debate before a closed parliamentary commission – the majors, complaining of "outright expulsion," threatened to boycott Quebec cinema screens unless some amendments were made to the bill. The U.S. consulate issued a letter of warning to the PQ government, mentioning reprisals, "possible countermeasures." Cultural minister Clément Richard, reading the signs of the times, decided to amend the bill slightly: accepting subtitled prints instead of dubbed versions and allowing the majors to distribute in the province, but only those films they have helped to produce (collectively about sixty films a year) or those for which they own world rights of distribution. Beyond that, Richard declared, Bill 109 would be compromised no further.

Though not quite Mozambican, it remained a tough bill – as stringent as recent legislation in Sweden. The U.S. embassy was "outraged," issuing an angry statement protesting that "such measures are especially troubling at a time when economic recovery is just beginning" and again threatening countermeasures. The majors' legal representative in Quebec, Jacques Laurent, told *The Globe and Mail* (June 18, 1983) that there was every possibility that the majors would pull out of Quebec. "It's questionable," he said, "as to whether it will remain economically viable for them to stay here. It's an unbelievable piece of legislation. The majors have made Montreal a premier centre for movies – a privileged centre – and if they pull out, it won't be any longer."

In the midst of the fulminations, Premier René Lévesque himself arose in the National Assembly to make an impassioned defence of Bill 109, saying that cultural industries are not like other industries and that Quebec was fully prepared to accept whatever U.S. reprisals might be enacted. On June 22, 1983, Bill 109 became Quebec's new Cinema Law.

Of course, Valenti complained bitterly to the press about the "precedential" nature of the law and their terrible worry that it might spread, like a virus, "throughout the world environment." But with the Quebec film industry celebrating throughout the summer of '83, and the Canadian feds applauding the feisty Québécois move, there definitely seemed to be something in the air – virus or otherwise. Why, even the CRTC seemed to have inhaled the revolutionary germ – making noises about actually enforcing year-round the 50 per cent prime-time Canadian content quota for TV broadcasters. Heady stuff for Canadian cultural nationalists. Perhaps a turning point for the Great White Screen.

Somewhere in all this, U.S. Ambassador Paul Robinson – whose embassy so vigorously protested Bill 109 – got on the phone to Sam Hughes, inviting him to that free-trade lunch. Things in the hinterland were becoming a bit too Mozambican. Time to rally the Canadian private-business sector, which traditionally has always been willing to sacrifice nebulous things like "culture" or "sovereignty" for more tangible stuff.

But what the hell, why not take the informed-paranoid's view of the situation? Maybe, just maybe, in the back of that ambassadorial brain-pan was the inkling that if you set the free-trade wheels in motion, not just the damned Cinema Law in Quebec, but every one of those protectionist cultural policies in Canada that hamper the U.S. entertainment business might eventually go down like bowling pins in the free-trade alley. And any moves to strengthen those policies, those "irritants" to the free-market forces, would be considered a sign of bad faith for the impending free-trade talks.

As Quebec settled down to take care of establishing the administrative side of its new Cinema Law – particularly the setting up of three new agencies responsible for various operations – it gradually became clear to all concerned that it would not be until at least April 1985 that the law could come into application. Revolution meets red tape. Meanwhile, Ambassador Robinson had gotten the free-trade ball rolling.

It rolled past the federal elections of 1984, with Sam Hughes quietly rounding up the business fold. It rolled over FIRA, which went down with the praise of the Reagan administration, "pleased at the encouragement of foreign investment and the removal of discriminatory treatment." And it rolled right into a meeting of the Canada-U.S. committee of the Chamber of Commerce, gathered in Calgary in October 1984. That, maintains Carol Goar, was the turning point for the private-business sector in terms of free trade. The powerful Chamber of Commerce committee decided to establish a permanent task force on Canada-U.S. trade issues.

Meeting quietly outside the glare of publicity, this private-sector task force has been chaired by David Braide, senior vice-president of CIL Inc., the large chemical company. Its forty or so members jokingly refer to themselves as "Ali Baba and the Forty Thieves," but in this context it seems more appropriate to call them the Braide Brunch. Their membership includes: John Allan, president of Stelco; Jake Warren, vice-chairman of the Bank of Montreal; Raymond Cyr, president of Bell Canada; Bill Morrow, president of National Sea Products; Bill Stinson, president of Canadian Pacific; Jim Black, chairman of Molson Companies; Tom Bell, president of Dominion Textiles; and George Urquhard, president of Enheat Inc. of New Brunswick.

With the new Mulroney government in place, they began pressuring for the free-trade deal inspired by Ambassador Robinson. As U.S. special trade representative Bill Brock had advised, the approach would have to come from the Canadians, and apparently the Braide Bunch has dutifully served that purpose. Along with the Business Council on National Issues (whose president had eaten the free-trade lunch in Rockcliffe), the Canadian Chamber of Commerce (ditto), and the Canadian Manufacturers' Association (ditto again), they began sounding out the new federal trade minister, James Kelleher, on a possible free-trade deal. By January 1985 Kelleher was issuing a discussion paper on the topic and promising nationwide consultations with the business community. Goar writes: "To his delight, the minister finds that much of the work has already been done for him. There is no need to set up a private-sector advisory group because the Braide task force is already in place. Kelleher adopts it as his own, noting that there is really no point in re-inventing the wheel." Behind the scenes, this task force has been advising the trade minister and Mulroney on free trade.

If we look at what we know of the membership composition of the Braide Bunch, it seems safe to assume that issues of cultural policy, cultural sovereignty, or even cultural industries would not be high on their agenda of free-trade concerns. The closest thing to Canadian culture represented therein is the stubby beer bottle. No, the Braide Bunch would not conceivably be advising Mulroney to go into free-trade talks with the goal of strengthening cultural policies and shoring up that one-and-a-half-billion-dollar entertainment trade imbalance. If anything, they might advise just the opposite: the removal of any such political "irritants" that might stand in the way of the talks. The informed-paranoid's view would suggest that Robinson could have been counting on precisely that when he set the wheels in motion: that the Canadians involved would be thinking of *everything but* the entertainment business when their eyes began to glitter about free trade, while for the Americans it would be a central issue.

Lo and behold, subsequent events suggest that such a reading might not be that paranoid after all. David Crane informs us that, in advance of the March 1985 Shamrock Summit, the Prime Minister's Office seriously considered a three-year suspension of Bill c-58 as a concession to Reagan. (That's the section of the Income Tax Act that fosters Canadian media by disallowing tax deductions for Canadian advertising dollars spent in U.S. magazines and border TV/radio stations – a measure opposed by the Conservatives when enacted in 1976.) At least two members of the U.S. Senate Commerce Committee have pinpointed Bill c-58 as anathema to free-trade discussions on other fronts.

But what about the MPAA? It wouldn't be like Jack "Boom Boom" Valenti to bashfully retire to the sidelines while a major Canada-U.S. summit on trade was in the offing. And if we look closely, there we find him and the MPAA involved in drawing up the list of the Top Six Trade Irritants for discussion at the 1985 Shamrock Summit. Included on the list was a topic close to Valenti's heart: the @@#$$*& Canadian cable-TV industry. Having cleaned up the cable situation in the United States by requiring domestic operators to pay royalties to MPAA members for the shows they retransmit, Valenti has been determined to see that similar royalties are dutifully paid by Canadian cable operators. In Quebec City on that March weekend, Valenti's friend Ron reiterated this MPAA concern while Brian practised singing on key.

Perhaps we'll never know if Quebec's Bill 109 came up for discussion at that 1985 summit, though the very fact of a meeting in Quebec might tend to raise the issue. Certainly the president himself, who in some way has never left Hollywood and so would rally around such an issue, has since been reported to have taken a personal interest in the matter. William Merkin, the U.S. trade official who specializes in Canada, has explicitly said that Canadian moves to limit U.S. control over film distribution would be targeted in the talks. But in March 1985, the distribution aspects of the Quebec Cinema Law were still mired in red tape, with prospects for another round of public hearings to come.

In the meantime, another issue had arisen on the entertainment front. Gulf and Western (parent-company for Paramount, member in good standing of the MPAA, owner of Famous Players theatres) was about to acquire Prentice-Hall Inc. of New Jersey and its publishing subsidiary in Canada. Hearing of Canadian plans to block the acquisition here, Gulf and Western's lobbyist Robert Strauss got on the horn to Allan Gotlieb, Canadian ambassador, and warned that the largest entertainment conglomerate on the face of the planet would adopt a "scorched-earth" policy towards Canada if the feds didn't comply. Gotlieb dutifully conveyed the message to Ottawa, advocating co-operation. Mustn't irritate the Yanks.

Yessirree, that free-trade ball was now really rolling. It rolled through the office of Bill Brock, U.S. special trade representative, who told the U.S. Chamber of Commerce in the spring of 1985:

> The failure of the [world trading] system to move has put the U.S. in the position where we have to contemplate defending our own vital interests. One of the ways we can do that is to take one or more countries and setting [sic] up a complete process by which we remove all trade barriers between us as an example of how good the world can be. The U.S. has to operate in its own self-interest and that means the priority has to be building up a global system.

Giving new meaning to the American song "We Are the World," Brock's words gave another push to the free-trade ball, which then rolled over the Macdonald Commission. While admitting that "If Canada and the United States were to move toward freer trade, large American-owned multinationals would benefit," the commission nevertheless took an obvious pro-free-trade stance, recommending "a leap of faith" on the issue. Meanwhile, in the same month that the Macdonald Commission Report was released, the United States was having no truck with "faith" or any other jingoisms when it came to trading. In September 1985, the Americans established a "trade strike force" to identify unfair foreign trade practices and make recommendations on how best to eliminate them.

As the busy month of September unfolded, another round of public hearings on Quebec's Cinema Law got under way, instigated in part by the MPAA. This set of hearings, conducted by one of the new agencies created by the law – the Régie du Cinéma du Québec, headed by André Guérin – was established especially to deal with Section 104 of the bill, which refers to the right of the régie to define the terms "producer" and "holder of world rights" for the purpose of granting distribution permits to alien operators in Quebec.

In advance of the hearings, Valenti complained to the press about the "very restrictive law" which "makes it very difficult for non-

Quebec companies to literally do business." But Québécois industry members were unhappy with the drafted definitions for completely opposite reasons. As *Cinema Canada* put it, the proposed definitions for "producer" and "holder of world rights" were so liberal as to be "opening the door to all the majors who either put up fifty per cent of the 'financial interest' in a film or held distribution rights for a film in North America and Europe. Given the circumstances, the majors couldn't have written a more accommodating definition." But at the hearings, the MPAA tried to water down the definitions even further. Every single brief from Quebec, however, argued for making the definitions more stringent.

As it became clear that the hearings were moving in favour of Québécois interests, the MPAA protested strongly. "We were told," says André Guérin, who presided over the hearings, "that they would intervene at the goverment level to oppose the regulations. There is no doubt that they had decided to fight." Universal issued a public statement that it would stop doing business in Quebec if the regulations were approved. As the hearings drew to a close, the MPAA members "were not pleased at all," says Guérin.

But in the autumn of 1985 Quebec was in the midst of an electoral campaign, and the Parti Québécois was not doing well in the polls. Though all the signs had been positive that the PQ cabinet would implement the regulations of the Cinema Law, suddenly on the eve of the elections the cabinet decided not to approve the regulations. Days later, on December 2, the PQ lost the provincial election in a landslide victory for the Bourassa Liberals.

As the dust cleared, the first press report about a possible cabinet cave-in due to U.S. pressure appeared in *La Presse* (December 6). The lawyer for the MPAA, Jacques Laurent, denied that U.S. interests had intervened in the cabinet decision. But two days later Gérald Godin (who in autumn had replaced Clément Richard as cultural minister) told *La Presse* that the Quebec cabinet had backed off because of direct pressure from the U.S. State Department, which had delivered a "verbal note" to the Quebec government threatening that American films would immediately be pulled from Quebec theatres – a move that would not terribly endear the Péquistes to the Quebec voters. Godin also said that a "written note" had been delivered to Ottawa, and that Reagan himself was taking a personal interest in the whole situation.

As the controversial cabinet cave-in became front-page news in

Quebec, Jack Valenti admitted that he had personally written to Lévesque, calling the Cinema Law "an expropriation of American interests" and threatening the complete "pull out" of the majors from the province. Valenti told *Le Devoir*: "I wrote to Lévesque like I write to many other prime ministers. I wrote to him because I was against a law which, in my view, is the most restrictive and protectionist that I know." Valenti here must have been speaking in hyperbole, for by comparison to the 1985 agreement signed between the government of India and the MPEAA, Quebec's Cinema Law is relatively tame.

But the MPAA cannot fathom foreign status for Canada. "I'm convinced," André Guérin told me, "that that's the major factor. They can't accept that Canada could be separate as far as cinema is concerned." Prime Minister Mulroney and Minister of Communications Marcel Masse both strongly protested this U.S. intervention into the domestic politics of Canada, though (strangely) their pointed remarks were carried only on Radio-Canada news.

Perhaps not coincidentally, at the same time that the Quebec cabinet was caving in to State Department pressure, Valenti was preparing an address to the U.S. Council on Foreign Relations. On December 4, 1985, he told them: "In many countries we are entangled in trade hedgerows, confidently erected by those nations who believe they can, with impunity, choke off the entry of films and TV material while they enjoy with profit and freedom the ample market of the U.S.A." First singling out Taiwan, Valenti attacked its film quota, its "bulky restrictions," its ineffective copyright laws. "All this," he said, "from a country with a ten-billion dollar trade surplus with the United States in 1984 and growing larger in 1985." Then he moved on to Canada, which, by the way, had a $20.4 billion trade surplus with the United States in 1984. Attacking the cable industry, the Quebec Cinema Law, and Canadian policy restrictions on U.S. film, broadcasting, and publishing companies that "are denied the right to open offices if they are not now in place," Valenti concluded his address: "We should begin the long journey toward turning the trade deficit around by moving on the front that can be more swiftly breached: market access to foreign countries of a scale equal to the hospitality which their goods and their businessmen find in our country." Because Valenti speaks for the U.S. entertainment conglomerates' interests, there should be little doubt about which "front" and "market access" he is referring to here.

But it is doubtful whether the Mulroney government has perceived the situation similarly. David Crane says that of the eighty-
four industry profiles prepared for the free-trade talks by Canada,
"none dealt with cultural industries." Marcel Masse, however,
appeared to fully grasp the situation. Just days after the Quebec cabinet cave-in, his office released the report of the Federal Task Force on
Film, which recommended nationalizing the entire film distribution
sector. But if Valenti was worried by this, he needn't have been, for
that free-trade ball was careening down the alley towards a strike. It
rolled over Masse's green paper on foreign ownership in the cultural
industries, which the government politely shelved. Then it rolled
over Masse's publishing policy, with the government allowing Gulf
and Western to acquire Prentice-Hall Canada. (Almost immediately,
Gulf and Western's Paramount Pictures raided Canadian "indie"
Norstar Releasing – taking away half its business by buying up the
rights to all films previously supplied to Norstar by Atlantic Releasing of New York.) And then it rolled over Masse himself, who was
shunted off to another portfolio. The Man Who Knew Too Much.

Meanwhile Jack Valenti and the MPAA continue to advise the U.S.
government on those "trade hedgerows" that stand in the way of the
"global system" so desired by the multinational corporations. For his
part, Simon Reisman, who has advocated the selling of Canada's
fresh-water resources to the U.S., seems equally poised at the bargaining table to trade off the country's cultural life-blood, if not by design,
then by default. He does not appear to recognize that in the last quarter of the twentieth century the world has fully entered a mass-media
age in which the U.S. entertainment business has the leading edge.
That this fact could be central to all aspects of international trade is a
possibility that escapes not just Reisman, but many Canadians.

Bill 109 remains on the books: a legal act whose proposed regulations the Bourassa government has said it will look into "for further
study." If all the cultural policy papers, research studies, task force
reports, green papers, white papers, and royal commission volumes
that have been devoted to the cultural industries in Canada were laid
end to end, there would be a formidable border between Canada and
the United States from sea to sea. As Reagan has succinctly put it:
"Thank God for Canada."

(1986)

☐ Jesus of Montreal:
Culling the Living Flower

"JESUS IS 'IN' these days," says the lawyer and career-planner to the protagonist Daniel in Denys Arcand's *Jesus of Montreal*. As the subject for film narrative, the story of Jesus has perennially been in, resurfacing in different eras and cultures to be retold according to a wide variety of emphases and *zeitgeists*. In recent times, *The Robe* is as different from *Jesus Christ Superstar* and *The Last Temptation of Christ* as *The Gospel According to St. Matthew* differs from Godard's *Hail Mary*. Each age and culture seems to generate its own film version of Jesus.

The infinite variations of these portraits don't come just from the varying personality, politics, and aesthetic vision of each director. The differences also spring from their unique cultural contexts. A society in which a significant number of swear words refer to the church is already well-steeped in the political critique of institutions that Arcand has honed throughout his career. By abandoning the impulse to make a Biblical epic (like Martin Scorsese's *Last Temptation...*), Arcand's film encompasses far more political territory.

Ernesto Cardenal, the Minister of Culture of Nicaragua, once stated with regard to Cuba, "The trouble with Castro's socialism is it's not Christian enough, because if it were truly Christian it would be more communist." That insight into the radical message of what is "truly Christian" permeates *Jesus of Montreal*, making it an extraordinarily complex meditation on the process of co-optation and institutionalization itself.

Arcand avoids the problem of Biblical realism by telling the story of Jesus as, on one level, a passion play put on in contemporary Montreal. An out-of-work actor, Daniel Coulombe, is hired by a Catholic priest, Father Leclerc, to "modernize" the play, which has run as a tourist attraction for some thirty-five years on Mount Royal. Daniel gathers other actors to collaborate on the new script. Their collaboration and interrelationships become another telling of the story of Jesus, on a second level.

On both levels Arcand incorporates much of the comprehensive research and rethinking of the historical Jesus and of early Christianity that has been taking place in Biblical scholarship over the last three decades, spurred by the discovery of the Nag Hammadi Codices in Egypt in 1945 and made available to scholars since the late 1950s. Those ancient codices (named after the village near which they were found) turned out to be Coptic translations of first- and second-century Gnostic scriptures that were considered heresy by second-century orthodox Christianity and were therefore excluded from the official New Testament. Not incidentally, that same orthodox strand of Christianity had become, by the fourth century, the official religion of the Roman Empire – a significant irony given the Christian sect's radical beginnings.

These other gospels and scriptures, most of which had been translated into English by the late 1970s, provide quite a different portrait of the historical Jesus and the early Christian communities than the one usually conveyed by official versions. As the academic theologian tells Daniel, while surreptitiously handing over research documents, there have been "archaeological discoveries, computer analyses of texts, new translations of the Talmud" – new research into Jesus' time that tends to trouble the institutionalized Church. With regard to Jesus, he says cryptically, "We're beginning to understand who he really was."

The emerging portrait in Gnostic scholarship suggests an historical Jesus who was a sexual being; a lover who treated women as equals, who danced with his disciples, who was steeped in most of the esoteric / magical traditions of the East and who was a highly political radical, challenging both the imperial powers of Rome and a collusionist rabbinical hierarchy that kept the people enslaved to Roman rule.

Moreover, the early Christian communities appear to have been fully non-sexist as well as widely diverse in their beliefs and practices: purposely devoid of dogma, since the prevailing Gnosticism emphasized inner knowing and personal understanding gleaned from one's own inner spiritual quest. To read *The Nag Hammadi Library*, as well as Elaine Pagel's explication of the texts in *The Gnostic Gospels*, is to enter a profoundly different scriptural vision. Indeed, feminist sleuths cannot help noting Peter's jealousy of Mary Magdalene, "whom Christ loved more than the others" – a jealousy that might account for the subsequent smear on her image. As feminist Biblical scholars have recognized, there is no basis for the prevailing assumption that Mary Magdalene was a whore. The most that is said of her past in the New Testament gospels is that she had been "possessed of seven demons" before Jesus' exorcism. And in the Gnostic scriptures, she is his closest disciple.

Thus, Peter's jealousy might also account for the historical splitting-off of the institutionalized Catholic Chruch based on papal succession and dogma, and the simultaneous suppression of Gnosticism. This "heresy" involved equality for women, lack of hierarchy and dogma, and a vision of the deity as both father and mother, with the female side of the dyad known as Sophia.

But such research and rethinking is dangerous in some circles. In handing over the contemporary research the academic theologian says to Daniel, "Please don't tell anyone. It will get me in trouble. You actors can say what you want." Such freedom turns out to be spurious, as Father Leclerc becomes enraged by the "modernized" passion play (which contains many Gnostic aspects) and demands that the actors return to his original version. The portions of it that we have seen, shown on videotape to Daniel early in the film are recognizably empty bombast: shallow images and sentimental clichés that are utterly hollow, but which convey an acceptable portrait of Jesus as preached by institutionalized Catholicism. When Daniel protests that their new passion play "works" (speaks to the people), Father Leclerc answers quite frankly: "I don't want it to work!"

Thus, Arcand highlights the radical message of Jesus by contrasting it with the institutionalized message of the Catholic Church (depicted as a virtually empty edifice). In their bitterness and scorn of the church, most members of the left who have a Christian background have thrown out Jesus' message as well and have raised their children without any spiritual heritage. In the film, the seventeen-year-old nymphet (the companion of the lawyer) says the passion play on the mountain is the first time she has heard the story of Jesus at all. But Arcand further recognizes that this spiritual vacuum has been

filled by the electronic media, which have become the new institutionalized "church," or in the Marxist phrase, the new "opium of the
people."

As a result, *Jesus of Montreal* is a brilliantly Godardian demystifi-
cation of the media, a sardonic send-up through deconstructive techniques of that new "religion" that preaches the most vacuous values,
summarized by the beer commercial being made in the film: "The
young crowd is here / We worship beer." By satirizing media and
media techniques, Arcand addresses the extent to which the media
church exploits and drains all meaning from modern life. But by
doing so, Arcand makes his major theme in *Jesus of Montreal* simulation itself: the prevailing *zeitgeist*. As the lawyer tells Daniel, "Some
ways of saying nothing go over so well. Look at Ronald Reagan!
Today, all you see is actors."

Arcand's decision to tell the story of Jesus, at the second level,
through the lives of actors in "showbiz Montreal," gives his theme of
simulation full reign. After all, it is the job of actors to simulate, to
play a role. But Arcand is making subtle distinctions between levels
of illusion-making, and the motivations behind each. The scope of
Arcand's project is actually encapsulated in the first few minutes of
his feature.

The film opens on a scene inside a rustic hovel where two men are
quarrelling. The man dressed in rags shouts in despair at the
wealthier other, "You said, 'Man must root out the idea of God from
life!'" The second man quickly leaves, while the ragged one, taking a
rope out of a chest, speaks in anguish to himself about suicide and the
loss of God. Putting the noose around his neck and tying the rope to a
rafter, he steps off the chair to his death. A burst of applause accom-
panies a cut to a long shot that shows actors on a stage, taking their
final bows.

Thus, what we at first assume to be a realistic scene in the film's
opening is revealed to be part of a play within the film: a play based on
Dostoyevksy's *Brothers Karamazov*. After the long shot of the actors
on stage, there is a cut to a medium shot of two members of the audience. The woman says to her companion with regard to the lead actor
(the man dressed in rags), "I want his head ... for my next campaign."
"He doesn't do ads," her companion answers. "I've heard that
before," says the woman.

Within these opening two or three minutes, Arcand signals his
style based on the Brechtian / Godardian technique of unmasking the

illusion-making process, alerting us to the simulations at work in every area of the acting profession. As well, he acknowledges that actors are the proletariat of a media industry engaged in head-hunting, with the ongoing temptation to "sell out." It is highly appropriate that Arcand tells the story of Jesus and his disciples, on the second level, as the story of a group of actors trying to survive with their integrity intact. The levels of allegory in the film all resonate around questions of what is real and what is unreal, what is meaningful and what is meaningless in an industry (and a society) based on simulation. As Daniel / Jesus gathers his colleagues from the acting community, Arcand subtly answers the questions in his wonderfully sardonic way.

After recognizing his friend Constance in Father Leclerc's video, Daniel finds her working in a soup kitchen. It's meaningful work, she explains, "Things have become so corrupt here." They then go together to a film studio where another actor, Martin, is engaged in a bit of hilarious voice-over work: simulating sexual passion for the soundtrack of a porn movie. He immediately quits the job to collaborate on the passion play.

The three find their next contact in another film studio, where actor René is delivering a voice-over narration for a special-effects film on the history of the universe from "big bang" to big crunch. Amidst all the pyrotechnics, René reads his script: "When the last soul vanishes from the earth, the universe will bear no trace of man's passing." After the take, he says to the director, with barely disguised scorn, "It leaves a lot unexplained."

The fourth actor-colleague is found during her starring role in a TV commercial for a cologne called "Esprit No. 7," whose ad is based on a Kundera novel. As everything becomes commodified, potential grist for the trendy media mill, the bankruptcy of meaning is contrasted to the passion play embodied in the life of Daniel / Jesus and his actor / disciple friends. Not surprisingly, Arcand depicts the story of Jesus driving the money-changers out of the temple as Daniel busting up the beer commercial audition, in which the women actors have been purposely humiliated. Interestingly, Arcand has this audition take place within the theatre set for the Dostoyevsky play that opened the film. Distinctions between meaningful and meaningless simulations are being delineated.

But Arcand goes further with this theme, recognizing that both the media church and the Catholic Church are steeped in illusions and role-playing. The "bad priest" character of Father Leclerc – a failed actor-turned-priest, who goes through the motions to keep his big apartment, his provided daily meals, his security – reflects the hypocrisy and emptiness of the church, in which decisions depend on not offending a board of directors, just as in the business world.

Where Arcand has taken the greatest risk is by thereby aligning both the media church and institutionalized Catholicism as simulations that substitute for, and actually oppose, the radical and real message of Jesus' words. In the film, both these institutions descend upon Daniel / Jesus' work to alter and co-opt it for their own purposes. But Arcand also simultaneously shows the transformative power of Jesus' message – a message that beaks the boundaries between theatre and life, between simulation and the real.

In taking this risk Arcand has subtly equated both the media church and official Catholicism with that despair voiced in the Dostoyevsky play. Arcand's techniques, which make us question our assumptions based on first impressions, could also be applied to that bit of dialogue in the play where the ragged man shouts at the wealthier one. At first, we might assume that the "you" referred to in the line, "You said, 'Man must root out the idea of God from life!'" refers to Marx, Marxism. Dostoyevsky was a contemporary of Marx, and the line itself conveys the stereotypical view about "Marxist atheists" and "godless Communists." But as with everything in this film, Arcand may be asking us to rethink this assumption as well.

Father Leclerc, angry about Daniel's passion play, rages about a number of things, including the fact that "Communists recite the Sermon on the Mount." It is right after this that he says of the passion play, "I don't want it to work!" Arcand's theme of simulations, of the co-optation of the radical message of Jesus (and spirituality itself) by the media church and official Catholicism, suggests it is these institutions that have essentially "rooted out the idea of God from life," opting for empty and meaningless spectacle that exploits deeply human needs, including spiritual needs.

Arcand thereby returns us to the original Marx and to the rethinking that has been taking place in Third World liberation theology – a movement at odds with official Catholicism. Just as Ernesto Cardenal recognized the radical message in what is "truly Christian," so other Third World thinkers have explored the close affinities between early Christian communities infused with Jesus' message and Marx's political critique. Mexican writer Jose Miranda (author of *Marx and the Bible* and *Marx Against the Marxists*) has traced the many New Testament references in Marx's original work and has persuasively argued that Marx (a baptized Christian) recognized that "early Christianity *was socialism*, and from that socialism is consciously derived the socialism of the Commune and that of the International founded by Marx."

The famous passage about "the opium of the people" has rarely been quoted in its entirety. When it is, it suggests a significant (if subtle) distinction between organized religion and embodied spirituality:

> Religious distress is at the same time the expression of real distress and the protest against real distress. Religion is the sigh of the oppressed creature, the heart of the heartless world, just as it is the spirit of the spiritless situation. It is the opium of the people. The demand to give up the illusions about its conditions is the demand to give up a condition that needs illusions. Criticism has plucked the imaginary flowers from the chain, not so that men will wear the chain without any fantasy or consolation, but so that they will break the chain and cull the living flower.

Marx's last sentence could apply to Arcand's *Jesus of Monteal*, which plucks imaginary flowers from both the media religion and institutionalized Catholicism to "cull the living flower" of Jesus' message.

(1990)

II
Mindscape

◻ Imagine ...

SOMETIMES IT STRIKES ME that our society is getting more and more graphic and literal. It's especially noticeable in stuff designed with kids in mind. There the unquestioned assumption seems to be that nothing should be left for the imagination, or even that nobody *has* an imagination any more.

You see it in places like Canada's Wonderland or Marineland, and any of the other popular theme parks, where explicit and detailed reproduction of reality is what's celebrated. You see it in kids' comics – heavy-metal *hommages* to magic realism. You see it in the popular scratch-'n-sniff stickers that all the kids collect: scratch the lemon sticker and smell "lemon." You see it in video-games, prized for their graphic depictions – right down to the little explosions on screen. There's even a board game out now for playing "Battleship," complete with little plastic replicas of all the boats in the opposing fleets. We used to play this game on graph paper, secretly locating our forces on our separate grids with simple Xs. Five Xs in a row symbolized a destroyer, for instance. All the drama of the game took place in the imagination.

Kids' toys, too, have become increasingly graphic over the years. Irwin Toys introduced Baby Alive in 1975 – a rather loathsome doll that wet its diapers. It was followed by a doll that not only wet but also developed "diaper rash," which could be "cured" by the accompanying nurse's kit. The $570-million-plus annual toy market in Canada has also been big on "character merchandising" – bringing out dolls and toys derived from TV and movies: the Cher doll, the Joey Stivic Baby doll, the Six Million Dollar Man doll, the E.T. doll, the Incredible Hulk doll, the Emergency ambulance, the S.W.A.T. car, etc.

In child psychology jargon, such toys are known as "highly structured toys": they have a very definite and detailed identity suggesting a specific function. The more highly structured a toy is, the less it invites imaginative play. The dolls modelled after TV or movie characters invite imitation of the characters' behaviour on screen. The battery-operated "action toys" leave little to do besides operating the on / off switch and watching.

Drs. Dorothy and Jerome Singer, psychologists at the Family and Television Research Center at Yale University, conducted a study in which children were given such TV-inspired toys, as well as "minimally structured toys": a rope, pieces of wood, a cardboard box – simple objects that could be used in various ways. What they found is that all the children produced a greater variety of imaginative play in response to the simple objects that can be found in any home.

Of course, this makes perfect sense. It's easy to pretend that a cardboard box is a boat, a cave, an airplane, or any number of things. It's harder to pretend that a model of the Spaceship Enterprise, complete with flashing lights, might be a tractor. It's also difficult to imagine an Incredible Hulk doll as anything other than an Incredible Hulk. You couldn't pretend it was a cowboy, for instance. For that, I guess, you'd have to buy the John Wayne doll.

Obviously, then, the more highly structured a toy is, the more it is restricted to a single use in play, and the more toys must be sold to meet all the needs of play. It is also probably true that the more highly structured a toy is, the more quickly it becomes boring to the child. So by 1983 U.S. advertisers were spending $600 million a year just on ads selling things to kids. The stuff that looks best on TV, of course, is the stuff that is highly structured and graphic. The average North American child watches eighteen thousand TV commercials a year. The toys children ask for, and receive, are largely the ones advertised on TV. And so the cycle continues.

What's most worrying in all this is what's happening to kids' imaginations. Teachers of young children often report that their charges don't seem to know how to play – an activity that directly springs from imagination. And teachers of reading are finding that kids are having major conceptual difficulties in this area. As one teacher put it: "When I read them a story without showing them pictures, the children always complain 'I can't see anything.' I have to really work to develop their visualizing skills."

If this makes you think of television, it should. What I think we're seeing, right through our entire culture, is the erosion of the imagination from thirty years of television. I will state it quite clearly: TV replaces the mind's eye.

"Imagination," writes Kate Moody in *Growing Up On Television* (McGraw-Hill, 1984), "is the capacity of the mind to project itself beyond its own perceptions and sensations." It is the picture-process of the mind, which can use concrete external stimuli as the raw material for new mental constructs and combinations. Imagination is the playfulness of the mind's eye, the ability to go beyond the limitations of the given reality. But imagination is much more than playfulness; or rather, our notion of playfulness must be extended to its full dignity. As Rose Goldsen writes in *The Show & Tell Machine* (Dell, 1978):

> Political thought, no less than any other kind, takes place in imagination. In imagination we move around the social system so that we can peer at social reality first from this vantage point, then from that one, each time taking our bearings from the different slant.... Social meanings emerge as we imagine the situation as it could otherwise have been (or be). The otherwise ... can exist only in imagination.

In other words, imagination is a truly revolutionary force, allowing us to conceive of alternatives. It is "radical" in the deepest sense of that word: transforming things at their root, opening up new possibilities, challenging and suspending (for the moment, or longer) the status quo.

According to authorities on child development, the prime time for the development of the imagination is between the ages of four and seven. It is a capacity we are all born with, but it must be given encouragement and opportunity if it is to develop. Much of its development, then, depends on environmental factors.

Those of us who had already passed through our preschool years before the advent of television around 1950 seem to have had more of a chance to develop "the mind's eye" than kids born into the TV environment. By their very nature, radio and books foster the creation of your own mental pictures, based on your individual life experiences and needs. Even illustrated children's books do not depict every action or every detail. There is room for inner visualizing by the child, room for variation within that visualizing. And each child's imaginative response is unique and is as valid as any other's.

But for the non-critical viewer, television pictures everything. Its prepackaged flow of visuals replaces the work of "the mind's eye." If TV viewing were merely an adjunct to other activities – like going to the movies on Saturday was for pre-TV generations – there would be little need for concern. But "the children of television" begin watching it as infants, and as preschoolers they devote more than twenty-five hours a week to it, on the average. Kate Moody states that it is precisely between the ages of four and seven that children's minds are most easily captured by TV viewing. Think of it: instead of millions of children off on their own personal flights of fantasy during their formative years, we have millions of children plugged in, for twenty-five or more hours per week, to the work of a few other people's imaginations. Moreover, as we have seen, much of children's non-TV playtime is also dictated by television through the toys it sells. Author Rose Goldsen has an excellent term for all this. She calls it "standardizing the terrain of imagination."

Those who think that special TV shows or channels for children are the answer may find another study conducted by Dorothy and Jerome Singer of interest. They decided to assess the effectiveness of a TV program specially designed to stimulate the imaginations of preschool children. They chose *Mr. Rogers' Neighborhood* and attempted to determine its effects, if any, upon children's imaginative play.

There were four groups of children involved in the study. The first group watched *Mr. Rogers' Neighborhood* every day for two weeks. The second group watched for the same period, but with an adult mediating the program's imaginative content. The third group watched no TV at all, but spent the time with a teacher who gave them exercises and games involving make-believe play and imagination. The control group of children watched no television and received no special adult attention. Then all four groups were observed at play.

The results revealed that the children exposed to the live adult and no TV viewing (group No. 3) showed the greatest increase in spontaneous imagination and pretend play. Those who watched the program with the adult intermediary present showed the next greatest gains. The other two groups showed little or no gains in their imaginative play. The study concluded that TV cannot stimulate a child's imagination nearly as well as a live person.

And here, perhaps, we come to the heart of the problem. I think all of us realize at some deep level just how demanding and challenging good parenting is. It in itself requires imagination – the ability to enter the world of childhood and understand, empathize with, the needs of children. Our society has never fostered good parenting. Its economic structure, in fact, dictates against it. Ask any parents if they have, or had, enough time and energy for their children. Ask yourself if your own parents had enough time and energy for you. The social and economic arrangements in our society make it almost impossible. This is not new. But what is new, over the last thirty years, is "the electronic babysitter." Children do not play, they are entertained. It is the difference between production and consumption. Those of us in our late thirties and older may not have had "live adults" to truly play with us, but at least we had our own "mind's eye" to make books and cardboard boxes come alive for us. The children of television have neither, it seems.

All of this was brought home quite vividly for me a few years ago when the Toronto Board of Education asked me to design a media curriculum for kids in their early teens. Teachers were finding, not surprisingly, that their students had no critical skills for dealing with the media barrage all around them. What made the project most interesting, however, was the fact that the teachers and advisors had made a crucial link between this lack of "media literacy" and another phenomenon noticeable in the classrooms. When asked to create products of their own imaginations (stories, drawings), the kids were almost totally at a loss.

Usually, all that these thirteen- and fourteen-year-olds could come up with were images or characters easily recognizable from television. They had no facility for imagining something uniquely of their own creation – something weird or wondrous, some strange artifact brought back from a flight of the imagination. According to their teachers, the kids couldn't think past the then-current TV clichés: a Fonzie, a muppet, bionic people, a cop with a 57-Magnum. Their stories and drawings seemed to be lifted intact from the TV screen.

What the Toronto board recognized at the time was that not only were the kids' imaginations sadly undeveloped, but that imagination and critical skills are thoroughly interconnected. Both have to do with being able to think of alternatives for a given reality. In designing the curriculum, I formulated an operating thesis: Without an imagination, it's virtually impossible to form a critical distance in terms of the media, and without a critical distance on the media, it's virtually impossible to exercise an imagination. This "vicious circle" is what the TV-generation seems to be caught in.

In retrospect, I guess I'd say that the curriculum turned out to be a kind of combination of groups No. 2 and No. 3 as described in the second study mentioned above. It included quite a few "remedial imagination" exercises geared to the kids' age level, as well as introductory exercises in media work and media criticism. I don't know if the curriculum is still being used. Given today's political climate, it would probably be considered a "frill" so I suspect that it is gathering mothballs next to curricula for dance or theatre arts.

I think of all this because the current climate would have us believe that "standardizing the terrain of imagination" has now been completed. The cultural / performance scene (TV, movies, theatre, music) is dominated by remakes, sequels, revivals, and reunions. On the political scene Margaret Thatcher has been re-elected with the slogan "There is no alternative"; Kissinger and Mondale have resurfaced for sequels; and the same old economic "cures" are being revived in new guise – "6 & 5," "Reagonomics," etc. I suspect we're supposed to think of society as being "highly structured" and thus not very amenable to imaginative tinkering and play – sort of like the toys sold to kids on TV. Actually, our social / political structures are more like cardboard boxes – they can be made into anything we want, given imagination ... if there's anybody out there who still knows how to play.

(1983)

☐ Framing Reality:
Thoughts on Soaps

A FEW YEARS AGO, while I was visiting Washington D.C., I did the conventional sight-seeing trip, stopping at various hallowed shrines – including the Lincoln Memorial. It was a lovely day, with spring in the air and that special quality of daylight that seems to be found only in D.C. on mid-March afternoons. Everything was perfect. Except that, a few paces to the right of Lincoln's knees, there was a bag lady parked with her metal shopping-cart piled high. Another tourist on the scene, laden with cameras and obviously wanting to take a post-card-perfect shot of the famed memorial, finally selected a vantage point from which (it was clear) the statue of Lincoln would be framed *sans* bag lady.

The dominant world-view in our society is much like that tourist. It frames reality in its own particular ways, including some things and excluding others. This dominant world-view purports to be the obviously "natural" and only way of seeing (therefore explaining) reality. But when we examine the boundaries of the frame – and especially when we know what has been excluded from the picture – we begin to see just how arbitrary, but politically motivated, are its dimensions. For example, until very recently it was possible to go through high school diligently reading one's history books (to use another "frame") and find no mention of women, blacks, or (except as part of a "hostile" landscape) Native peoples. Clearly, we must always ask: who frames reality, how do they frame it, and who benefits from this particular way of seeing things?

One of the most useful ways of answering these questions is to redraw the given frame: making it larger and more inclusive so that what was marginal or absent before can now be seen as part of the bigger picture.

This redrawing of the frame is precisely what radical groups are doing when they speak for the oppressed. By making present and visible what was formerly excluded and absent, they break the old frame and thereby completely change the picture. The dominant society may pretend for a while not to notice the reframing – sort of like the tourist trying to make-believe the bag lady wasn't there – but ultimately the larger picture, the new dimensions of the frame, will prevail.

In many cases we can find examples of alternative ways of seeing, different ways of framing reality, already existing within the subcultures of the oppressed. But we must be prepared to look in the most unlikely places.

Which brings me to daytime soap opera – a TV programming form often despised and dumped on by just about everybody, including feminists. But since daily soap opera has been popular with women viewers for three decades, it's worth our while to try and see what's in it that may be of use to challenge patriarchy, redrawing the dominant frames. Though this form of TV storytelling contains much that is silly, antifeminist, and just plain awful, daytime soap opera (or daily serial narrative) is also a totally unique narrative structure, unlike anything else on TV. As a form it expresses, I think, a different framing of reality, a different way of seeing and experiencing the world. Interestingly, Latin American countries have also long had their own indigenous daily soap operas – one of the few forms of indigenous TV drama within the barrage of U.S. program imports. In certain ways, daily serial narrative expresses a world-view common to the oppressed.

The most remarkable thing about daily soap opera is its historical scope. Many of the shows have been running continuously since the early 1950s, a phenomenon of longevity that even *The Tonight Show* can't match. And in these longest-running TV shows, many of the original characters are still part of the ever-unfolding story, and if not them, then certainly their progeny or their legacy within the fictional towns of their settings. I interviewed Erwin Nicholson, producer for *The Edge of Night*, a while back during the making of episode No. 6,400. "You see, in daytime," he said, "let's put it this way: there's just one big middle. Our beginning was twenty-five years ago. Now we're doing the middle, and hopefully there will be no end." Daily soaps have a frame that is multigenerational, in which the past always resonates within the present. In fact, a recurring theme in daily serial narrative is that one can't escape the past. While this is sometimes made overt in the story content, the structure itself necessarily contains the past in its ever-expandable middle.

By contrast, virtually everything else on TV is ahistorical, at least within its own frame. Sitcoms and action-adventure series (episodic narrative) have a kind of weird amnesia. A given program does not refer to events in a past one, so there's no historical continuity from episode to episode. And characters generally do not change over time in the sense of learning cumulatively from past events. Sitcoms and crime series contain no historical sense.

This is primarily because the dominant narrative structure selected for TV is that of classical drama, which has a clear-cut beginning, middle, and end. During the allotted time of the drama, some conflict is initiated, intensified to a climax, and then resolved. This structure works well for individual, self-contained dramas such as made-for-TV movies. And it worked well back in the "golden age" of the 1950s when U.S. TV was doing live, one-of-a-kind dramas like *Twelve Angry Men* or *The Miracle Worker*. But what is truly weird is that when TV turned from doing live, individual dramas, to doing filmed, episodic series – where the same characters reappear week by week – it took the classical narrative structure and stuck it on a programming premise that asks for different treatment.

The result is the continuing episodic series in which nothing and no one changes, in which the only continuity from episode to episode is the recurring sets, the recurring characters, and their unchangeable behaviour. Archie Bunker, the "lovable bigot," may soften and mellow his viewpoint during the course of an episode, but we know that next week he will reappear just as irascible as ever: as though this week's confrontation really meant nothing.

All narrative functions in terms of the expectation of what is to come. Will Matt Dillon catch the bank robbers? In classical narrative, this expectation is rewarded. The climax and denouement serve to resolve the difficulties and answer the question. During the half-hour or hour-long program, things are put right again, all questions are answered. This structure is basically reassuring: it contains a return to order, at least a resolution of the disorder created by expectation itself. But it seems to me that when this structure is used with characters who reappear week by week unaffected by past events, the implication is more than reassuring: it is insistent upon the status quo. It says, in effect, that no matter what happens, nothing will change. By excluding historical continuity, episodic narrative draws a rigid frame around the present, telling us that the past cannot affect it.

The network news is also presented along the lines of classical drama. Each item is given its own self-contained little beginning, middle, and end and is presented as though it had no real connection to – or explanation in – the past. Each item is rigidly separated off from every other item, as though what happens in Beirut, for example, has no connection to a change in the domestic price of oil, for instance. And each item (and the news in general) assumes that the spoken words of politicians are to be conveyed to us without really interrogating or examining their hidden nuances, subtleties, and larger context.

Daytime soap opera, or daily serial narrative, is *not* based on the structure of classical drama. With its ever-expandable middle (and no end in sight), expectation is never-ending. Resolutions are always deferred, new questions are always being introduced. Will Bill find out that his wife's sister's baby is really his by artificial insemination? Will his wife submit to her sister's blackmail attempts, or will she finally let Bill know the truth? We tune in tomorrow not so much to find out the answers as to find out what further complications will be added to the questions, what new wrinkles will be given to our anticipation. If Bill discovers the truth, will this lead to another nervous breakdown, causing him to go back to Springfield General where his ex-wife and illegitimate daughter are both doctors and sworn enemies?

(I never promised you *The Cherry Orchard.*)

What is interesting here is the form, and the world-view. If episodic narrative (sitcoms, crime series) is obsessed with re-establishing order and rigidly framing the status quo of the present, daily serial narrative celebrates change, complications, and complexity. According to its frame or world-view, the one thing we know is that events will make a difference to what happens in the next installment. Everything can change, including characters. Daily soap opera, with its huge historical scope, its complexity of continuing and interwoven story-lines, and its large constellations of interrelationships, poses a world-view in which there is no such thing as a final resolution and no such thing as "the status quo." In this structure, there is no privileged main character whose "status quo" represents the whole. Rather, we see here that everything and everyone is immediately or remotely affecting and being affected by everything else.

Daily soap opera presents a frame that is far more inclusive, larger, than any other on TV. Through it, one experiences the given world as historical, interconnected, and ever changing.

Because it is constantly recapitulating or retelling its own past, daily serial narrative seems to take two steps forward and one step back. This is reflected in its use of language or style of dialogue. Daytime soap dialogue is almost torturously repetitious, as characters try to explain what they mean, or elaborate on their feelings, or retell in different words an emotional experience from the day before. It is hard to describe soap's unique dialogue, but it is obviously different from the style of dialogue heard on prime-time.

TV language at night is quite pertinent, to the point, and non-repetitious. There are few pauses, few gropings for words. The dialogue is clearly geared to helping advance the narrative towards the climax and the restoration of order. Words do not stand in the way of this advancement, they help it. We might say that on prime-time, words quite simply mean what they say. TV's night-time language is presented as almost naively beneficent – always accomplishing its goals, communicating effectively, and impeding nothing.

But in daytime soap opera, dialogue is quite purposely layered with nuance, hidden meanings, pregnant pauses, repetitions, and rewordings which suggest that language is something to be examined and analyzed: something untrustworthy that must be explored and listened to carefully. Historically, women have been denied the power of the Word. Stereotypically cast in the role of listener, they have developed a sensitivity to the nuances and subtleties of language – learning to read between the lines, so to speak. This alertness to language (especially in combination with facial expressions and bodily gestures) is a key element of soap opera. Arguably, it is a major strength of women themselves, an aspect of their differing world-view, their larger, more inclusive framing of the world that refuses to see things as fixed, unchanging, unconnected, resolved, and unquestionable.

Despite all its shortcomings (and there are many), daily soap opera contains unique differences, ways of redrawing the frames by which to view reality. Through their historical scope and long-range continuity in which the past keeps resonating in the present, their assertion that things always change and events always have long-term repercussions, and their conscious questioning of the spoken word, daytime soaps provide us with some useful tools by which to examine other things in the dominant society.

(1984)

☐ A Chip off the Old Block

OVER THE PAST year or so there has emerged in the mass media what can only be called the Computer Bandwagon. Since early 1983 the media have become filled with news articles, feature stories, and, of course, advertising devoted to the wonders of the computer – especially the "personal" or "family" computer. In March 1983, *The Globe and Mail* instituted its weekly "Technology" section, highlighting computerization. In autumn 1985, CBC-FM's *Arts National* began its new "Friday Night" program, including weekly coverage of "high tech." The major North American news magazines, including *Maclean's*, have published cover stories dealing with the computer, while many daily newspapers now offer computer columns as a standard feature. *Psychology Today* devoted its entire December 1983 edition to the computer, and in February 1984 *Chatelaine* published its "Plain-English Guide to the Personal Computer." Even that bastion of New Left journalism, *Mother Jones*, ended its investigation into computerland ("Fast Times For High Tech," December 1983) with the recommendation – "If you can't beat it, buy it."

Several things are worrying about this Computer Bandwagon. The most obvious is the feeling of *inevitability* that surrounds it. The media seem to unquestionably assume that computerizing the home is the next inevitable step in social evolution. It is as though everyone – journalists and consumers alike – has accepted the slogan by which Apple Computer Inc. advertises its hardware: "Soon there'll be just two kinds of people. Those who use computers and those who use Apples."

According to my recent research, only *Maclean's* reporters Gillian

MacKay and James Fleming ("At Home with IBM," November 14, 1983) have dared to challenge this basic assumption. They quote a computer consultant as saying: "The home computer market just has not taken off. The reason is simple: what can you use them for? I don't know." And they go on to state:

> Much-touted uses like home banking, personal budgeting and catalogue shopping via television sets have failed to rouse widespread interest; indeed, Ontario's Infomart venture into computerized home shopping, VISTA, died amidst failing retailer support late last month. John Bear, author of *The Computer Wimp*, cites the story of one Toronto man who was so desperate to find new uses for his $4,000 personal computer that after he had indexed his addresses and Christmas lists he turned to cataloguing all his neckties.

But such practical, down-to-earth reportage is rare in media coverage of computerization. More typical is the thinly disguised enthusiasm of *Psychology Today* in its special computer issue last December. Editor Douglas Gasner writes: "While the god in the machine may be a lower-case entity, it is nevertheless a formidable god, sometimes maybe even an ennobling one." And in the same issue Neil Frude excitedly states in his article "The Affectionate Machine": "It can be anticipated that computer systems will be future friends and intimates as well as colleagues."

Which brings me to the second worrying thing about the Computer Bandwagon – the anthropomorphizing of these pieces of machinery. This is immediately apparent in the ads for personal computers, which commonly ascribe human characteristics to them. The ad for the Apple IIe and III shows a smiling man cuddled up to his computer, with the headline: "How To Make Friends With a Computer." (The copy tells us that it's "just a matter of you getting to know your personal computer personally.") Texas Instruments' ad for the TI-99/4A Home Computer declares it "The One That Can Grow With You." The ad for the Commodore 64 tells us that "It Writes, Rates, Creates, Even Telecommunicates," while Xerox's 16/8 computer is "The Only Computer That Can Walk And Chew Gum At The Same Time" (meaning it can do two tasks at the same time). Atari advertises its 800 XL Home Computer with the slogan: "We Made Them Smart Enough To Know You're Only Human." And IBM launched its "little newcomer in the growing family of IBM personal computers" – the PCjr – with a picture of a Charlie Chaplin look-alike (more about that later) pushing a baby carriage, and the headline: "Announcing A Proud Addition To Your Family."

Perhaps copywriters assume that by anthropomorphizing computers, they will make them more acceptable to the general populace, more readily able to be integrated into family life (like "cute" little R2D2 in *Star Wars*). Whatever the motivation, it clearly mirrors the thinking of computer experts themselves, who seem to look upon their creations as much more than pieces of hardware. Says Alan Kay, Atari's chief scientist (sometimes called "the father of the personal computer"): "Although the personal computer can be guided in any direction we choose, the real sin would be to make it act like a machine." Brian Gaines, an expert on human-machine interaction, states: "Sympathy and understanding are traits that we might hope for in people, and in requiring them in computer systems, we are clearly beginning to accept the computer as a 'colleague' rather than a 'tool.'" Patrick Huyghe, researcher in artificial intelligence, writes: "So many of the activities of the computer resemble human cognitive processes that the comparison between man and machine has never been more apt."

This industry-wide refusal to view the computer as simply another tool or machine raises suspicions of male "womb-envy" (perhaps first noticed as a masculine trait by Mary Shelley in her novel *Frankenstein*). In any case, the anthropomorphizing of the computer is accompanied by a simultaneous mechanizing of the human. Within the computer ethos, the human brain is described in terms of a machine, and it is found to be wanting, deficient. This mechanizing of the human is usually very subtly done. It can be found in the metaphors and models used to explain how the brain works. For example, in his article entitled "The Hardware of the Brain" (see what I mean?) in the *Psychology Today* computer issue, John David Sinclair attempts to outline the differences between computer and brain functioning. He explains that the basic units of a computer are the transistors, which act as switches with two positions: open or closed. When the transistors are closed, electricity flows through them. When the transistors are open, the signal does not get through. These two states, open or closed, correspond to the 1 and 0 binary system that digital computers use.

The brain, however, functions through synapses, which are also "like switches" but which have *more* than two states. The brain's synapses can also be partly open and partly closed, allowing gradients of strength in their signals and not just the totally open or totally closed positions found in transistors. From this, Sinclair concludes: "Synapses are thus more like loose connections than good switches. Having a brain with about 100 trillion loose connections may be partly responsible for our sometimes fuzzy thinking." Obviously, the machine is to be the measure of all things. In comparison to the binary (either/or) efficiency of the digital computer, the functioning of the brain appears "fuzzy."

Our patriarchal culture has always valued abstract digital logic, separating thinking from feeling so that emotions or contextual awareness doesn't mess up the strictly "rational," "scientific," and efficient objectivity it considers the be-all and end-all of thought. Not surprisingly then, computer experts themselves tend to equate the binary, digital mode with thinking *per se.* Says MIT's Sherry Turkle: "Our anxiety about the computer is based not so much on whether computers could ever think like people but on whether people have always thought like computers." Another MIT computer expert, Marvin Minsky, states: "I think that what we have learned is that we are probably computers." Speak for yourself, Minsky.

This overvaluing of digital logic has led to an even more worrying trend in the computer ethos: the impulse to deify the computer, to ascribe God-like qualities to it. Again, we can see this in some of the ads. The Xerox computer is shown floating in the sky, backed by majestic clouds – an iconography borrowed from medieval depictions of God-the-Father. The Commodore 64 computer ad includes a lapel button that says: "I adore my 64." The Atari 800 XL slogan – "We Make Them Smart Enough To Know You're Only Human" – implies a greater-than-human intelligence at work. When even the editor of *Psychology Today* can write unselfconsciously of "the formidable god in the machine," we know we must be in mythic territory.

Charles Ferguson writes, in *The Male Attitude*:

> The machine, if fully developed, offered Man the prospect that he might become as important as woman in the life process. This was part of the vision and the imagination. With the machine he could produce. *Like an ancient diety,* it would enable him to do what he could not do otherwise.... Except as menials, there would be no woman in the process of production ... just as there was no man around in any significant way at the birth of a child. (emphasis added)

The "ancient deity" implicit in the machine is, quite probably, the patriarchal God of the Old Testament: ruthless lawgiver of "thou-shalt-nots" and harsh judge over a strictly demarcated binary (either/or) code of living. Indeed, as depicted in Genesis, this God's process of producing all creation is strikingly non-feminine and non-organic. God simply says: "Let there be light," etc. As Charles Ferguson writes of the Genesis creation myth: "There was no concept of conception, no gestation, no fetus, no growth in uterus, no birth. Rather the job was done by fiat: Let there be!" Carol Ochs, in her book *Behind The Sex of God* (Beacon, 1977), compares an earlier matriarchal creation myth with the Genesis version, and says of the latter: "The supreme god no longer creates from the body but must prove that he can create from the spirit or 'by word alone.'" Moreover, Genesis not only erases the feminine principle as progenitor, its version actually inverts it – having Adam subsequently "give birth" to Eve from his left side.

By the time of the New Testament, the Gospel of John (1:1) tells us: "In the beginning was the Word, and the Word was with God, and the Word was God," thereby echoing and reinforcing the idea that the source of all creation is an abstract principle operating in terms of digital logic. Not surprisingly, our Judeo-Christian heritage abounds in the suppression and exploitation of all that is non-logical, non-digital, non-verbal.

Arguably, it is the force of this heritage that may be behind the impulse to deify the computer. Certainly this unique machine is the most recent, and most impressive, example of the rule of digital logic. And to the experts and supplicants, the computer must seem – like the Old Testament God – to create by fiat: Let there be!

By subtly deifying the technology, the computer industry evokes the resonance and weight of patriarchal religious authority and also perpetrates a kind of grand mystification of its whole industrial ethos. An example of this can be found in the article by Robert Arnold Russel in *Saturday Night's* April 1984 issue. In his cover story, "One Year That Changed The World," Russel argues convincingly that the year 1975 was a turning point in the mass-market introduction of digital, computerized, "smart" technology. However, he concludes the piece with this passage (which summarizes his position, and, in a way, that of the whole computer industry): "It was in 1975 that the materialistic, nationalistic, polluting, squandering, brutal industrial age began to yield to a more *spiritual*, global, conserving, information economy. The world changed forever in 1975, and the year may well come to be studied and honoured." (emphasis added)

Russel conveniently ignores the fact that Malaysia, Taiwan, and Singapore are teeming with Silicon Valley sweatshops where teenage women toil away bonding microchips at less than $3 a day for their North American employers. Moreover, his argument that computerization has brought a "structural change" to society only mystifies the extent to which computerization is simply patriarchal capitalism's thinking and methods taken to a more efficient level. His notion of "globalism" is fraught with the same kind of obfuscation that surrounded McLuhan's concept of the "global village." (As we all know, "global" means "American" in such contexts.) And who is to say that computers are more "conserving" than any other mode? They seem to use a helluva lot of electricity.

In other words, there's little reason to believe that the "information economy" (read: computerization) is any less "materialistic, nationalistic, polluting, squandering, brutal" than the industrial age. (If you're wondering about polluting, talk to VDT operators about low-level radiation and to engineers about ozone-layer depletion in the silicon process.) But the tip-off in Russel's final passage is his use of the word spiritual. Like others fascinated by computers, he must pay homage to the god in the machine.

To remove this spiritual aura that surrounds computerization, perhaps it is useful to look at one last advertisement – which effectively reveals the human distortions and manipulations of information inherent in "the information economy." IBM's media campaign for its latest personal computer – the PCjr – uses a Charlie Chaplin look-alike variously wheeling a baby carriage (carrying the "proud addition to your family") or plugging in the computer, with the headline: "How To Plug Your Family Into Modern Times." The allusion, of course, is to Chaplin's 1936 film Modern Times – which was actually a semi-Marxist indictment of patriarchal capitalism's mechanistic, technological oppression of the workplace. The IBM ad does some interesting but obscene things with this allusion and with the Chaplin icon.

IBM copywriters appear to assume that our memory of the actual movie will by now be vague and hazy, so their ad can use the resonance of the allusion for the company's own purposes. Accordingly, they lift the words of the movie title – which the company must assume have by now lost the sardonic edge Chaplin gave them – and use the denotative meaning of these words to summarize the era we live in: "modern times." Within the same operation in the ad, IBM appropriates the popular image of Chaplin and neatly subverts it – using the icon to endorse and serve the very ideology that Chaplin challenged.

This shameful distortion and subversion should forewarn us of the dangers inherent in handing over more and more territory to the computer. The industry is very big on memory. It enthuses over the computer's random-access memory (RAM) which it measures in kilobytes (K) and uses as a major selling feature. But, as we see in the IBM ad, memory can be quite random indeed. Not only facts but also iconographic resonance can be shifted and distorted to suit and serve the needs of "the information economy."

Faced with the widespread media push towards computerization, the mystification of the industry, and the deification of the technology, we need to recognize the computer as the result of, and the ultimate expression for, patriarchal capitalism's world-view and values. We must place limits on the extent to which we allow the computer to take over our world.

(1984)

☐ A Lament for Supergirl

SUPERGIRL DEAD!... screams the banner headline of the *Daily Planet*, the Metropolis newspaper for which Clark Kent moonlights when he's not off battling crime as Superman. Great Hera! Could it be true? Can superheroes really die?! Even more startling, has DC Comics actually snuffed one of its major creations?

The answer is starkly depicted on George Perez's magnificent cover for issue No. 7 (October 1985) of DC's *Crisis on Infinite Earths* – the twelve-part series that started in January and is radically streamlining DC's multiverse. There Superman stands, crying in agony and holding the lifeless body of his beloved cousin Kara (alias Linda Lee Danvers, alias Supergirl) in his arms. Behind him, the entire galaxy of DC superheroes has gathered to mourn the death of one of their own – killed while gallantly saving Superman from the evil Anti-Monitor, Master of the Anti-Matter Universe. Who would have thought DC editor Marv Wolfman would go this far in his efforts to simplify the DC morass of parallel worlds and proliferating characters! But something had to be done. In recent years, the company has even resorted to publishing comic-book encyclopedias to identify its confusing array of alternate universes, superheroes, and villains. Wolfman says the problem started in the 1950s when DC Comics developed two worlds: Earth-1 and Earth-2. Earth-2 became the domain for the original, aging DC heroes created in the late 1930s and early 1940s: Superman, Wonder Woman, Batman, and the others. Earth-1 was the parallel world for their new, ageless identities created in the 1950s: identities granted additional superpowers and slightly different costumes. But, says Wolfman, "Over the last 25 years, the writers sort of got carried away and invented all these new earths: Earth-3, Earth-4, Earth-x, Earth-s."

To stem the confusion, DC's team of editors came up with the idea for *Crisis on Infinite Earths*, timed to coincide with DC Comics' fiftieth anniversary. The series is not only dramatically paring down the infinite earths to just one earth, it is also crippling, retiring, and even killing off some of the superheroes. "We had 60-year-old characters wandering around on these different earths," says Wolfman. "It was so confusing!"

But Supergirl was only twenty-three. And unlike the Earth-2 Batman, who met his demise early in the *Crisis*, she had no ageless counterpart on Earth-1 to continue in her stead. Supergirl was truly singular.

Shocked as I am by her demise, I realize I should have expected this. After all, when DC Comics suspended publication of *Supergirl* with the September 1984 issue, the cover showed her battling Future-Man, who cackles defiantly: "You are the Past, the Dead Past!" And though Supergirl manages to change Future-Man back into Professor Metzner (her former employer), the final panels of that issue showed her tellingly subdued by other strange forces. Her old boyfriend Richard Malverne suddenly returns and gathers Linda Lee in his arms. As his mouth merges with hers in the very last panel, our Supergirl manages one final utterance: "Dick! I ... MMMMPHHH!"

"Supergirl's demise will strengthen Superman, our best-known hero," explains Wolfman when I call to ask a plaintive "why?" "She had the same powers as Superman, the same origin, so she was diminishing his powers by being so similar. Superman is a part of American mythology. He was created in 1938. Supergirl, on the other hand, was created in 1958. She came last and never was as popular."

Well, it's a clear case of "last hired, first fired." Even in the world of superheroes, there are certain grisly realities that can't be altered by one's superpowers. Ever in the shadow of her more auspicious cousin, Supergirl's career was what we might call "checkered." Launched several times over the last twenty-three years, Supergirl's Linda Lee Danvers had tried teaching, movie acting, and in her most recent incarnation (1982) became nineteen again and entered Chicago's Lake Shore University as a student and part-time secretary. But she could never settle on the right niche for herself. Maybe Chicago just wasn't her kind of town. Moreover, her superalter ego went through what Wolfman describes as "an incessant number of costume and hair changes" until finally settling on the trendy red headband for her newly permed blond hair and the Superman-style leotard with flared mini-skirt.

Saddled with such an ongoing identity crisis, Supergirl neverthe-less managed to keep up with her schoolwork and also battle arch-vil-lains like Decay, Ms. Mesmer, Brains, and Blackstarr. Those readers who complained that her rogues' gallery lacked credibility seemed to overlook the fact that our Maid of Steel was also grappling with more subtle threats like Richard Malverne and passing Psychology 101. But when called to fight against grim Decay or any of the other villains menacing the campus, Supergirl never hesitated to give her all.

One may argue with Wolfman's belief that "When the fans see how Supergirl is eliminated, they will not be disappointed," but it is true that she achieves a moment of poignant glory. As the forces of Anti-Matter threaten to kill not only Superman but also the entire Mul-tiverse, Supergirl rushes into the centre of destruction, thinking: "Be true to yourself ... Be the best you are able ... Don't ever give anything but your best." Even Dr. Light, watching Supergirl in action, is moved to reconsider her own superheroine motives: "Sh-She is a hero, totally selfless and concerned only with others. While I have wasted away my life with selfishness."

Batgirl's eulogy, broadcast on wGBS-TV during the memorial ser-vices, serves as a fitting summation of Kara / Linda Lee Danvers / Supergirl: "... A hero is not measured by what her power may be, but by the courage she shows in living and the warmth she holds in her heart."

Supergirl is dead. Long live Supergirl. As the grieving Superman utters: "I live on. Hurt, but not disillusioned."

(1985)

❏ Invitation to a Gagging:
Forbidden Images and Friendly Icons

The South African press, despite its lip service (in the past) to media
freedom, has never been free; it has been restricted by its publishers or
the state. Censorship is a noose that has tightened as the apartheid
state has become less secure. The death rattle of media freedom hardly
raises an eyebrow now. Whites, who often have reacted with fury to
media criticism of their apartheid lifestyle, now have the media they
deserve: an emasculated complication of trivia that pays little attention to the tragedy that their country has become.

– Charlene Smith

IT IS FRIGHTENINGLY eerie to watch the news, read the newspapers,
and learn almost nothing of what is really going on in South Africa
since the state of emergency (the second one in months) was imposed
by President Pieter Botha on June 12, 1986, in advance of the tenth
anniversary of the 1976 Soweto riots. We hear rumours of more than
three thousand people (including union and church leaders, as well as
at least twelve South African journalists) arrested by the police and
state security forces in these first weeks, of "isolated" killings in the
black townships, of some sit-down strikes by black workers since the
June 16 "stayaway," of a new curfew imposed on dozens of black
townships, of a series of bombings in the cities. But primarily what
we learn is the extent to which the South African and foreign press
have been effectively gagged by the white minority regime. That in
itself has become the major news story.

In terms of the outside world, the press gag is obviously based on
that old cliché: out of sight, out of mind. By making unlawful the
transmission of anything but the most innocuous imagery and facts,

the South African regime apparently assumes that we, outside the country, will forget or lose interest in South African news and the fate of its oppressed, that we will come to believe the "more human face" of apartheid that its PR efforts are dedicated to erecting. Botha and company are counting on the collective amnesia that is such a significant part of the media age, with its passing journalistic fads and its rapid turnover of news. As the world lurches from crisis to crisis, the white minority regime assumes that, in time, the attention of the press and the outside world will shift elsewhere to the next hot story. Unfortunately, this tactic has worked with other regimes in other places and other times, and it could work again.

Within South Africa itself, the press gag seems to serve a somewhat different function: that of protecting and maintaining the white South African belief-system, which surely must include the perception of themselves as good, fair, God-loving, Christian people. By obliterating from the media those facts and sights that could challenge this self-perception, the press gag is both sign and symptom of the forms of denial operating in the white psyche. To grasp the truth of this, we need only consider what, under the law, are the tabooed images.

It is illegal for any photographer, radio broadcaster, or TV cameraperson to film or record "any public disturbance, disorder, riot, public violence, strike or boycott, or any damaging of any property, or any assault or killing of any person." It is also illegal to film or record the police and state security forces carrying out their assigned enforcement duties, which are increasingly totalitarian in scope. Thus, the whites (already geographically distant from the scenes of eruption) are further spared the mediated sight of their own collective hatred and violence finding expression on the bodies and minds of the black "others." The television screen, that most vivid conveyor of images into the sanctity of the home, must not be allowed to impinge upon that other, psychological screen: denial.

Since this dynamic of seeing / not seeing is structurally so central to both the press gag and the apartheid belief-system itself, one particular image must be underscored in our brief analysis, especially because of its long-term repression in apartheid society. Since 1964 it has been illegal in South Africa to publish any photographs or drawings of Nelson Mandela – the leader of the African National Congress imprisoned these past twenty-four years for "terrorism." Obviously this decades-long repression of one visual icon, the graphic representation of the face of one man, indicates the extraordinary degree of psychological resonance and symbolic power that has formed around this single signifier. Undoubtedly the repression itself has contributed to this symbolic resonance: an accumulation of both white dread and black hope projected onto the simple lines of a face. That the man himself, Mandela, remains unseen within his prison cell surely adds to the symbolic power of the unseen icon.

The forbidden image of Mandela, then, must be included with, and in some sense must summarize, those other images that are taboo: the images of black rebellion in the townships, the images of white state violence in action, the imagery of suffering, oppression, death, destruction, and tragedy that erupt at the margins of the closed, white neighbourhoods. All this, in both representational and psychological terms, seems to have been pushed off the screen of consciousness in the collective white psyche.

By the very fact of the extremity of taboos surrounding this material and this imagery, we can assume that there is a structural counterpart – an *acceptable* opposite pole of imagery – that is equally extreme in its popularity for white South Africans. Counter-balancing the forbidden, unseen image of Mandela (that most repressed of icons), there must be another image, fully accepted and even loved, that stands visible in the light of popular adulation.

South African writer Charlene Smith has characterized her country's media as "an emasculated complication of trivia" that ignores the dark sides of its own reality. It has always been my belief that trivia of any sort deserves close scrutiny: that it is precisely there, in the seemingly innocuous and insignificant leisure-time diversions of a society, that one can find important clues to societal workings and dynamics that have been rendered less than conscious, but which operate beneath the surface nonetheless. Entertainment is never just entertainment. Always, it speaks far more than it says or sings, dances, belches, laughs. Not surprisingly then, it is within South Africa's "emasculated complication of trivia" that we find the acceptable icon that structurally opposes the repressed image of Nelson Mandela.

Since the winter of 1985, the top-rated televison series in white South Africa has been, and continues to be, *The Cosby Show* – featuring that (supposedly) cute, cuddly, upper-middle-class black family known as the Huxtables. To make sense of this mind-boggling fact, we need to try to see what is going on in the series, and especially in the character of Heathcliff Huxtable (played by Bill Cosby), that makes it so fully appealing to white apartheid viewers. Like two sides of an archetype, the images of Heathcliff Huxtable and Nelson Mandela must, in some sense, be seen as opposite.

In the weekly dilemmas that structure its plots, in the roseate tone of its sensibility and unreality, *The Cosby Show* is a complete throwback to 1950s sitcom humour: dealing with cute little domestic hassles of the nuclear family, problems of upper-middle-class consumption and spending, apparently endearing little communication breakdowns between parents and children, etc. There is virtually no acknowledgement in the show of the difficulties for even a wealthy black family in a white society, nor is there anything to suggest that the Huxtables, in their designer clothes and opulent home, are in any way *atypical* of most blacks.

Heathcliff Huxtable is more than a successful doctor and family man, he is the apparently acceptable version of the black father in this 1980s remake of *Father Knows Best*. Surrounded by the lavish domestic set, with all its signs of wealthy consumption and taste, Huxtable is thus fully placed within the structure of the larger society, whose values and systems he obviously upholds. As father, he is kind and jocular, playful and understanding, at ease with his wealth and position, guiding his little flock with a firm hand along the labyrinths of TV-life. Of course, as father he is also leader, and what this black father-leader "knows best" is thus worth focusing on.

Heathcliff Huxtable is a family physician: a role that carries with it, besides the obvious wealth, a number of significant symbolic nuances. This role becomes especially important to our understanding of Huxtable's popularity in white South Africa. It is apparent that the structural opposition between the repressed image of Nelson Mandela and the popularity of the Huxtable icon can also be expressed in the terms: "terrorist" / doctor. Here we begin to sense the psychological and ideological usefulness of *The Cosby Show*.

While the image of the terrorist is threatening and disturbing, the image of the doctor is soothing and calming. The doctor heals wounds rather than causing them. The doctor nurtures people in their pain rather than contributing to their pain. The doctor facilitates birth rather than inflicting death. Ultimately, the doctor symbolizes nurturing and life, while the terrorist symbolizes revenge and death.

As black father-leader, Heathcliff Huxtable is thus very appealing to the guilty white psyche. In a white society where the role of blacks has been limited to that of caretaking, domestic service in white households, and laborious servility for others, it must be profoundly wish-fulfilling to see that black role raised to its height in the ultimate caretaker – the doctor: nurturing and soothing. In a society that must somewhere feel the heavy guilt of decades of apartheid, it must be satisfying to see weekly the image of a black father-leader whose personality and vocation itself have nothing to do with revenge and destruction. In a society whose white regime daily evokes the rage of the oppressed, it must be a relief to gaze upon the face and possessions and life-style of Heathcliff Huxtable: the image of a black man clearly not oppressed and obviously not threatening. What black father-leader Heathcliff Huxtable "knows best" is that there is no racial oppression, and whatever subterranean levels of guilt may throb in the white psyche, the doctor's compassionate calling promises the soothing avoidance of any reprisals.

By contrast, the repressed image of Nelson Mandela represents the dreaded alternative black father-leader who "knows best" that there clearly is racial oppression through which blacks are kept poor, uneducated, excluded, and fully victimized, and that apartheid must be overthrown, by violence if necessary. The forbidden image of Mandela speaks not only of the real situation of the blacks, but also of the terror circulating in the white psyche: a terror of black rage, and a terror of facing one's own inhuman cruelties to that black race. Since none of this can be faced – and the press gag effectively keeps it all out of sight – The Cosby Show serves to reiterate every week that none of it need be faced: that there is no racial oppression, that in fact the Huxtables are better off than many whites, that there is no real reason to change anything.

Through the popularity of The Cosby Show, which is the top TV hit in our society as well, we and the white South Africans are indubitably linked at the level of pop culture tastes. Whether we like to admit it or not, the Huxtables must be as reassuring to us, at some deep level, as they are to the white minority regime.

(1986)

◻ On Night Heat

"TWO WOMEN KILLED in one week. Every woman expects to be number three.... A new fear, and there was enough fear already." So intones the Walter Winchell-type crime reporter / narrator whose column loosely informs *Night Heat*, CTV's new prime-time series that has president Murray Chercover raving about "a new phase" in the network's "evolution." I watched Episode No. 2 of the twenty-six programs slated for the Tuesday 10 PM time-slot. If (as I suspect) it's any indication of what's to come, then CTV may find itself in trouble.

Not that the series isn't "brilliantly done." There's no question that Lantos and Roth's RSL Entertainment Corp. knows how to make a cop-show. The episode I saw had all the right moves as far as the formula's conventions are concerned: fast pacing, strong police characters (Scott Hylands, Jeff Wincott), tight story-line, lots of tension, eerie shadows and creative lighting, foreground / background action and visual tension within the frame, widely varied camera distances (from extreme long-shot to extreme close-up) that create intensity, ominous musical underscoring, etc., etc. *Night Heat* even wowed a jaded late-night U.S. audience when it played occasionally on CBS-TV's midnight time-slot in the spring of 1985.

But I recall reading a few murmurs in the U.S. press about the series' violence towards women. Episode No. 2 (shown on September 17, 1985) left little doubt.

Sure, I know ... it's difficult for any crime show to choose victims these days. Or criminals, for that matter. Some organized protest faction will inevitably find fault with their group's portrayal – whether it's white-collar businessmen protesting TV's depiction of corporate-gangster types, or Vietnam vets angry over the stereotyping of them as psychopaths, or women demanding that program-makers raise their consciousness about female stereotypes, or Blacks and Chicanos and Native peoples refusing to continually play the "heavies." What's surprising is that, in this climate of viewer sensitivity, no one has bothered to suggest that the crime show formula be retired as no longer socially viable. Apparently there is some unwritten television law that states that cops and criminals stories shall forever be of supreme interest on prime-time.

Given this, there *are* certain limitations that can be supported. One of them has to do with a kind of obsessive quality that often comes through in (male-made) crime show series. Episode No. 2 of *Night Heat* is a prime example.

Hylands and Wincott are on the trail of a murderer of women, a psychopath who specializes in hara-kari-style eviscerations of his victims. In the course of the program, we learn that there have been fifteen such killings – a shocking enough figure and mental image. But that isn't enough for *Night Heat*. Before the sixteenth victim is found, the police characters must discuss in detail the wounds found on the previous corpses by which they were "drained of blood almost instantly." After the next victim, Merry Young, is discovered, we are treated to 1) an on-scene reference to the grisly state of her body, 2) a reporters' scrum at the police office in which the journalists demand more details about the mayhem, with plaintive cries that "we heard the bodies were practically eviscerated," 3) a follow-up scene in which Hylands graphically demonstrates the movement of the murderer's knife "in, up, across" the woman's torso, 4) a computer check of previous victims which necessitates another description of the killing style wherein the knife "goes up and over the left breast."

By this point one begins to suspect that the program-makers are unconsciously revealing and revelling in their own fascination with violence towards women. It's the old Cecil B. DeMille approach: indulge in sin for three-quarters of the movie, then righteously punish at the end. But in this case, before the climactic ending, we get to see two more women charmed by the smooth-talking murderer (and Chuck Shamata is certainly convincing in the role), with one of them dangling helpless on the safety net of the CN Tower as the knife-wielding psychopath waits for her to give up her attempt to escape and come down to his waiting arms.

If we take the message in such a story beyond the obvious truisms that 1) there are dangerous psychopaths around, and 2) the police catch them, we come up against the recurring and deep-seated message that it is women's ontological state to live in fear for their very lives. The obvious traces of obsessive emphasis on this message in programs like Episode No. 2 of *Night Heat* unmask the program's overt concerns. In fact, in the highlighted scenes for the following week's *Night Heat*, a man strikes a woman across the face – leading me to strongly suspect that Episode No. 2's obsessive hostilities towards women were more than a momentary aberration in the series. Lest we innocently believe that, as the Shamata character says, it's just "a little backwards step between the sexes," we might look a bit closer at this genre.

George Gerbner and his colleagues at the University of Pennsylvania's Annenberg School have been studying the effects of violent TV programming (particularly crime series) since the early 1970s, making annual "violence profiles" for each U.S. network's schedule and interviewing thousands of TV viewers from all walks of life. What is most interesting about their work is that they have found that the most evident effect of violent programming is the distinct climate of fear it fosters in those viewers who watch a lot of it.

Regardless of age, education, or income-level, these "heavy viewers" (watching four hours or more of TV daily) consistently overestimate the extent of crime in the cities where they live, as well as their personal chances of being criminally victimized, and continually harbour exaggerated fears about the immediate world in which they live. This "mean-world syndrome" is strikingly absent in those interviewees who live in the same cities under similar sets of circumstances, but who watch little television. Gerbner told me in an interview that if viewers are afraid of their immediate environment, they will stay inside their homes – abandoning the city streets to a small minority of the populace which does engage in criminal acts – and in such a way does widespread fear contribute to urban crime.

The indications of this research are profound, raising basic questions about the extent to which crime series (a staple in formula programming ever since *Dragnet*) have contributed to Fortress America, have fuelled the drive for right-wing "law 'n order" measures, or have added to the deterioration of America's inner cities through the fearful flight to the suburbs. Though such questions can't be answered definitively, they are at least worth pondering, especially when Canadian networks and production companies automatically adopt this TV formula and fit it to Canadian locales.

More specifically, Gerbner's research reveals that women are the most prevalent victims in crime series. Correspondingly, those "heavy viewers" who are female turn out to be the ones most terrified to go out into the cities where they live.

"A new fear, and there was enough fear already," intones the *Night Heat* narrator. If CTV wishes to add to the climate of fear, especially by indulging in violence towards women in what seems to be *Night Heat*'s obsessive fashion, then viewers could make their own lives less stressful by simply turning the program off.

(1985)

☐ Real Men on the Campaign Trail

ON BOTH SIDES of the border, Elections '88 hit a vile new low in campaign rhetoric and posturing, with Boy Talk and Macho Mouth innuendo characterizing "political debate" in the last gasp of the twentieth century. Masculinity emerged as the real subtext of both the U.S. and Canadian federal elections. The winning strategy adopted by most of the venal pigs running for office was to talk like a Real Man.

In the United States, the Democratic challengers began their campaigns by trying to outmuscle one another and stay clear of "the sissy factor." Bruce Babbitt declared himself the first to "stand up" for America; Albert Gore Jr. tried to talk tough on arms control; and Michael Dukakis, the eventual nominee, boasted about being "firm" and resolute in guiding Massachusetts' economic turnaround.

Republican candidate George Bush was haunted by "the wimp factor" going into the campaign, but even more serious in the early days of the race was his tendency to botch just about every sentence issuing from his mouth. Call it "the dimwit factor."

In February, when Bush lost badly in the caucuses of the farming state of Iowa, he explained the loss by saying that people were too busy to vote for him because "they were at their daughters' coming out parties." Later, when asked by the press how he planned to address the drug problem, Bush answered, "I'm going to be coming out with my own drug problem." But his best blooper occurred at a Republican rally in Twin Falls, Idaho, in May. Boasting about his years with Ronald Reagan, the vice-president said, "We have had triumphs, we have made mistakes, we have had sex." In the shocked silence that followed, he quickly corrected himself to say, "We have had setbacks." As Bush later explained, "I don't always articulate, but I always do feel."

With both "the wimp factor" and "the dimwit factor" stalking Bush, his chief media director, Roger Ailes, recognized, at least halfway through the campaign, that some drastic image-revamping was called for. Real Man opponent Dukakis was scoring points off Bush's bloopers, garbled syntax, and damaging off-the-cuff remarks. Time to bring in the big guns.

Former White House speech writer Peggy Noonan, responsible for many of cowboy Reagan's most memorable flights of rhetoric, was rushed in to doctor the candidate's terrible foot-in-mouth disease. And simultaneously, his team of political imagemakers recognized that it was time for the Gunfight-at-the-OK-Corral phase of the campaign. Under remedial coaching, Bush began to swagger and engage in some he-man tough talk. His epic Real Man showdown with CBS anchorman Dan Rather was supposedly an indication of his masculine sparring and resolve. His refusal to discuss the Iran-Contra scandal was meant to indicate that this Real Man was not about to be pushed around by the press. But suddenly "the dimwit factor" struck again. "I will never apologize for the United States of America – I don't care what the facts are," he vowed, trying to affect a Clint Eastwood squint behind his glasses.

In the final months of the campaign, the U.S. candidates tried to look like posers at Muscle Beach, sprinkling their rhetoric with manly images of sexual potency, aggression, and, most of all, the repudiation of anything feminine. To cover their bland ineptness and their records as little more than insipid geeks, the U.S. presidential candidates latched onto Macho Mouth as the solution, cranking up their heroic postures as Real Men – strong, firm, resolute, aggressive, and domineering. No wonder the voter turnout on November 7 was the lowest since 1924. Less than 40 per cent of eligible voters even bothered to make a choice between these two poor excuses for manhood.

In Canada, Brian Mulroney took a cue from the U.S. Macho Mouth style early in the game when he claimed, on October 13, that "Our opponents are selling timidity and the concept of a little Canada." It sounded big and tough, with the Conservative leader, backed up by a $24-26 million federal government "information" campaign on free trade, leading the pack. During the televised debates, Mulroney led with the chin, seeming to pride himself on the fact that he doesn't consult with women's groups on issues like day-care. It was typical Macho Mouth style: distancing one's self from the dreaded taint of women's influence. He also tried to appear tough on issues like free trade's threats to Canada's social programs, asserting that "I think the best social program is a job."

But the day after the debates, with 72 per cent of the population agreeing that Turner had won the televised contest, Tory popularity suddenly started to wilt in the polls. Within days Tory standings had drooped noticeably, while a resurgence of the Liberal party thrust dramatically upwards on the polling charts.

The immediate effect on Mulroney was evident. He suddenly regressed from Macho Mouth to Boy Talk, a younger version of the same thing but with a twist. The difference is primarily to be found with reference to women, and it is like the difference between a six-year-old boy and a twelve-year-old boy. A six-year-old may think girls are "yucky" but still needs to cling to mummy's skirts from time to time. A twelve-year-old boy wouldn't be caught dead doing that.

So, just three days after the debates, Mulroney retreated from his bold foray into Macho Mouth. At a rally in Kingston, when he and Flora MacDonald were booed by a large group of anti-free-trade protesters, Mulroney shouted back: "Any time, any time ... I'll take you on any time. Flora and me!" When the heckling continued, he retaliated: "I'll tell you what my mother would do with you – she'd wash your mouth out with soap!"

It was a pathetic moment, and Tory strategists and the pro-free-trade business forces must have blanched in horror. Scrambling frantically to save the plunging Tory popularity and the odious, servile free-trade deal, Canada's business sector realized it was crucial to get some Real Men out on the campaign trail. They advised quickly that the Mulroney government send out the big guns. Soon Michael Wilson, John Crosbie, Jake Epp, Don Mazankowski, and Simon Reisman were out on the campaign trail, slinging he-man insults and going into hyper-gear with the jabbing forefinger. In the midst of the torrent of rhetoric about "liars," "traitors," "scaremongers," "cowards," and "wimps," it was apparent that the whole basis of the campaign had moved away from the issue of free trade and over to an entirely different footing, so to speak.

Nonetheless, under pressure, John "The Mouth" Crosbie regressed to some Boy Talk of his own. "I'm not going to be mambypamby [when] I disagree with a deliberate attempt to deceive the Canadian people by those in the NDP and Liberal party" who are "security blanket seekers. They go home at night and put their thumbs in their mouths and worry about what is going to happen to them the next day."

Assisted by the Wilson-Crosbie-Epp-Mazankowski-Reisman role-models, Mulroney got back into the Real Man saddle and rediscovered his Macho Mouth. In assessing the opposition, Mulroney referred to the NDP's Svend Robinson, a declared homosexual, with a sniggering remark at a November 2 rally. "Wouldn't that be something," he snickered, "Svend as minister of defence. I'll tell ya that would make one fine ministerial meeting." The remark went over so well that he used it again the next day at another rally. When reporters later suggested to him that he had made a slur, Mulroney coolly answered, "So what?"

Meanwhile, Canada's business sector started talking tough to save free trade. The Canadian Alliance For Trade and Job Opportunities, a business lobby group that ultimately sank more than $5 million into pro-free trade advocacy advertising campaigns, started to really pump iron rhetorically in the days after the TV debates. Their November 3 four-page ad in thirty-five newspapers across Canada, entitled "Straight Talk On Free Trade," effected a combination of patriarchal authoritarianism and Hemingwayesque prose, with punchy, short sentences dismissing all argument. On panels and press conferences, Alliance spokesmen Peter Lougheed, David Culver, Thomas d'Aquino, and Lorne Walls came out fighting like rabid skunks, snapping and snarling at opposing views and implying that anyone who questioned free trade was obviously not a Real Man.

On November 7, the Consumers Association of Canada pulled out of the Alliance, claiming that it was "a business lobby" and not the "non-partisan" organization it purported to be. Consumer spokesperson Tom Delany added that many businesses that opposed the free-trade deal had been "neutralized" by the Alliance's efforts, "which question their masculinity" if they have concerns about their ability to compete under free trade.

The terrible irony about all the Macho Mouth and Boy Talk by pro-free traders is that the deal itself makes Canada completely subservient to the United States in virtually every area of life. In other words, our Real Men (including women like Barbara McDougall) used Macho Mouth and tough-guy posturing to sell Canadians on a deal that actually wimped-out completely in terms of Canada's best interests. While it sounds like some political version of S&M, with our Real Men standing firm in their resolve that the country should be shafted, it's clearly a sign of the times. The dreaded "wimp factor" has addled the brains of both politicos and electorate alike.

Maybe we should invoke the child labour laws to get these dangerous little boys out of office and out of our hair. With Bush and Mulroney at the helm on both sides of the border, and with Macho posturing as the accepted mode for "credibility," society is headed for, in Bush's memorable phrase, "deep doo-doo."

(1989)

□ Packaging the Populace: Polling in the Age of Image Politics

> When a television director once suggested to Harry Truman that his tie was inappropriate for TV, Truman stared pityingly with those blue eyes for about ten seconds. "Does it really matter?" he asked. "Because if while I'm talking about Korea, people are asking each other about my necktie, it seems to me we're in a great deal of trouble."
>
> – Edmund Carpenter

SOME FORTY YEARS after this exchange between Truman and an unknown TV director, things have changed. Now a "focus group" would be convened, well in advance of the telecast, to determine the appropriate colour symbolism and patterned motif, the shape and precise knot of the presidential tie to match the intended mood of the televised speech. The results of an in-depth, psychographic survey would be shown to Harry, indicating that 42 per cent of the upscale, influential populace consider this particular tie troublesome.

The contemporary media advisor would answer that of course such things really do matter, that in the age of image-politics they can make the difference in the perceived credibility of any political leader. Indeed, a complex apparatus of media expertise exists primarily to ensure that such tiny details do not sabotage the smooth unfolding of the political will. It is as though during the past forty years of television's rise to sociopolitical hegemony, things like Truman's tie (Was it polka-dotted? A bow-tie? A polka-dotted bow-tie?) have expanded to fill the entire screen of our collective, imaginal brainpans. And yes, we are in a great deal of trouble.

But the term "image-politics" can be misleading, especially because it tends to direct our focus to effects rather than causes. Thus,

137

the term makes us think of things like John Turner's speech-coach during the '88 election, or George Bush's cowboy hat and hang 'em high rhetoric, mouthed to combat the wimp and sleaze factors plaguing him in the early days of his campaign. The conventional understanding of the term "image-politics" was nicely summarized in autumn 1988 by media consultant Patricia Adams: "Mulroney is so damn well packaged that you could turn him around and expect to see a list of ingredients on his back."

But the real basis upon which image-politics necessarily proceeds is the coded images in our heads. As veteran U.S. political media advisor and adman Tony Schwartz puts it: "The goal of a media advisor is to tie up the voter and deliver him to the candidate. So it is really the *voter* who is packaged by the media, not the candidate."

To understand the full implications of this tantalizing statement – which applies equally to both consumers and voters in contemporary life – we must delve into the dismaying complexities and hideous obfuscations of that key linchpin and primary mediator between the public and the power-bloc: the pollster. Over the past two decades, in-depth attitudinal polling (otherwise known as "psychographics") has become absolutely central to every aspect of public relations and business-as-usual, especially political business-as-usual.

In the current era of the "sound bite," the "process event," the "photo opportunity" and "image doctors" for every corporate and governmental media event (sometimes euphemistically known as "communications"), attitudinal polling is the crucial first step in a sequence of events designed to address the images in our heads. Not surprisingly, the layers of mystification surrounding the politics of polling are as thick as the leather of Allan Gregg's trademark jacket.

The telephone interviewers hang up their backpacks and athletic tote-bags, their umbrellas and Eaton's shopping bags, and gather in the posh sixth-floor meeting room of Decima Research Ltd., Gregg's polling firm, located in the Rosedale area of uptown Toronto. It's 5:00 PM, the time when most people are finishing the daily grind, but for the fifty-or-so members of the Decima telephone staff – many of them high school and university students – the working "day" is just beginning.

The supervisor hands out the evening's questionnaire. This time it's an attitudinal survey being conducted for the major chemical

companies, who want to know how Canadians feel about their industry. A quick glance at the graffiti scrawls in any urban area would provide an answer, but the companies are interested in a far more
detailed and in-depth psychological grasp of the public attitude. Not
just the numbers pro and con, but the mind-set behind the opinion:
the feelings, fears, beliefs, mental images, bits of information and
knowledge, the media clichés, and the prevailing attitudes that generate the respondent's opinion.

The supervisor goes through the questionnaire section by section,
pointing out the potential trouble-spots in the twenty-three-page survey, and she informs the crew that the optimal time for completing
this particular in-depth probe is thirty-seven minutes per respondent.
Obviously, to get a good representative sample of more than a thousand completed surveys, the crew is going to be dealing with this particular questionnaire for a couple of nights running.

As the briefing finishes, the interviewers pick up their sharpened
pencils and their stacks of questionnaires and retire to their individual cubicles, where a long list of phone numbers waits beside each
phone. The numbers have been randomly selected by computer, but
they all accord with the base-line demographics sample frame chosen
for this survey: urban middle class. Across Canada, the first round of
fifty telephones starts to ring. "Hello," says the Decima interviewer
in each cubicle, "today we're talking to people in your neighbourhood
about issues facing us all."

Decima Research Ltd., chaired by Canadian polling *wunderkind*
Allan Gregg, is part of the massive and sophisticated polling apparatus that has been erected across North America since the early 1970s.
Official pollster for the Tory party, and with an impressive battery of
corporate clients, Decima is the leading company in Canada specializing in psychographics: meticulous profiles of consumer / voter attitudes matched with conventional demographic data (sex, age, race,
income, education, occupation, and location).

"I try not to use the word 'psychographics,'" Gregg tells me. "More
simply, people have a shared psychology and shared beliefs, that's
all." Nevertheless, five nights a week, every week of the year, year-in
and year-out, Decima (and similar companies) telephone thousands
of people who are willing to bare their psyches to some telephoning
stranger during a forty-minute probe.

The phenomenon itself would be worthy of analysis for what it may indicate about societal anomie and / or the telephone as terrorist weapon of modern-day marketing, but more important is the question of what happens to the resulting psychographic data. The answer is that it is the first step in a chain of media events that are now entirely typical of our times.

An historical example from the early days of Decima's ten-year rise to success indicates the sequential elements in the chain. In the summer of 1980, the Ottawa lobbyist for the Canadian Petroleum Association, Jamie Deacey, hired Decima to conduct a survey of the public's attitude towards the oil industry. Gregg's resulting probe revealed that, by and large, Canadians perceived oil companies as rich, greedy, untrustworthy tax-dodgers that could not be counted on to supply Canada's energy needs. While these results may have been somewhat shocking for the corporate sponsor of the survey, the findings were crucial for taking remedial action.

The association launched a national advocacy advertising campaign in newspapers, magazines, and television – fronted in the early years by former CBC-TV newsman Ken Colby. The ads extolled the virtues and achievements of the oil industry and particularly addressed (for the purpose of remedying) those weak points in the institutional image revealed by the attitudinal survey. Colby's familiar presence (his "recognition factor," to use the jargon) was useful for lending an aura of objectivity, and even news value, to the ads.

Meanwhile Decima continued to poll for subtle shifts in public opinion during the initial ad campaign. This allowed for the fine tuning of imagery and language used in subsequent ads so they would speak to the concerns and beliefs of the desired demographic constituency. Similarly, the psychographic data was useful for designing other aspects of the PR campaign, especially the "news management" side: press conferences, press releases, speeches by corporate spokesmen, and photo opportunities to generate favourable press coverage. As John Sawatsky reports in his book *The Insiders*, the result of this lengthy but dedicated PR campaign (dutifully tracked by Decima for its client) was that "the oil industry's 'honest' rating rose from 32 to 54 per cent in three years."

What must be emphasized about this now typical chain of events is that attitudinal survey findings do not necessarily lead to any real changes in the sponsoring client's actual behaviour. Feedback from the public vis-à-vis the oil industry, for instance, did not noticeably generate any industry housecleaning in those problem areas uncovered by the survey. Instead, the housecleaning was directed at the perceptions in the public mind: the images in our heads. Paraphrasing Tony Schwartz's dictum, we could say that it was the consumer-citizenry that was repackaged by the media campaign and delivered over to the corporate client.

Thus, the rise of psychographic polling has generated a standard sequence of events for corporate and governmental PR activity: 1) conduct an in-depth attitudinal survey; 2) mount an advocacy ad campaign that remedies any image-problems revealed; 3) track throughout the ad campaign to fine tune for opinion shifts; 4) take other PR steps (including "news management") to help alter perceptions; 5) keep on polling to stay on top of things.

This process has now become typical of every high-powered public relations endeavour. The first step is always to find out how the public feels about something. For example, in 1985 Decima began conducting in-depth attitudinal polling on the issue of free trade. "In 1987," says my Decima deep-throat (let's call her Silkwood), "we did a long survey on free trade – you know, a twenty-three-page questionnaire. We interviewed way over a thousand people on the phone, probing their hopes and fears, their opinions and beliefs about the free-trade deal. It was awful," says Silkwood, "I know it was being done to help somebody write propaganda, whoever was sponsoring the survey. What people don't know is that these attitudinal polls are the basis for propaganda."

Nevertheless, psychographic polling is now so commonplace that in Canada it has even become a kind of weird and twisted form of pop-culture ritual, thanks largely to our "punk pollster" wearing the earring and the leather jacket.

In 1989, for the fifth year in a row, Canada's weekly newsmagazine devoted virtually half of its first issue of the new year to the *Maclean's* / Decima Poll – twenty-three published pages of numbers, charts, statistical data, and personal interviews gathered by some fifty *Maclean's* staff members and the polling expertise of Decima Research Ltd.

This massive annual cover-story – "A Spotlight On Canadians," in the January 2, 1989 issue – takes up far more pages than *Maclean's* would ever devote to any news story during the rest of the year. Editor Kevin Doyle explains: "For one thing, it provides the most comprehensive post-election analysis of voters and voting patterns, based on

1,500 interviews, ever done in Canada. For another, it is one of the first attempts to measure changes in the attitudes of Canadians as the world rushes toward the end of one century and prepares to begin another – and a new millenium."

But there's another angle from which to view this gargantuan *Maclean's* / Decima Poll. It is a component part in the buildup of the necessary psychographic data base – national in scope and increasingly long-term – through which trends in the public psyche may be accurately pinpointed and targeted.

"*Maclean's* is one of our clents," says Gregg. "We do the poll for them. We say the data is ours and the information is theirs. But look. We already have a huge data base. We will merge census data, we subscribe to *InfoGlobe*, we access all kinds of data. But the most important, for our purposes, is always the up-to-the-minute data. The *Maclean's* poll provides historical context." In this sense, the annual survey is a spin-off of Gregg's tutelage under the most important pollster in the United States.

Hard to believe, but it's only a dozen years ago that Allan Gregg was Allan who? That was before Richard Wirthlin, pollster for Ronald Reagan since 1970, started a joint venture company in Canada and uttered a prophetic remark. "Allan," he said, "we're going to make you the number one pollster in this country. You watch."

Back in the mid-1970s, political polling in Canada was still in a primitive stage: focusing primarily on so-called "horse-race polls" (who's ahead) and relying on U.S. pollsters and political advisers for campaign strategy. The Progressive Conservatives, for instance, had perennially hired Bob Teeter (pollster for Nixon, then Ford, then Bush) to oversee their campaigns. But the feeling within the party was that Teeter tended to simply recycle his last Republican campaign strategy when advising the Tories.

At the same time that the Conservatives were becoming disenchanted with Teeter, a young university student arrived to work in the research office of the Tory headquarters. Allan Gregg impressed his superiors with his abilities and political savvy, and in the summer of 1978, Bill Neville, top Conservative Party strategist and advisor, nominated Gregg for an exchange program sponsored by the U.S. State Department.

Gregg applied for a ten-day consulting tour across the United States to interview and learn from the leading U.S. pollsters and political consultants. The State Department approved the idea and made arrangements for Gregg to meet the top guns in the field. On his whistle-stop tour through Washington and Texas, Gregg encountered the cream of the crop. But it was in California that he met *la crème de la crème* in a coterie of political advisors including Peter Hart, Pat Cadell, Lance Torrence, Matt Reese, Stu Spencer, and Richard Wirthlin.

It was Wirthlin who impressed Gregg the most. When it came to polling, nobody in the late 1970s Western world had a better grasp of the intricacies and techniques of the business. Certainly nobody else could even come close in terms of those three primary keys to the polling science: simulations, targeting, and tracking. And equally important, nobody had a more thoroughly detailed, psychologically convoluted, and demographically correlated national data base than Richard Wirthlin. By the time of Gregg's visit, Wirthlin had cranked up his Santa Ana polling apparatus to a fever pitch: poised to launch his Main Man right on course to the Big Enchilada.

Roland Perry's study of the twenty-year Wirthlin-Reagan collaboration, *Hidden Power* (Beaufort, 1984), reminds us that polling is an offspring of military "wargaming," which found high-tech formats in the late 1950s via computer developments. Military and political scientists at the Pentagon glommed on to the marvels of the technology for running complex simulations of battle: giving numerical weights to factors like population densities, opposing military strengths, precedents in battle, specific environmental conditions – thereby creating scenarios that could be quickly analyzed to yield probability outcomes. Wargaming by computer allowed for detailed, moment-by-moment adjustments to changing factors in the Cold War political scene.

Big business immediately saw the usefulness of such techniques for developing marketing models and strategies. When the new line of more accessible hardware, like the IBM 360 series, came on the market in the mid-1960s, business was already primed to engage in its own form of wargaming. For example, a company could run a wide range of production variables, demographic factors, market situations, and "what if?" scenarios to calculate probable outcomes. (What if we introduce a new brand of breakfast cereal into the market next year? Is the market saturated? Can it stand another competitor if we position our product for the adult market? What if our price per item is two cents lower than the nearest competitor? What if we pitch it to the female "pink collar" market? What if we launch in August? etc., etc.) The computer could handle such factors by correlating weighted numerical equivalents: spewing out model outcomes for each scenario.

Richard Wirthlin had helped develop such market simulation models for business during the experimental years, and he quickly recognized the potential usefulness of such strategies and marketing techniques for the political arena. In 1969 he started his own company, Decision Making Information (DMI), and began to build up the necessary demographic data base. Besides accessing every available statistical agency in the country, DMI hired a large crew of telephone interviewers for attitudinal survey work covering a wide range of consumer / voter issues, concerns, and beliefs.

By the time he joined Reagan's team of political advisors during the 1970 California gubernatorial race, Wirthlin was perfecting his "Political Information System" (PINS) – a complex mass of psychographic data on specific target groups across the country. PINS is based on five key elements: up-to-the-minute attitudinal survey work, fixed demographic information, historical voting patterns for every county in the United States, continuing assessment of political party strength in each state, and subjective analysis by Wirthlin's team.

"For 20 years," states Roland Perry, "Wirthlin has computer-filed his own polling data in the hundreds of campaigns he has run for Republicans, along with quantities of census figures, information from 37 federal departments, voting history figures from every county, and extensive market survey work for scores of American businesses." As a result, says Perry, "Wirthlin's computers can provide him in an instant with the political preferences and behavior of 110 categories of the American electorate."

In 1970, this computer targeting was a pioneering strategy in political campaigning and was used by Reagan's team to tailor ads, speeches, and direct-mail for specific audiences. By the time of Reagan's first presidential race, targeting had become so refined that it could pinpoint the prevailing psychographics of individual city neighbourhoods.

Another technique that Wirthlin borrowed from consumer marketing to apply to the 1970 campaign was tracking. It was this technique that most impressed Gregg during his 1978 visit. In the product world, once that new breakfast cereal is launched, it must be closely followed to provide feedback on marketing strategies. (In which individual stores within the fifty major markets is it moving? Which TV time-slots are delivering the desired consumer groups? What effect is the special display on supermarket shelves having? How is our product-recognition factor? What do focus groups feel about the words "high in fibre" on the package? etc., etc.)

Wirthlin recognized that tracking would help a candidate's team know whether specific speeches, events, and "news management" techniques were having an effect on the public or not. This could be determined best by daily attitudinal polling to precisely graph the ongoing course of a campaign. In the United States tracking has now become so standard that it is used continually, while the pollster's client is in office, to monitor his or her performance. "It's like turning on the television set," says Wirthlin. "We leave it on all the time. We don't take our finger off the pulse."

In the mid-1970s Wirthlin also began using the technique of simulations to develop predictive models for political strategy. This allows the team to run a variety of "what if?" scenarios before and during the campaign, reacting in advance to possible moves by the opposing candidates, possible developments on the international scene, possible changes in the stock market, or possible outcomes of TV debates. This technique provides a variety of futuristic scenarios and countermoves to help keep the campaign on top of developing action.

While Wirthlin was perfecting his polling techniques with an eye towards the 1980 presidential race, a few other changes were occurring that would boost pollsters to a place of (backstage) prominence. First, corporate business had become fed up with its dismally low "honest ratings" in the polls and blamed it on a hostile press. The first to take decisive PR action was Mobil Oil in 1973. The weapon of choice was the advocacy ad, based on attitudinal survey findings and designed to address demographic constituencies without going through the filter of adversarial reporters. By buying time and space in the media to speak their corporate minds on a wide range of political issues, companies could engage in some "news management" of their own. By 1980, U.S. business was spending more than $1 billion per year on advocacy ad campaigns.

Second, in the mid-1970s the U.S. Census, a division of the Department of Commerce, developed a service that sold complex demographic data about the population to polling companies like Wirthlin's DMI. The data filled in whatever gaps existed in Wirthlin's PINS system and opened up a new national data base for market researchers and pollsters across the country.

Third, in 1976 the U.S. Supreme Court ruled that political candidates may spend unlimited personal money on their campaigns, and "unaffiliated groups" can finance their pet candidates without any restrictions on spending – as long as their activity is not authorized by the candidate's official party organization. As a result, special-interest groups quickly began forming their own "political action committees" (PACs) to lobby for their own private agendas and to finance political campaigns. As Joseph Fanelli, president of the powerful Business-Industry PAC, stated early in the game: "We're interested in electing people with the right philosophy." Between 1976 and 1982, PAC funding for candidates jumped from $22.6 million to $80 million. By 1986 the figure had soared to $342 million, with the average U.S. political candidate for office receiving more than three times as much money from PACs as from a party organization.

This, then, was the political scene that greeted Allan Gregg during his 1978 tour of the top U.S. political pollsters and advisors. It was all a vile travesty of real democracy but, as writer Hunter S. Thompson would say, these things happen. And behind the scenes, busily gathering the data on the vulnerable citizen psyche, was the pollster, whose psychographic profiles provide the basis for fine tuning every political and corporate marketing strategy.

As Allan Gregg could see, there was nothing quite like it in Canada. The first step was to erect a decent polling apparatus, because tracking, especially daily tracking, was the key to every successful campaign

In the late 1970s there was another Canadian impressed with Wirthlin's work. Tom Scott of Sherwood Communications, an ad-exec and top honcho among the Ontario Tories, had quickly sized up the polling inadequacies of Bob Teeter and decided that it should be possible to build a Canadian polling company to operate in the private market and be on call to the Conservative Party.

Scott talked to Wirthlin and the two agreed to start up a fifty-fifty joint-venture company in Canada. With Sherwood Communications providing the start-up money and Wirthlin's DMI providing the state-of-the-art computer technology, polling methodologies and expertise, Decima Research Ltd. was created. While the idea was being struck, Scott convinced Wirthlin that Allan Gregg would be a worthwhile partner, not only because of his obvious abilities but also to avoid that old "Bob Teeter syndrome," wherein a U.S. pollster was running the show. Wirthlin agreed and Gregg was cut in with a one-fifth share.

Wirthlin moved his vice-president of administration from California to Toronto and sent a technical wizard to get all the hardware – the big phone banks and computers – up and running. There was also the necessary business of tutoring Gregg. While Wirthlin was the ideal mentor, Gregg was the ideal student. Abandoning his dream of starting a rock band, Gregg began to develop an innate flair for the subtleties and intricacies of the polling business. As Gregg later observed: "No one can analyze data faster than I can. I just crunch it up." Very soon Wirthlin was assuring his eager student about his prospects, that he could soon be "the number one pollster in this country." Decima opened for business in July 1979 sporting the most sophisticated polling hardware, software, and expertise the country had ever seen. Meanwhile, Wirthlin had a little job to do back home. The polls were showing that people thought his presidential candidate-client might just nuke everything in sight once in office.

Decima did $800,000 of business in the first year, $1.8 million in the second, and $2.4 million in the third. Despite this healthy growth, investors lost half-a-million dollars. Part of the loss came from Decima's financing of *Decima Quarterly* – a report of research-survey findings sold by subscription to corporate and government marketers for $24,000 a year. No doubt modelled after the similar quarterly developed in the United States by Patrick Caddell (private and Democratic Party pollster), Gregg's publication provided the attitudinal survey results of polls conducted every March, June, September, and December. By conducting in-depth polling interviews with 1,500 Canadians four times per year, *Decima Quarterly* gave marketers a psychographic profile of changing attitudes, insecurities, values, and beliefs across the country on a wide range of issues.

In the first three years of Decima's operation there were only two subscribers to *Decima Quarterly*, thus making it a massive drain on the company's resources. But Gregg's idea was simply ahead of its time for Canada: by 1985 there were fifty-two subscribers together paying a total of $1,248,000 for the publication. Nonetheless, during the early years both Wirthlin and Sherwood Communications decided to sell their shares in the company to Kinburn Capital, a holding company involved with Public Affairs International Ltd. (PAI).

At that time PAI was a fast-rising PR company specializing in government relations for corporate clients. It had been involved with Decima as a research partner for the *Decima Quarterly*. The feasibility (and efficiency) of a company that combined a polling arm and a lobbying arm was evident to everyone. By 1983 PAI president David MacNaughton, PAI vice-president Michael Robinson, and Decima chair Allan Gregg bought back Decima and PAI from Kinburn. It was a very smart move. By 1985 the PAI-Decima partnership was pulling in $17 million annually.

During the early 1980s a number of significant changes were occurring in the Canadian scene that greatly helped Decima's rise. Not coincidentally, these changes were also coalescing around the push for free trade – that volatile issue that became the focus of the 1988 federal election. Throughout the 1980s both government and corporate sectors in Canada recognized the wonders behind the new sequence that had caught on in the United States: psychographic polls / advocacy ads / tracking / fine tuning / news management / desired public perception.

The first step was the formation in 1976 of the Business Council on National Issues (BCNI), a lobby group representing 150 blue-chip corporations in Canada. By the early 1980s, the BCNI had become a "virtual shadow cabinet" (in the words of critic David Langille), skilled in government relations to the point of determining policy behind the scenes. At the same time, its member corporations jumped on the advocacy ad bandwagon to improve image problems revealed in the polls and to promote their own sectoral agendas. By 1982 an estimated 20 per cent of *The Globe and Mail*'s advertising revenues was coming from advocacy ad campaigns, with the figure on the rise.

Meanwhile Decima was starting to do a brisk business, as Canadian corporations caught on to the value of its polling activity and research. The 1984 election revealed the benefits of Gregg's polling apparatus for the Tories, especially his ability to do daily tracking throughout the campaign, while the opposition pollsters limped behind with their weekly and/or spot-polling procedures. Business also noted this distinctive feature of Decima, which was far in advance of any other outfit in Canada. Says Gregg: "Daily tracking is very important for picking up the edge on things like policy and news management. But it's really important for organizational purposes. I can do five hundred interviews a night during a campaign. Over five nights that gives me a huge sample size – 2,500 interviews all within the same sample frame. That gives a very complete picture of what's happening across the country riding by riding. Tracking is basic for fine tuning an election-projection model."

In 1984 another change occurred that would be significant to later developments. As the result of an appeal under the Charter of Rights by the National Citizens' Coalition, the section of the Canada Elections Act that had previously controlled activities and spending by special-interest groups was struck down. Spending by political parties and candidates remained limited by law, but there were no longer any curbs on spending by special-interest groups, nor were they under any obligation to disclose the sources of their financing.

In retrospect we can see that all these factors came together during the 1988 election. In the final four weeks of the campaign, following the TV debates, an influx of advocacy ads, corporate and Tory news management, and a blitz of direct-mail marketing and corporate employee-relations tactics turned the tide for the pro-free-trade forces and for Mulroney himself. There is little question that Gregg's polling abilities were central to an election in which one out of every four voters changed his or her mind at least once during the campaign.

Part of the fallout of that 1988 election was an obvious flurry of corporate takeovers and mergers, leading to some mighty large corporate bodies in that reverse fat farm called free enterprise. Decima has been involved in its own corporate moves – proving that it doesn't just merge data.

In February of 1989 the Decima-PAI partnership teamed up with Hill & Knowlton, the largest independent public-relations firm in the United States. Ironically enough, Hill and Knowlton's polling arm is Richard Wirthlin's DMI, meaning that the former mentor and investor had now taken over Gregg's outfit.

"As of the third week in February," crows Gregg, "Decima-PAI, which specializes in government relations, and Hill and Knowlton [which specializes in every form of public relations] are under the same roof. We are the only company in Canada which will now be able to deliver *full service* for a client."

"Does this mean you'll be designing advocacy ads?" I ask.

"This means doing advocacy ads, corporate image, speech writing, contacts, media relations, news management, *full* service. The thing we heard most in the past was clients would say to us: 'We did all this [polling] research and then we didn't do something with it.' Now that has changed."

I can hear the excitement in Gregg's voice and I know why. Hill & Knowlton has been doing PR for nearly sixty years and has a tremendous clientele worldwide: governments, multinationals, industry associations, political parties, you name it. "We are providers of services," Gregg is saying, "and they are looking at their suppliers to come with them ..." I tune out momentarily while he's talking. I've just flashed on something else my Decima deep-throat told me: that attitudinal surveys are two-tiered.

"During the week we survey the populace," Silkwood had said. "But on weekends a different staff comes in. They telephone individual corporate executives at home, by name, to get their attitudes and opinions on issues. That's a different data base."

You don't have to be Richard Wirthlin to guess what happens with *that* polling data. It helps to maintain accord between corporate movers-and-shakers and policy decisions of the party in power. That, indeed, is the essence of government relations: PR to effect and impact on government planning and thinking in advance of decisions. With Hill & Knowlton under the same roof, Decima will be accessing corporate desires worldwide, as well as fine tuning their PR strategies at every level. Meanwhile the pollsters will keep their fingers on our psychographic pulses, registering every blip, dip, peak, twist, and vagary in our prevailing mind-set, so that *full service* can be provided for clients.

"Start a rock band!" I want to say to Allan Gregg, who's now recounting his polling successes in Israeli and Australian elections. "Be a *real* punk," I want to interrupt. But I bite my tongue. I know that things have advanced far beyond the input of just one pollster. An awesome image arises in my mind: Richard Wirthlin's data bank, twenty years in the making, merging with all the accumulated psychographics data of Decima Research Ltd. Full service indeed.

(1989)

◻ Reclaiming the Body:
Beyond Media

His disciples said, "When will you become revealed to us and when shall we see you?" Jesus said, "When you disrobe without being ashamed and take up your garments and place them under your feet like little children and tread on them, then will you see the Son of the Living One, and you will not be afraid."
    – "The Gospel of Thomas," *Nag Hammadi Library*

BACK IN THE early 1970s, a particularly illuminating joke circulated among North American Native peoples: "Question: What is cultural deprivation? Answer: Being an upper-middle-class white kid living in a split-level suburban home with a colour TV." Like most good jokes, it penetrates to a core of truth. We in the overdeveloped countries are not accustomed to thinking of ourselves as in any way "deprived," especially with our electronic media seemingly bringing the entire world into our living rooms. Nevertheless, from a different cultural perspective and set of values, white western society is profoundly bereft of the fundamentals that give meaning to life. In the midst of our obscene, unlimited consumerism, we are, paradoxically, perhaps the most deprived people on the planet.

Focusing on the "deprivations" of affluent white Westerners may seem politically incorrect. Nonetheless, doing so is important because those deprivations are at the root of a world-view and a way of "life" that are profoundly destructive to the planet and to all other peoples and living species. Our addiction to technological "progress" and unlimited consumption is the sign of a deep, unmet hunger and loss within. What we have lost – in part as inheritors of the Judeo-

Christian patriarchy – is bodily wisdom: we have lost the body itself as the measure and ground of being.

One of the key insights of contemporary feminism, in its critique of the patriarchal system, is its recognition of the schizoid divisions that characterize the dominant world-view, and especially the splits between spirit and matter and between mind and body. Those of us born into Western – or Westernized – society inherit a prejudice that calls body and matter the "realm of the Devil," grossly inferior to spirit and mind. Even in an age that no longer consciously believes in gods and devils, the lingering fear and hatred of the body and matter are readily apparent in our wholesale destruction of the planet for the sake of a mental ideal called "progress." Patriarchy's hierarchical ranking of mind and spirit over body and matter can be traced, in the Christian tradition, to the Garden of Eden cosmology, in which body and matter become the locus of the dark, feminine Eve-Satan collusion, resulting in original sin and the "fall of man."

The ironically named Age of Enlightenment (which in fact coincided with the historical period of witch-burnings, the onset of the slave trade, and the plundering and decimation of traditional peoples) heralded a seeming salvation through science from the dark realm of matter. Cartesian dualism posited the human (that is, white male) mind as outside of nature, which was henceforth perceived to be a mechanism or clockwork. The denial of life to other species, the planet and the cosmos itself, accompanied by the denial of fully human status to women and people of colour, reflected the continuing fear of body and matter. The triumph of the scientific paradigm of mechanism over vitalism oriented the western world towards the "need" to conquer nature, which as a category included the body, the feminine principle, women, and peoples living in so-called "primitive" harmony with the biosphere.

In the twentieth century we have yet to heal the mind / body, spirit / matter splits that accompany patriarchy. Indeed, rapid technological development, including the development of the electronic mass media, have further deepened the prevailing schisms. Surrounded by media stimuli, simulacra of the real world, we are in fact a society suffering from sensory deprivation. As the ground of being, we have replaced the body and its direct sensory feedback with the technologically reproduced image. But our new ground of being is an illusory one.

Not surprisingly, insight into the white Western world-view comes from those who have not adopted it. Lame Deer, a Sioux elder, has observed, "I think white people are so afraid of the world they created that they don't want to see, feel, smell or hear it. The feeling of rain and snow on your face, being numbed by an icy wind and thawing out before a smoking fire, coming out of a hot sweat bath and plunging into a cold stream, these thing make you feel alive, but you don't want them anymore. Living in boxes which shut out the heat of the summer and the chill of winter, living inside a body that no longer has a scent, hearing the noise from the hi-fi instead of listening to the sounds of nature, watching some actor on TV having a make-believe experience when you no longer experience anything for yourself, eating food without taste – that's your way. It's no good."

Just as the Native joke names colour TV as central to our "deprivation," so this Sioux elder wisely recognizes that watching TV an average of seven hours a day immerses us in media "experiences" that are in fact neither real experiences nor experiences of the real. "You no longer experience anything for yourself" is the key phrase in Lame Deer's stark critique of our society.

How, for example, does one experience a cow? A realistic photograph of a cow, or a tape-recording of her sounds, or the two combined, might tempt us to think that we know what a cow is. But the face-to-face reality of shared space with another being can never be conveyed through media, no matter how realistic. We experience a cow only by being in the presence of an actual cow. Direct sensory experience is an entirely different realm of knowledge from mediated "experience." An actual exchange of bodily information, a meeting of auras if you like, takes place in the self's real experience of any other, whether that other is a person, animal, or living milieu. Our media approximations are pale, paltry substitutes for such powerful exchanges. Indeed, there is no exchange whatsoever, which is one of the reasons why our media culture can be seen as a culture of sensory deprivation.

But the electronic media have also altered our sensorium in subtle ways. Marshall McLuhan recognized that the primacy of media disconnects the senses. "Media tend to isolate one or another sense from the others," he wrote. "The result is hypnosis." In our culture, where the favourite media are film and especially TV, the separation of vision from the other senses, the isolation of the eye from the bodily ground, contributes to the fragmentation of the bodily whole. We remain fascinated by the image, especially the moving image, and hypnotized by the spell of its "realism." The simulacrum has become more appealing than the real thing because it does not ask for an exchange between perceiver and perceived.

We are only now beginning to consider seriously the effects of media-saturated culture on our bodies and our relation to the real. One significant clue to those effects can be found in our virtually insatiable habits of consumption. This compulsion to consume more and more of everything suggests a pathological emptiness, a sort of black hole, at the core of our being. The body has its natural satiation points, its limits to consumption, its dialectic between hunger and fulfilment with internal feedback loops that maintain the necessary homeostasis. But a society cut off from the body and grounded instead in the mediated image has no sense of limits, no sense of "enough." Indeed, the loss of the body as the ground of being fuels the "need" to consume endlessly.

Robbed of bodily grounding in a society predicated on spirit / matter, mind / body dualism, we seek to fill this emptiness with substitutes that only exacerbate the problem. Out of touch with our bodies, immersed in media simulations, and consuming the planet's resources at a frenzied pace, we nevertheless remain deprived of the "original blessing" that is incarnation itself.

As McLuhan observed, the media age is an age of disembodiment, in which "people kill to find out if they are real." A more readily apparent phenomenon is that people buy to reassure themselves of their own reality. Lame Deer has suggested, "Sometimes I think that even our pitiful tarpaper shacks are better than your luxury homes.... You are spreading death, buying and selling death." Television is a "technological cataract" that has helped us to "see" the necessity for machine supremacy, and especially death technologies, with more than $2 million spent every minute on nuclear weapons. In our fascination with technologically reproduced images, we have become similarly mesmerized by technology in general, seeing it as the sign of progress regardless of its effects on the ecosystem or even on personal health. Indeed, we have come to consider human beings as inferior to machines. As a recent electronics ad states: "To err is human. That's why we test with robots."

Most frightening, however, is the extent to which we are transforming the world itself into a "flesh-free" simulacrum. We are eliminating some ten thousand species every year, sacrificing the forests and lakes to our notion of technological progress, reducing the very diversity of life to a homogenized byproduct of laboratory science through developments in biotechnology. Our "crucifixion" of Mother Earth (to use Matthew Fox's term) is fuelled by patriarchy's desire to replace it with a more perfect replica: a controllable machine-world that is more "efficient" than the imperfect realm of nature.

By numbing our senses, robbing us of our bodily ground of being, and training us to "see," "hear," and even "think" like machines, the electronic media have been part of this agenda. It has become difficult even to imagine a solution to any of our problems that is anything but another technological fix.

A recent pilot project in a large Canadian hospital provides a vivid example. The project involves hospitalized newborns and infants whose working parents are unable to make daily visits to their offspring. Rather than work out a solution with employers and parents that would facilitate frequent visits, or a paid leave of absence to meet the emergency surrounding the infants' needs, or even an arrangement combining paid leave and in-home crisis care, the hospital is experimenting with a media "solution." Videotapes of the mother's face and voice are played and replayed to the crying infants, who appear to be soothed by these simulacra.

If we think about this project in terms other than efficiency, disturbing questions arise. No one knows whether, by tricking the sensory input of the infants, the machine videotapes will cause disturbances to sensual and psychosocial development. Nor does anyone know the extent to which parent-infant bonding will be enhanced or impeded by the tapes. Nevertheless, the project reveals a propensity to think in terms of technological "solutions" and to consider realistic media as replacements for the real.

The challenge is to reclaim the body and its wisdom, including the planetary body and the wisdom of the biosphere, by overcoming our dependency on technology, including the mass media. This reclamation is necessary for the healing of the spirit / matter, mind / body splits that permeate our world-view. Once we fully recognize that all matter and living things are sacred, we can no longer exploit the planet or kill it off to feed our own emptiness. Simultaneously, once we return to our senses, rediscovering the simplicity of our unmet, but real, bodily needs, we will begin to build on the solid foundation of real bodily ground to fill the inner emptiness. The original blessing of our own unique and individual incarnation waits to be embraced and experienced. As the Jesus of the Gnostics recognized, when, like little children, we become unashamed of our embodiment, then we will find the cosmic Wisdom revealed.

(1989)

☐ Trouble in Mondo Condo: Deciphering PEN's Unconscious Agendas

> Most of us operate outside the mainstream of European and first-world cultures, and we rejoice in and respect our differences as we emerge from the shadows of exploitation, oppression, discrimination and sexism. We know there are no valid models to imitate, least of all in the mainstream of Western tradition and the systems it has generated.
>
> – From a statement to PEN by The Next Generation participants

AT THE 54th International PEN World Congress (September 23-October 1, 1989), the paradoxes and contradictions were swarming thick as "no-see-ums," making any analysis of what went down from September 23-26 (the Toronto portion of the event) a daunting challenge in both dialectics and tact. The assignment had "proceed with caution" signs bristling everywhere in its path, so I will state immediately that this Congress was successful for a whole host of reasons, but especially because it highlighted, in unavoidable detail, contradictions that are absolutely central for our society to examine.

Betty Friedan noted that "Consciousness is the first stage of every revolution." I would add that conciousness is necessary at every stage of change, and the Toronto segment of this Congress revealed precisely those areas where consciousness is necessary. Any event that can accomplish this in four short days deserves praise. Thus, the trouble in Mondo Condo was nothing less than an opportunity for growth in consciousness for everyone: organizers, participants, demonstrators, and public alike.

One obvious paradox (though by no means the first in sequence) was the mind-boggling incident outside Roy Thompson Hall following the PEN "gala," in which PEN organizer and incoming president

June Callwood, outraged by demonstrators carrying signs that read "Canadian Women of Colour Locked out by PEN's Invisible Ink," told them individually and collectively to "fuck off." Callwood, introduced on at least one public occasion as "the Mother Teresa of Canada," thereby challenged her public to balance their perception of her with a less saintly dimension.

When this news story appeared in *The Globe and Mail* on the morning of Tuesday, September 26, it prompted Congress organizer Graeme Gibson, President of the Canadian Centre (English-speaking) of International PEN, to issue an immediate press statement, which opened with these words:

> As one of the organizers of the 54th World Congress of International PEN, *I regret the attention paid to a small group of protesters.* I am also concerned that this matter will obscure the serious issues we have addressed in our four days of meetings in Toronto, and will continue to address for the rest of the week in Montreal. [Emphasis added]

Thus, by day four of this Congress (held for the first time in Canada), we had a spokesperson for an international organization that works doggedly around the world for freedom of the press and freedom to dissent announcing his "regret" about the press coverage given to this protest. As I say, the contradictions were swarming thick as "no-see-ums." Only in Canada, eh?

There have been six other PEN World Congresses since the World Congress held in the United States in 1986. At that Congress Norman Mailer insulted women writers, and Margaret Atwood took up the challenge, promising that Canada's 1989 Congress would be "bilingual and bisexual." The most recent Congress was held in Holland in May of 1989.

"Was that a huge affair like this one?" I asked Sarah Thring, who had attended the 53rd International PEN World Congress in Maastricht, Holland. "It was a smaller program," she answered. "Two days of panels and evening readings." Besides PEN delegates, there were "a few other guests of honour and some Dutch writers. The literary sessions were only open to Congress delegates, while the two evenings of readings were open to the public." By contrast, Canada's Congress was, she explained, "the most ambitious program that has ever taken place in the history of PEN," with six hundred delegates and invited guests, and "the largest public participation ever scheduled."

It seems, then, that it's only in Canada that a PEN World Congress has ever taken on such megaproject proportions. That decision itself raises questions about unconscious agendas, complicated by all the other signifiers at work in this event. Besides imitating Toronto's hideous penchant for festival inflation – this one, squeezed in between the Festival of Festivals and the Wang International Festival of Authors – the Congress reflected an upper-middle-class bias. This was reflected in the choice of venue (Harbourfront, that vile corridor of affluence and scandal that triggers the gag reflex in any decent member of what's left of the Left), in the gala at Roy Thomson Hall (the building itself is a signifier of Canadian upper-middle-class ostentation), in the ticket price per event ($7 for anything in the Brigantine Room or the Premier Dance Theatre), in the selection of mainly media celebrities as panel moderators, and in the whole aura surrounding the event, which seemed to lack only diamonds on the soles of its shoes.

Perhaps all this was summarized by a quote in Marc Glassman's piece for *Metropolis* (September 21) in which a member of the organizing committee predicted confidently that this Congress was going to be "the greatest literary party of the decade."

The first problem in organizing any party is the guest list, a decision-making process that is an equal-opportunity offender in any context. For Canadian PEN, which began to plan this event two-and-a-half years ago, one thing must have been immediately clear: the guests of honour (117 in total, as it turned out) would not include Norman Mailer. Otherwise, the selection process seems to have proceeded quite smoothly until January 1989, when Toronto PEN members David McIntosh, Patricia Aldana, and Ronald Wright recognized that there was a certain hole in the guest list, an absence that, like any deepening void in the universe, threatened to suck the glitz right off this party in the making.

As McIntosh tells it, "We recognized that at least 70 per cent of the invited guests were established, senior writers" – writers who, in his words, "had already lived through their battles for freedom of expression." Moreover, that guest list conveyed "the impression that issues of freedom of expression happen elsewhere, outside of Canada." But according to McIntosh, by January of 1989 "there was no money on hand" at PEN to use in filling this significant gap in the program.

Nevertheless, McIntosh went ahead in the spring and began the daunting task of selecting writers and finding sources of alternative funding to invite seventeen primarily minority and Native writers in their twenties and thirties from twelve countries including Canada. To finance this "experimental program," called The Next Generation (consisting of two literary panels and three free public readings at the Water's Edge Café), McIntosh tried to find "sources of funding within the countries where these writers live": Nigeria, Guatemala, Mexico, Jamaica, Kenya, South Africa, New Zealand, Australia, Canada, England, and the United States. He also generated some private donations from people in Canada, "specifically for this project."

Meanwhile, the (shall we say) non-experimental part of the Canadian PEN organizing committee was working with a budget of $1.2 million – provided by every level of government in Canada and by corporate sponsors such as Labatt's, Southam, *Saturday Night*, and McClelland and Stewart.

With a split in the seam of the pants of this event already under way by spring, it's not surprising that there was trouble in Mondo Condo, and that the trouble tended to expose the unconscious white, liberal, middle-class mainstream agenda in the party planning. But even if the demonstration outside Roy Thomson Hall had never happened (and been reported), that agenda was stamped all over this Congress and was recognizable to many of its participants.

Arguably, Canadian PEN organizers fell into the trap of what cultural historian Daniel J. Boorstin has called "the pseudo-event," hoping to make a media splash with their "greatest literary party of the decade." Not recognizing that this very goal would expose the limitations of their progressive intentions, they opted for all the signifiers of spectacle, thereby revealing their own unconscious biases. The blame, however, must be laid primarily at the feet of bourgeois feminism, which over the past twenty years has rarely been able to think beyond the issue of sex and gender to countenance issues of race and class in its political understanding. Even more problematic, white middle-class feminism has typically assumed that climbing up the Establishment ladder to success is not only everyone's goal but also the sign of revolutionary progress. As a friend of mine put it, "Bourgeois feminism encourages us to want a bigger slice of a rotten pie."

Over at the Water's Edge Café, Black Canadian poet Dionne Brand put it more succinctly. As a speaker on The Next Generation panel called "Freedom of Expression and Access to Audiences," Brand stated: "If the mainstream media ever praises my work, I'll have to rethink what I'm doing." The best part of this 54th International PEN World Congress was that the seventeen participants in The Next Generation (ghettoized in every way at this Congress) expressed complete disinterest in joining the mainstream, acute awareness of the co-opting potential in media systems, vital commitment to their work as a political force for change, and obvious solidarity with one another. They also gave their audiences riveting and real examples of literary work forged in the crucible of political struggle here and now. As usual, most of the vital energy was happening at the edge, while over at dead centre in the main event of the Congress, there seemed to be a concern that this Party proceed without any glitches.

This was especially noticeable in terms of the impression detected by David McIntosh in the original guest list, that "issues of freedom of expression happen elsewhere, outside of Canada." In Literary Session 1, "The Writer: Freedom and Power" moderated by Barbara Frum, panel member Margaret Atwood used the occasion to say that she always feels "like a jerk on these panels" because, by comparison to whatever happens to writers in other countries, "we have it easier here." Instead of informing her audiences about the unique forms that silencing and censorship take in Canada – forms that are politically connected to the harsher measures taken in other countries and that include racism in the publishing industry, lack of outlets through media colonization, tax harassment, libel suits, RCMP surveillance and pressure, self-censorship under structures of corporate ownership, and, at times, imprisonment of writers – Atwood spoke of Canada's "post-colonial culture" through which "we now have an audience for literature in this country." Acknowledging that the next step in Canada is access for minority and Native writers, Atwood nonetheless conveyed the impression that freedom of expression is really not an issue in Canada.

That impression was subtly reinforced in other panels. For example, in Literary Session 3, "Creating Mythology" moderated by Michael Ignatieff, Canadian panel member Timothy Findley told his audience that "Writers in this country have taken on a role as spokespersons for Her Majesty's loyal opposition. Our voices are heard." But it was even more apparent in the choices made among those senior, established writers not selected from Canada to be guests of honour.

For instance, in Literary Session 8, "Private Conscience and State

Security," moderated by Adrienne Clarkson, the panel members were Chinua Achebe (Nigeria), Duo Duo (China), Harold Pinter (England), Miriam Tlali (South Africa), and Tatyana Tolstaya (U.S.). While these panelists provided fascinating answers to the question posed – "Does the perceived national security of the state take precedence over writers' sense of their responsibilities?" – the decision not to include a Canadian on this panel implied that the question is not relevant here. I, for one, immediately thought of Ian Adams and his novel *S: Portrait of a Spy* – a vivid example of how that question worked itself out in Canada's own relatively recent past. Similarly, any of the many writers imprisoned during the War Measures Act in Quebec would have challenged the airbrushed picture of Canada being conveyed to the public at this Congress.

In retrospect, that picture seems even more curious because, behind closed doors in the Assembly of Delegates, some Canadian issues of freedom of expression were being raised. In the host of resolutions passed by the PEN assembly, there were two dealing specifically with recent events in Canada. One resolution condemned the laying of a criminal charge against Doug Small, Ottawa bureau chief for Global-TV News, in the events surrounding the Wilson budget leak. The other resolution addressed the case of Elaine Dewar, the investigative journalist whose work has been deemed unacceptable to the Reichmanns.

Why, then, was there such a concerted effort to convey an impression of Canada (at least during the public portions of this event) as not just glitzy but a model of freedom of expression for all to see? I suspect the answer has to do with middle-class liberal notions of "freedom" and "democracy," notions that were being signalled (and subtly challenged) in other moments during the main event. As Susan G. Cole recognized in her piece for *Now* (September 28), during Literary Session 4, "Power and Gender" moderated by Mary Lou Finlay, a moment occurred just after Cuban writer Nancy Morejon had explained the process by which her poems had come to be published in her country. In Cole's words, "Finlay pushed in and asked, 'Do you criticize the revolution?' Morejon replied, 'Oh no.' Then, seeing Finlay's knowing nod – a gesture of dismissal of communist-style censorship – Morejon looked her in the eye and said, 'That would be betraying myself.' "

A similar moment occurred during Literary Session 8 when moderator Adrienne Clarkson asked panel member Duo Duo (in exile from China) to "tell us what our freedom looks like to you." Reminding her that "I've been away [from China] only a hundred days," Duo Duo then graciously reassured Clarkson that "freedom here is realized."

Pondering what seemed to be a certain self-congratulatory agenda going down in the main event, I also noticed that some guests of honour were patiently, subtly, and very politely making delicate little pricks at the (unconscious) middle-class liberal assumptions underlying the Congress. Nigerian writers Chinua Achebe and Wole Soyinka were particularly skilled at this, with Achebe reminding his audience (and Clarkson) that "You have to understand the complexity of the world. The world is not the free and the unfree. There is the great excluded, and the excluded are beginning to disrupt things." Similarly, Soyinka noted pointedly that "Third World intellectuals, unlike their counterparts in the First World, tend to examine more critically their own mythologies than do those in the First."

This difference found expression during Literary Session 8 in a comment that might have seemed a non-sequitur had I not attended Literary Session 1 the day before. During the opening literary panel Atwood had made a literary allusion to the Hans Christian Andersen tale, "The Emperor's New Clothes," when she stated, "All over the world it has been the writer's function to say 'The emperor has no clothes.' " The following day Chinua Achebe picked up the allusion and expanded it: "The emperor masquerades in many clothes," he said. "One problem in the West is that it's less easy to see the emperor."

As soon as he said it, I knew that he knew the ending of that Andersen tale (which Atwood may have forgotten). The emperor, exposed and embarrassed in all his naked vainglory by the words of the child, becomes rigid and defensive: commanding that the parade of his now naked power go on, and that his lords-in-attendance continue to carry the non-existent train of his non-existent royal robe. So much for the power of the writer in this choice of metaphor. But when one looks at the Andersen tale as a message about the conscious/unconscious dialectic (the inflated ego momentarily punctured by spontaneous reality), then this simple tale, twice alluded to in this Congress, provides a necessary insight.

Arguably, at this point in history, every progressive person on this planet is being asked to recognize personal and societal contradictions (best expressed in that saying, "You can talk the talk but can you walk the walk?"). There is no shame in this process, but there is a sting: at which point, as the tale warns, the impulse is to become rigid and defensive, refusing consciousness, refusing change, refusing to let go of an inflated power-agenda.

The most difficult challenge is to live through the sting. To stand naked in one's own human unconscious fuck-ups, recognizing that in this last gasp of the twentieth century it is impossible to be politically correct at every level, but that an increase in consciousness is always the desired goal. Since consciousness is the very terrain of the writer, it is not surprising that, even in the midst of this PEN megaproject, consciousness-raising was the real agenda behind everything that happened during the 54th International PEN World Congress.

(1989)

◻ The Temple of Fashion

"THE ACT OF ACQUIRING has taken the place of all other actions, the sense of having has obliterated all other senses," the British art critic and cultural historian John Berger observed in his 1972 book *Ways of Seeing*. By the mid-1970s, acquisition had achieved the status of a new religion in the West. The appearance of a new advertising buzzword, *spirit*, was a clear signal of this development.

Once Coca-Cola had merely claimed to add "life" to our lives. Now everything from a cola through a department store and a hotel chain to a fashion designer began to make even bolder assertions. In slogans such as "the Pepsi Spirit," "Simpson's Spirit," "the Spirit of Hyatt," and Yves Saint-Laurent's "New Spirit of Masculinity," advertisers proclaimed the new religion of buying. More recently, the world *soul* has entered the advertising lexicon as another religious additive to enhance acquisition.

In such a context, shopping malls have become the cathedrals of our time: vast horizontal-Gothic places of worship that draw the faithful together in communal rites central to the new religion. While the Prime Movers in this religion are the TV God and its consort, the advertising industry, the shopping cathedrals are themselves temples of technomagic where steps move effortlessly beneath one's feet, doors open automatically, celestial Muzak hymns permeate the atmosphere, and the wave of a credit card completes the sacred transaction. Isolated from the mundane reality of urban existence, the shopping mall is sacred space, climate-controlled and patrolled, devoted to the ease of acquisition: the meaning of life in the postwar West.

This religion has evolved its own holy days (such as Boxing Day solstice) and holy seasons (Back-To-School octave). It also has its important sites of pilgrimage (in Canada, the West Edmonton Mall and Toronto's Eaton Centre), although every North American city has its lesser malls where the same litany of brand names holds out the promise of salvation. Nevertheless, this is a religion in which both faith and good works are necessary. This facet of the religion is nowhere more apparent than in the domain of Fashion, whose side chapels in each shopping cathedral remind us that last season's profession of faith is up for renewal.

According to the arcane hermeneutics of the Fashion Bible, one risks damnation by last year's colour or the slightest oversight of tie, lapel, or faux nail. Thus, the Gospels according to Armani and Alfred Sung, Ralph Lauren and Christian Dior are continually being reinterpreted for our edification and enlightenment. While slogans such as Calvin Klein's "Eternity for Men" and Alfred Sung's "Timeless" collection evoke an eschatological promise signifying the end-time of shopping, it is a central tenet within the religion (and certainly dogma in Fashion) that our indulgences are never plenary. "Shop Till You Drop" is the vulgar – but correct – grasp of this aspect of consumer theology.

Fortunately, the high priests of Fashion (particularly the college of ecclesiastics gathered at *Women's Wear Daily*) continually disseminate guidance on each chapter and verse of the Fashion Bible. Their perennial lists of "Best Dressed" and "Worst Dressed" remind us that even those not banished to the purgatory of obscurity risk hellfire by sinning against Fashion commandments that are perpetually under revision.

For this reason, there exists a wealth of inspirational literature and illustrated texts to assist us in our salvific efforts. *Vogue, Esquire, Gentleman's Quarterly,* and *Flare* provide not only the necessary iconography for the consumer aspirant's meditation but also details on those Fashion sins (venial and mortal) that can impede our progress. The pages of such inspirational texts also offer devotional readings on the lives of the Fashion saints: popular saints of the past like St. Marilyn and St. James Dean; current beatified exemplars like Madonna and Billy Idol; and our living martyr to Fashion, Elizabeth Taylor. But such devotional reading and contemplation are only preparations for the greater liturgies of the mall.

Window shopping brings the congregation into closer proximity to the Fashion priesthood and the means of redemption, but before we enter any of the mall's side chapels there is usually an impressive form of statuary to mediate our passage. Modern mannequins have evolved with the mall itself, becoming increasingly elaborate, detailed, and even startling in their effect.

The old form of mannequin (like the old form of storefront) was, for the most part, simply uninspiring: its wig askew, its coiffure outmoded, its facial expression vague and nondescript, its limbs akimbo or missing, its stand ridiculous or pathetic. Only by the greatest leap of faith could the consumer attain the proper buying spirit through a glance at such a guardian of the portals.

The new mannequins, on the other hand, are appropriate statuary for the impressive cathedrals that surround them. Figures of anatomical perfection, these statues with their erect nipples, painted fingernails, detailed eye makeup, stunning hairdos, high cheekbones, and long sinewy legs remind us at a glance just what it is that we, as mundane Fashon consumers, aspire to. While the male statuary is somewhat less intimidating, it too bespeaks the contemporary codes of the Fashion cult: chiselled jaws, muscled but sleek torsos, long-legged figures of power.

But it is the faces of the new statuary that are most significant in their religious function: aloof, haughty, disdaining, beyond appeal. Inspiring neither solace nor prayer, these figures at the portals are part of the shrines of envy and are meant to inspire a certain measure of fear.

To gaze at one of these detailed figures is an oddly unsettling experience (though in truth they are meant to be only glimpsed in passing). Typically, the statue is posed so that its haughty gaze is directed above or away from us, as though we were quite obviously beneath contempt. At the same time, the statue's fetish of forever-perfect and hyperrealistic detail cruelly reminds us of our own imperfections. Whether we are fully conscious of the effect or not, we enter the chapels of Fashion subtly diminished and suitably envious.

Such feelings enhance the redemptive power of the array of apparel within. Each article of clothing promises to increase our status and transform us in turn into objects of envy, in our own eyes and the imagined eyes of others. Here, the numinous brand name confers its accretion of socially envious connotations, religiosity, and sacred trust. This veneer laid upon mere cloth by the high priests of Fashion is necessary for passing through the challenging ritual of the changing room.

Within this confessional enclosure, one is confronted by the atten-
dant mirror revealing all the sins of the flesh that mar one's progress:
the cellulite thighs, the body hair, the paunch, the girth, the less-
than-perfect contours reminding us that the spirit is willing but the
flesh is weak. Making promises to join the modern-day *flagellantes* in
a daily workout routine, we proceed to put on the desired article of
clothing that promises to miraculously transform our lives.

The moment of beholding ourselves dressed in the desired brand
name has also been prefigured and prepared by the statue at the
chapel's portal. Like it, we must harden our gaze, overlook that small
inner voice of protest about the price, and focus on a future vision of
ourselves as the envied possessor of this article of apparel that most of
the faithful will have already seen (and desired) in the inspirational
Fashion texts. We know that the envious others will recognize at a
glance that we have joined the elect.

Where once it was possible for the faithful to identify, from a
momentary glimpse, the habit of a Franciscan friar or Benedictine
nun, so now the congregation is steeped in the familiar cut and style
of various designer looks. Indeed, one can dress oneself entirely from
head to foot in Ralph Lauren or YSL, Lee or Esprit. As the most dedicated of the Fashion faithful realize, it is the brand, not the cloth, that
clothes us. So the slogan says, "Life's Necessities: Food, Shelter and
Lee Jeans."

As we become the objects of our own devotion, the high point in
the shopping mall liturgy approaches: the transforming ritual of the
credit card. Through its instantaneous magic, we momentarily
redeem ourselves and enter the ecstasy of acquisition, consuming
and consumed by the bliss of possession.

It is precisely this ease of acquisition that is fundamental to the
new religion. The technomagic of the credit card is in keeping with
the whole aura of effortlessness that pervades the mall. Indeed, the
many objects on display seem magically conjured out of nothing to
fulfil the promise of advertising images' sleight-of-hand. For all
intents and purposes, these millions of objects seem to have no origin,
no history of labour and creation. Only the shopping agnostic would
think to consider such questions as: who made these things, and
under what conditions?

For example, most of our brand-name clothing is made by Third
World garment workers, primarily women, who are grossly under-
paid and exploited by North American contractors paying as little as

ten cents an hour for the labour. In the export-processing zones of the Philippines, Thailand, Hong Kong, Mexico, Indonesia, and dozens of other countries, non-unionized workers typically work sixteen-hour days for the most meagre of wages, assembling the host of products that fill our malls. Even Canada's high priest of Fashion, Alfred Sung, employs Hong Kong labour to work at a fraction of Canadian wages in sewing the apparel of the elect.

But the religion of acquisition excludes any knowledge of the actual work that goes into the making of our products. For most of the consumer faithful, these millions of objects simply appear "as seen on TV" or in the photo magazines: as though untouched by human hands, as though the image itself (like an idea in the mind of God) had somehow spawned its progeny, as it were, "in the flesh." Like Doubting Thomases, we touch and buy their tangibility to reaffirm our faith. Thus, while some have dubbed this new religion the Church of Perpetual Indulgence, it may more accurately be described as the Church of the Wholly Innocent: wilfully apolitical, purposely unknowing, steeped in the mystification and technomagic of our time.

(1991)

III
Landscape

☐ Canada Dry:
Pipedreams and Fresh-Water Politics

OVER THE LAST year-and-a-half, an odd silence has descended on the issue of water diversions and exports, which reached a peak of media coverage and speculation in that banner year of 1985 with Mulroney's now infamous interview in *Fortune*, his appointment of Simon Reisman as Canada's free-trade negotiator, the signing of the Great Lakes Charter, the election of Robert "Megaproject" Bourassa, and the report of the Canadian Federal Inquiry on Water Policy. Since then, a great shower curtain of obscurity seems to have been pulled across the entire issue, coinciding with the behind-closed-doors policy on the free-trade talks and much of Canadian-U.S. relations in general. As usual, we have no real idea of what is being decided for our future. And yet, Mulroney's stance on water export has long been apparent. Before he wisely decided to maintain a Velcro-lips public-relations silence on the matter, he indicated to reporters that one of the most attractive foreign-investment opportunities in Canada is the abundant supply of fresh water, and he told *Fortune* writer Rod McQueen, "I'm favourably disposed to anything that improves our relationship with our neighbour. If it [water export] happens to make good economic sense and improves the environment, why not?"

But that was 1985, so why reopen a topic that sets the Canadian public's teeth on edge, sends blood pressures soaring, and just makes everybody as unhappy as hell? Well, primarily because a cluster of events has been occurring throughout the neoconservative eighties that makes the prospect of fresh-water export from Canada more likely than ever. South of the border, some significant changes are falling into place that coincide with the Mulroney (and the many Mulroney cronies') mind-set. The way things are going, the Americans won't even have to ask for Canadian water diversions. The wheelers-and-dealers north of the border will go ahead, just as they've done with hydroelectric power, and set things up to provide the resource as an exportable commodity. As Pollution Probe's Kai Millyard told me, "The Mulroney government and the private sector are enthusiastic about the possibility [of water export] with free trade coming."

If you've been following demographic patterns lately, you may have noticed that in population size the U.S. sun belt has expanded over the last twenty years from about a size thirty-two to somewhere in the neighbourhood of a size seventy-eight, and the elastic in its polyester waistband is clearly straining. All those resettled Northerners, with their new ten-gallon hats and their RVS parked in the driveways and their kidney-shaped swimming pools out back behind the split-levels, are starting to feel a certain itch. Not the itch that sent them speeding down Interstates 35 and 25 and 71 in their silver Airstream trailers and Dodge motorhomes in search of Paradise. No, this is a different itch. It's the rasping itch in the throat called thirst. They found Paradise in the sun belt, sure enough. But in many places that Paradise turned out to have an average annual rainfall of about 16.2 centimetres – hardly enough to give a decent bath to a chihuahua.

This scarcity of resource, compounded by a massive influx of sunseekers and relocated industries, has not been accompanied by a lifestyle of conservation appropriate to the desert – say, that of the Hopi Indian. There are highly populated areas of Texas and California that are slowly but surely sinking into the underground abyss created by pumping out the subterranean water-table. The city of Houston, which has long sucked massive amounts of water from beneath its gleaming skyscrapers, has already slid several feet into the underground cavern that is opening up below the spreading metropolis. Even though farmers across the sun belt are increasingly abandoning the concept of irrigation-dependent crops, and in many cases are simply letting the tumbleweeds take over in parts of Arizona and Texas, the new urban sprawl more than makes up for the previous demands of crop irrigation on a scarce supply of water.

Over in Florida, sixty years of tapping underground fresh-water supplies, exacerbated by tourism and resettlement, are gradually drying up the Everglades and have led to that bane of retirement living: giant sinkholes that suddenly open up and swallow whatever Winnebagos, Chat-and-Chews, K-Marts, and Cadillacs happen to be parked above them. As the sinkholes proliferate, so does the seepage of ocean water into the groundwater-table, making unfit for consumption the small reserves that remain.

The massive shift of population and industry to water-scarce states has already resulted in a series of water wars and heavy-duty skirmishes that have broken out across the sun belt: pitting region against region, state against state, cities against state governments, neighbour against neighbour. You've got southern California fighting northern California, with the former accusing the latter of outright stinginess in refusing to divert water down to where most of the population lives. You've got L.A. itself fighting the folks of Owens Valley, Mono Lake Basin, and the Sierra Nevadas who are just plain sick and tired of providing 80 per cent of the city's drinking water. You've got California royally teed-off at neighbouring Arizona, which won in court the right to divert the Colorado River and thereby take half the water previously used by thirteen million sun-worshippers in the lower third of the state. You've got southern Florida fighting northern Florida, whose county governments don't want their tourist-rich neighbours tapping into the Suwannee River. You've got New Mexico fighting mad at Texas, with the city of El Paso sticking pipes into the neighbouring state and pumping water over the state line to slake the powerful tortilla-thirst of its own citizenry. A bit further north, things aren't much more harmonious.

In 1981, South Dakota sold water rights to the Missouri River to a coal-slurry-pipeline company, Energy Transportation Systems, for the tidy sum of $9 million a year. The company is building a pipeline from Wyoming's Powder River basin over to electric-power plants in Arkansas and Louisiana, using 20,000 acre-feet of Missouri River water each year to run the project. When the federal Department of the Interior approved the transaction, its wisdom prompted the down-river states of Iowa, Missouri, and Nebraska to file suit to stop the pipeline.

Depending on who you talk to, the whole mess has either been clarified or exacerbated, or clarified in an exacerbating manner, by U.S. Supreme Court rulings in the early 1980s, that determined that it is unconstitutional for any state to place a ban on water export across state lines. According to the august court, such bans are a restriction on interstate commerce. These rulings made it legal, for example, for the city of El Paso to stick those pipes in neighbouring New Mexico, and for South Dakota to sell the Missouri River to a private company for diversion elsewhere.

The Supreme Court rulings are significant for three reasons. First, they indicate that water is perceived as a commodity like any other, subject to laws of supply and demand and whose man-made transference or sale from state to state cannot be restricted. Thus, the rulings opened the door for both diversionary thinking and the perception that water, as a commodity, is yet another resource from which the megabucks might be made. Second, those court decisions subtly subvert conservation-style thinking. Rather than carefully husbanding your own local resources, if things get tight you can look elsewhere for water. Third, the most obvious elsewhere to look for water within the United States is the Great Lakes. Though the Great Lakes are internationally shared, Canada has virtually no legal say about what the United States does with Lake Michigan, that falls entirely within U.S. territory and which already has the Chicago diversion pumping one billion gallons per day out of the lake and over to the Mississippi River basin by way of the Illinois River.

When the U.S. Supreme Court ruled in 1982 (Sporhase vs. Nebraska) that state bans on water diversions to other states are unconstitutional, the decision sent reverberations right across the continent and set off a flurry of economic activity. Sun-belt states started looking at a variety of diversion proposals, including one to build a pipeline between Lake Superior and the Missouri River basin, so that water normally flowing into Lake Erie would flow south. Indian bands across the country filed more than fifty lawsuits to reclaim water rights lost to the white man more than a century ago. And private industry started seeing dollar signs in every glass of water. As Environment Canada's water expert Richard Pentland told me, "Right now the big thing [in the United States] is the buying and selling of water rights, with farmers selling off to private industries." As the trend in water use switches from crop irrigation (whose costs in some areas have tripled in the last five years) to urban / industrial use, private corporations are quickly buying up the rights to resources already strained to the limit. In the process of consolidating their legal holdings, private industry may well begin to apply pressure for diversions from water-rich states – encouraged by those Supreme Court rulings.

In the United States in the 1980s, then, some significant factors are falling into place. That twenty-year shift in the population from north to south, which has more than doubled the population of sun-belt states, has not only placed an incredible drain on water resources, but is also about to be reflected in the coming reapportionment of

Congressional seats, giving water-scarce states more voting power than they have ever previously held. That political shift, coupled with the Supreme Court rulings, will have a significant impact on future water policy. In more immediate terms, both those phenomena will undoubtedly affect the fate of a specific U.S. federal moratorium due for re-evaluation in 1987. After twenty years in place, its imminent demise or renewal will signal much about the current status of the American way.

For most of the past century, the American way has been three parts U.S. Army Corps of Engineers, two parts unabashed greed, and one part massive psychological denial. As a recipe for water use, this one has been a disaster in ecological terms ever since the 1902 U.S. Bureau of Reclamation launched its project of settling the west by forcibly making the desert bloom. After more than sixty years of reversing rivers flowing the wrong way, of bombing, damming, and rechanneling waters into parched regions made to blossom and boom with water-dependent crops and thirsty populations, the U.S. Congress suddenly experienced an influx of sanity. In 1968, after years of funding megaproject feasibility schemes that would reach right up into Canada and turn the continent into a large facsimile of Venice, Italy, Congress said: Enough already! No more of these expensive, environmentally stupid megaprojects for water. We got the Central Utah Project under way, we got the Central Arizona Project under way, and that's it! We gotta learn to conserve!

Congress placed a ten-year moratorium on federal funding for engineering studies devoted to major inter-basin water transfers: a measure geared to put a damper (so to speak) on the Brobdignagian pipe-dreams of corporate engineers. In 1978, Congress renewed the moratorium for ten more years. The 1987 decision on whether to reopen federal funding for such studies will indicate if water-megaproject thinking is back in vogue in the U.S. centres of power. Both Pollution Probe's Millyard and Environment Canada's Pentland say it's not, that the big water-diversion schemes aren't gonna happen. A less optimistic view is found in Michael Keating's book, *To The Last Drop* (Macmillan, 1986). Keating writes, "Just because they are outrageously expensive does not mean that diversions will not happen. Senator David Durenberg of Minnesota told a 1984 water conference in Toronto, 'The first principle of water policy, in my country at least, is that rational thinking does not apply.'"

An even less optimistic view would have the reader consider the following factors. The last round of fifties-style water-megaproject activity is now coming on-line in the United States. When Americans see the "success" of such things, they tend to get enthusiastic about doing some more. The Central Utah Project, conceived in 1956 and more than thirty years in the making, is due for completion by 1988. It consists of twelve gigantic artificial reservoirs, 220 kilometres of tunnels, canals, and aqueducts, three power plants, nine pumping stations, and twenty-one kilometres of dikes bringing water hundreds of miles for irrigation, urban / industrial development, and electric power. Down in nearby Arizona, they recently completed the first leg of the Central Arizona Project (CAP) in a two-hundred-mile concrete canal linking the Colorado River with Phoenix. Started in 1968, and the federal government's most expensive water project ever, the CAP will, by 1991, extend that canal 335 miles across the desert right to Tucson. Through a series of dams, twelve tunnels, four pumping stations, and presumably enough concrete to pave the moon, each year the CAP will deliver enough water to cover 1.5 million acres with fresh water a foot deep.

But even as the Phoenix dignitaries gathered for the opening ceremony on November 16, 1985, and watched as the tap was turned on and this new branch of the Colorado River coursed through their waterworks, they were reminded by their state representative, Eldon Rudd, that this extraordinary feat of engineering could still not meet their ever-increasing needs. "The time is going to come in the not-too-distant future," said Rudd to his blue-chip audience, "when we are going to be looking for water again, and today is the time to start looking for it." See what I mean? And then you've got the Reagan factor.

"Small Is Beautiful" is not a motto likely to be framed and hanging in the Reagan White House. A nation willing to plunk down $3 trillion for a gargantuan Star Wars video-game made real might well consider $200 billion for a few earthly water canals as petty cash, and very petty in terms of environmental impact. That's the price tag affixed to NAWAPA – a massive water-transfer scheme first proposed in 1964 and one which, under the Reagan administration, has been taken from the shelf, dusted off, and revived in certain political circles on both sides of the border. The North American Water and Power Alliance (NAWAPA) is a proposal by the Ralph M. Parsons engineering firm of Pasadena to divert water from the Yukon, Laird,

Fraser, Peace, and Columbia Rivers for use in the United States, Mexico, and Canada. It would create a reservoir five hundred miles long and ten miles wide in the Rocky Mountain Trench in British Columbia, connect that reservoir by canals across the Prairies and over to the Great Lakes, and also feed water down through the water systems of the U.S. Southwest. Following the election of Reagan, the Pasadena firm claimed that there was renewed interest in the scheme in the sun-belt states, but also in British Columbia, where certain political and financial sectors are not averse to turning much of the lower part of the province into a great big water tank.

The other part of the Reagan factor is what must be called a renewed hostility towards the environment. Under Reagan, a significant portion of the U.S. public has been encouraged to think (as does their esteemed leader) that pollution comes from trees and other vegetation, that acid rain is not a problem, and that "extremist environmentalists" are the real threat to the American way, which exists to ensure that corporate polluters must be free to do whatever they wish for the sake of business. This mind-set has allowed much of the U.S. public to remain comfortable with (or innocent of) the fact of some 32,000 toxic chemical waste dumps scattered across the country, 16,000 of them threatening the drinking water of their communities (and ours, in many cases). The Reagan factor also appeals to that portion of the American psyche that might be termed species-hubris: when push comes to shove, all those little terns and gulls and blue-feathered water-skimmers can just go flock themselves. And if they're Canadian terns and gulls and water-skimmers, well who cares?

And then there's the Ogallala factor.

The high-plains states – Nebraska, Kansas, Oklahoma, west Texas – have long been known for their abundant production of beef cattle, sorghum, alfalfa hay, cotton, corn, and wheat. This abundant production is fully dependent on the Ogallala Aquifer – the world's largest underground reserve of fresh water, stretching out some 16,000 subterranean square miles. For more decades than one cares to count, the aquifer has had at least 170,000 irrigation pumps rammed into its innards, which every year suck out the equivalent of the Colorado River to keep the wheels of agribusiness moving. In one of the few federally funded engineering studies allowed to bypass the engineering-study moratorium, the United States Army Corps of Engineers checked into the remaining reserves of the old aquifer in 1976. What they found, like some proctologist peering into ancient, unfathomable depths, was that there is hardly enough water left down there to shake a length of pipe at.

Laid down over the millenia, the aquifer had been reduced, in less than half a century, to an estimated three quadrillion cubic metres of water and was being sucked out at a 1977 rate of twenty-seven billion cubic metres a year. Theoretically, that would mean the aquifer should last another hundred thousand years or so. Unfortunately, the theory would apply only if the reservoir was equally spread out beneath the surface. As it is, there are already places where the irrigation pumps are spitting up nothing but sand, especially in the southern regions and largely thanks to the voracious needs of agribusiness.

Water stats about food are both eye-opening and mind-boggling. It takes 14,935 gallons of water to grow one bushel of wheat. Counting all the irrigation necessary to raise the corn to feed the steer, one steak is the equivalent of 3,500 gallons of water. For every egg you break for Sunday brunch, 120 gallons of water have gone down the gullet, so to speak. The water demands of agribusiness are awesome, and increasingly so. When the corps re-emerged from its subterranean scrutiny, it recommended that the Ogallala Aquifer be filled back up. One surefire way to do that, they said, was to divert water over from the Great Lakes.

A dozen years later that recommendation, which is still reverberating through the brain-pans of the high-plains populace, brings to mind another political event worth watching in 1987-88. We'll watch it anyway, but it's important to see it from a particular water-related twist. Currently the smart money is on Robert Dole as the probable Republican presidential candidate for 1988. Robert Dole is the senator for Kansas, and Kansas is smack-dab in the middle of that region completely dependent for its economic survival on the disappearing Ogallala Aquifer. John Carroll, an American specialist in Canada-U.S. relations, warned in 1983 that as the aquifer gets sucked dry, the states dependent on it "will become panicky." Already he said, "they are starting to look north."

Canada has obviously been cursed with the kind of climate that makes sun belters and high-plains drifters shiver with dread. On the other mitten, Canada has been blessed. Canada has 90 per cent of the continent's surface supply of fresh water. Canada has nearly 20 per cent of the *world's* total supply of fresh water. With one-tenth the population and industry of the United States, Canada has twice as much available surface and underground fresh water. Canada is perceived to be so waterlogged that Americans wring the map of Canada out before they spread it across the conference table and eye all those big and little blue lakes – some of them haven't been named yet, for crissakes! – and all those watery blue veins running up and down, over and across a territory simply splattered with big and little blue lakes. The rasping itch in the throat grows.

But perhaps more important than the U.S. perception of Canada's water-abundancy is the Canadian perception of it. In the immortal words of Quebec's Robert Bourassa: "If there are surpluses, why don't we sell it instead of wasting it? The choice is between pure waste or making an important benefit for the economy of our country and the well-being of our citizens." By the mid-1980s, this mind-set was catching on. As *Fortune's* Rod McQueen wrote of the Mulroney interview, "No one [in the United States] has seriously proposed shipping Canadian water to the Arizona desert or elsewhere, and no one knows if such a sale would be feasible. But Mulroney seems to invite offers." You're thirsty? Did I just see you wet your lips with your tongue? Here, drink James Bay.

A bandwagon of sorts started forming around Newfoundland engineer Thomas Kierans (brother of former Liberal cabinet minister Eric) and his proposal to dam James Bay, make a fresh-water lake out of the twenty rivers flowing into it, divert that water by a 167-mile GRAND (Great Recycling and Northern Development) Canal to Georgian Bay, flush the water through the Great Lakes, and pipe it down to the sun belt. Brian Mulroney gained the leadership of the Conservative Party in 1983 partially on the strength of his backing of Kierans's idea. In his book *Where I Stand*, Mulroney indicated that megaprojects like the GRAND Canal and other massive hydroelectric developments in Quebec and Labrador would be the means "that would bring a wave of astonishing benefits to the whole region." Later, however, a Mulroney aide stated, "Although Prime Minister Brian Mulroney supported the [GRAND Canal] scheme in 1983 when he ran for the Conservative Party leadership, since he became prime minister he has no position on it." The word "maybe" must have been left off the title of Mulroney's book.

Robert Bourassa included a chapter on Kierans's GRAND Canal in *Power From The North*, the manifesto on James Bay Phase II that helped to sweep him back into power in 1985. There Bourassa baldly stated that "water is a good, like any other, and can be bought and sold." For his part, Simon Reisman, after talking with Thomas Kierans, had a "flash of inspiration" that Americans "might be desperate for water. I realized that we ought to look at this as a developing resource in relation to trade. America's interest in trading with us has always been linked to something else they wanted from us. I felt water should be looked at in economic terms."

By 1985 several of the continent's major engineering and construction firms had formed a consortium known as the GRAND Canal Company (GRANDCO): the SNC Group of Montreal, the UMA Group of Calgary, Underwood McLellan Ltd. of Saskatoon, Rousseau, Sauve & Warren Inc. of Montreal, and Bechtel Canada Ltd. of Toronto (son of U.S. Bechtel – the world's largest engineering firm). GRANDCO has Louis Desmarais (brother of Power Corp.'s Paul) as its president, and supporters like Arthur Bailey and Duncan Edmonds, who (like Desmarais) run powerful Ottawa consulting firms. As Richard Pentland puts it, "These are all major companies that are influential in political and financial circles."

What attracted them is, of course, the economic potential. Thomas Kierans explains, "If I go down to Arizona today and look at a piece of land on which there is no water, the value per acre is in the area of fifty cents to five dollars. If I put dependable water on it, it jumps to about $50,000 an acre. That's the wealth. That's where we're going to get paid from." A different factor has attracted Atomic Energy of Canada Ltd. (AECL), which provides research assistance to GRANDCO and has a representative sitting on GRANDCO's board of directors. In AECL's case, the allure is the nuclear power plant to pump the water up and overland to Georgian Bay.

Not many people outside GRANDCO currently think that Kierans's canal is ever going to materialize, although Kai Millyard concedes that "private pipe-dreams have a way of becoming public nightmares." Its whopping $100 billion price tag puts it beyond the pocketbooks of even mega-megaproject boosters (but if there's enough interest in $200 billion NAWAPA, this one might look like a bargain). The more important point, though, is this: what's to stop it? What's to stop Canadian wheelers-and-dealers from going ahead with this, or any other water export plan they might think of, including export by tanker (already under consideration by several private companies, at least five of them in British Columbia and one in Mulroney's own riding)? The answer is: not much. In terms of the Great Lakes, certainly not the Great Lakes Charter.

In 1983, a task force appointed by the governors of Illinois, Indiana, Michigan, Minnesota, New York, Ohio, Pennsylvania, and Wisconsin, as well as the premiers of Ontario and Quebec, proposed a Great Lakes Charter to protect their waters from the greedy schemes of the sun-belt *nouveau riche*. After all, 80 per cent of all Canadian and 40 per cent of all U.S. iron and steel industries are on the lakes, and it takes 60,000 gallons of water to manufacture a single ton of steel. Moreover, given the nuclear power plants dotting the region, it takes more water than all the municipalities of western Canada use in a day to run the smallest nuclear power plant for a twenty-four-hour period. No way were those governors and premiers gonna let those sun belters take any water. After two years of study and consultations, the charter was signed in the spring of 1985 by the region's politicians, who called it "a strong signal to the sun belt." Just what kind of a signal, however, is still open to debate.

The Great Lakes Charter is sorely compromised by two significant facts. First, states and provinces have no authority to make treaties that are legally binding, so whatever the charter had to say was primarily a public-relations exercise. Second, those U.S. Supreme Court rulings on interstate water transfers meant that the charter could not forbid diversions. In effect, then, all the Great Lakes Charter really says is that its signatories agree to consult with one another if any proposed diversions surpass two million to five million gallons per day. Moreover, the charter sets up a system of permits whereby such diversions may be implemented.

Not surprisingly, a year after its signing, the environmental group Great Lakes United announced in February 1986 that Great Lakes water was more vulnerable to diversions than ever, what with at least five of the co-signatory states passing legislation that allows permits for "justifiable" diversion, and with Canadian wheelers-and-dealers jumping on the GRAND Canal bandwagon. At virtually the same time the Great Lakes Charter was being signed, MP Bill Blaikie (Winnipeg-Bird's Hill) wrote to Pollution Probe: "Any way you look at it, the idea of massive water exports to the U.S. is assinine. Regrettably ... things seem to have gone from bad to worse as a variety of federal and provincial politicians seem anxious to jump on-side with the prime minister in favour of such massive exports."

Equally rude, two months after the signing of the charter, the state of Ohio had introduced Bill 709 in the state legislature, calling for a 120-mile canal to connect Lake Erie and the Ohio River basin (the final link in the Great Inland-Waterway). At the same time, Ohio

Congressman James Traficant introduced Resolution No. 1519 in the U.S. House of Representatives, calling for federal funding to study this Ohio River Canal Project. Traficant's resolution was co-sponsored by more than thirty U.S. Congress members, including some from New York, Indiana, Illinois, and Wisconsin. So much for Great Lakes Solidarity.

Meanwhile, New York was having its own water troubles.

In the middle of the drought of '85, which had New Yorkers facing fines of $500 for watering lawns and washing their cars, a thirty-three-year-old environmentalist and river-keeper on the Hudson, John Cronin, noticed something remarkably odd. Exxon supertankers were quietly dumping their salt-water ballast and reloading with Hudson River water. He began to follow these supertankers in his eight-metre boat during the summer, watching them dump and reload, dump and reload. Finally, Cronin reported his findings to the authorities. The ensuing investigation revealed that Exxon had been scooping up water from the Hudson ever since 1977 and transporting it down to Aruba, whose government was pleased to buy it for some $5 million rather than build an expensive desalination plant.

Exxon paid $1.5 million in an out-of-court settlement to avoid legal hassles. But then New York State decided to get tough. There was, after all, an unpopular drought in progress. Environmental Commissioner Henry G. Williams announced in September 1985 that, from then on, operators of large vessels like the Exxon supertankers would have to pay $100 for a permit to transfer water out of the state. Governor Cuomo signed the bill, thus setting up a regulatory precedent for the legal handling of water withdrawals by corporate interests. Exxon has since dutifully paid for the $100 permit and continues to dump and reload, dump and reload, transporting water down to a grateful Aruba. A few months after the signing of this permit bill, but with no indication of satiric intent, New York City Mayor Edward Koch's 1986 task force on water concluded that a major new source of fresh water would be needed to solve the city's perennial shortage. Included in the recommendations was a proposal to build a tunnel from Lake Ontario to the Big Apple, by which a billion gallons per day might be diverted.

Given such trends and developments, it would be really nice to have a Canadian federal water policy firmly in place. The closest thing we've got is (wouldn't you know it) a report by a commission – the Federal Inquiry on Water Policy (the Pearse Commission), which decided in September 1985: "We should be prepared for [export] proposals in forthcoming years, but we cannot now predict whether they will be beneficial to Canada or not. We have therefore concluded that it would be imprudent for the federal government to reject all exports out of hand." Moreover, the commission struck a somewhat favourable note with regard to export by tanker, suggesting that such a means poses few environmental concerns, provided of course that the federal government passes "legislation to require anyone who proposes to export water to obtain a license."

The absence of a federal water policy tends to leave the matter in the hands of the provinces, and here we are confronted with what may, in fact, be the big loophole.

Michael Keating points out that Canada internally "diverts more water than any country in the world, but very few of us realize it." Already there are at least fifty-four water diversions in place across the country, most of them being used to create giant reservoirs for provincial hydroelectric plants. The most obvious is the first phase of Bourassa's James Bay Project, begun in the 1970s, which flooded an area of Quebec the size of Nova Scotia. As Manitoba, Quebec, British Columbia, and other provinces hitch their economic stars to massive hydroelectric power exports to U.S. utilities, they are damming and diverting more rivers and creating ever greater reservoirs that encompass thousands of square kilometres. While our provincial politicians go ahead and turn the country into a series of great big water tanks, the feasibility of simply selling that water south will grow. After all, the environmental damage will have been done, so why not make a profit off it? *The Globe and Mail* itself has pointed out:

> There is a physical connection between electricity production and water export in the simple fact that a dam built to capture the energy of falling water usually needs a large reservoir behind it. And that reservoir can be used to divert water out of the watershed, if the economic need for water becomes greater than the need for electricity.

At this point, Alberta readers might be reminiscing about events in the early 1980s, when NDP leader Grant Notley exposed the Lougheed government's plan to divert northern rivers to meet southern Alberta needs without precisely mentioning water diversion to the public. Documents leaked to the NDP revealed that dams under construction were located precisely where they would be needed for a massive interbasin transfer scheme – a scheme so costly that, as

Notley reasoned even after the Lougheed cabinet killed the project, it would make sense only if the Conservative government was considering exporting water to the United States. Not surprisingly, the scheme depended on a big PR effort. One of the leaked government memos recommended "two full years of public relations activities to develop further acceptance by the public toward diversion and water development."

As events unfold over the next few years, don't expect water diversions to be called water diversions by politicians and wheelers-and-dealers. We live in the age of Orwellian newspeak, when the MX missile is renamed "the Peacekeeper" by Reagan, and when Thomas Kierans himself calls his canal project "water recycling" and refers to the GRANDCO consortium as "environmentalist."

As corporate industry continues to poison and foul the Great Lakes, there may well be growing appeal for a scheme to flush out the lakes with fresh water from the north. David Lees has reported in *Toronto Life* that there are 164 toxic-waste sites on the U.S. side of the Niagara River. "Every day almost ten tons of toxic chemicals are dumped in the Niagara River, but while the problems created by this – like the problems associated with acid rain – are predominantly Canadian, the source is almost exclusively American." Rather than actually solve this problem, which threatens the drinking water and health of forty million people, corporations and politicians may be holding out for a scheme like the GRAND Canal, which is pitched as a way of bringing "new" water down to the Great Lakes and thereby cleaning them up for everyone. This may account for the interest in Kierans's idea expressed by politicians in Minnesota and New York, an interest that might be translated as encouraging the dumb Canadians to solve U.S. pollution and water-shortage problems. According to the wheeler-dealer mind-set, the way to solve one environmental problem is to compound it with another even more astounding and spectacular. That's "progress."

(1986)

☐ Speaking the Unspeakable: Understanding Ecofeminism

Whatever is unnamed, undepicted in images, whatever is omitted from biography, censored in collections of letters, whatever is misnamed as something else, made difficult-to-come-by, whatever is buried in the memory by the collapse of meaning under an inadequate or lying language – this will become, not merely unspoken, but *unspeakable."*

– Adrienne Rich, 1976[1]

DARING TO SPEAK the unspeakable is what characterizes every liberation movement, and in our time we are witnessing an extraordinary collective phenomenon of new naming, renaming, unburying, remembering, and rethinking in virtually every field of thought and endeavour. This challenge to patriarchy in all its forms is coming from every oppressed people on the planet. As Nigerian writer Chinua Achebe has put it, "The great excluded are starting to make trouble."[2]

Not only are we starting to make trouble, but we are also making links among ourselves and among previously disparate and isolated disciplines, fields, facts, and phenomena: links that certainly do trouble that privileged point of view from which most thought has been thought (and most words written) over centuries. As previously excluded voices struggle out from under oppression and imposed silence, their contributions change the entire picture.

Consider, for example, Eduardo Galeano's trilogy, *Memory of Fire* – a telling of the past five hundred years of history from a Latin American point of view.[3] By filling in what had previously been unnamed, undepicted, omitted, censored, misnamed, buried, and unspoken,

Galeano has not just challenged the prevailing historical portrait conveyed by most First World accounts, he has given all of us some missing pieces of that fragmented jigsaw puzzle called patriarchy.

As we put that puzzle together, we are able to see its picture as entirely arbitrary: a world-view that benefits only a tiny few, at the expense of most other beings on this planet – and the planet itself.

Over the past dozen years or so, but especially during the otherwise dismal 1980s, a great number of pieces of the puzzle have been added, leading to a critique that goes right to the core of the Western patriarchal paradigm. Part of that developing critique has been the rise of "ecofeminism," which, in essence, bridges the gap between ecology and feminism: strands of analysis that have existed side by side over past decades without necessarily intertwining. Thus there have been any number of environmental analyses and books that illuminate the processes of ecological degradation, but which fail to make the connection between planetary exploitation and other forms of social injustice and inequality. Similarly, any number of feminist texts have explored the politics of patriarchal society without broadening and deepening the focus to include the exploited planet. By making explicit the connections between an unjust and mysogynist society and a society that has exploited "mother earth" to the point of environmental crisis, ecofeminism has helped to highlight the deep splits in the patriarchal world-view.

As women have long recognized, our oppression is primarily based on body-difference. Our women's bodies, which bleed, conceive, give birth, and lactate, have been perceived under patriarchy as "closer to nature" than the male, closer to the animal realm, and we have thereby been deemed "inferior" to men. The second wave of feminism in this century necessarily rejected this patriarchal projection by asserting that "anatomy is not destiny" and by struggling for equal opportunity in all professions, for control over our own bodies, and for social change in a deeply misogynist world – struggles that obviously continue.

It may be fair to say that ecofeminism has taken the critique deeper to ask: Why is it that men feel "superior" to nature, cut off from the natural realm? Why is it that men perceive their own bodies as *not* "close to nature," not even part of nature? By thereby changing the framework of analysis to highlight the mind / body split so central to patriarchy, ecofeminism reveals the basic fault line in the patriarchal zeitgeist.

That fault line is hierarchical dualism. Where there is only difference, Western patriarchy perceives not just "opposites" but a hierarchical relationship between the opposing terms. Thus, patriarchy's perception of the female as subordinate and inferior to the male is recapitulated in the culture / nature dichotomy wherein non-human species and the Earth itself are perceived as subordinate and inferior to "mankind." Focusing on this prevailing anthropocentric view, Elizabeth Dodson Gray writes in *Green Paradise Lost*:

> Ultimately, the problem of patriarchy is conceptual. The problem which patriarchy poses for the human species is not simply that it oppresses women. Patriarchy has erroneously conceptualized and mythed "Man's place" in the universe and thus – by the illusion of dominion that it legitimates – it endangers the entire planet.[4]

Gray and others have traced the conceptual "error" in the West back to the three-thousand-year-old creation myth expressed in the first three chapters of Genesis: with its command to "subdue the earth" and "have dominion over" all living beings; and its narrative which "explains" male dominance in Chapter 2 through Adam's creation first, his naming of all reality, his birth of Eve from his side, and the Eve-Serpent collusion.

As creation myths go, Genesis is a relatively recent one, recorded when patriarchy was still in the process of becoming entrenched. The ancient Hebrews did not invent patriarchy – which was well under way at least a thousand years before Genesis was recorded – but they too were caught up in its zeitgeist.

While there are undoubtedly profound meanings in our Genesis myth, it has traditionally been understood to mean that Eve and the wily serpent were responsible for the "Fall of Man." By yielding to temptation and then tempting Adam to eat the forbidden fruit, Eve is perceived to have caused the wrath of Yahweh, resulting in Paradise Lost. But if we ask what the "Fall of Man" was, we recognize that it was a fall into consciousness – specifically consciousness of the body. Genesis tells us that after eating the fruit, Adam and Eve "knew their nakedness" and hid from Yahweh, who angrily asks: "Who told you that you were naked?"

Thus, at issue in the first three chapters of Genesis is body consciousness – the gaining of carnal knowledge or the knowledge of embodiment, incarnation. As the result of this supposed transgression, the angry Yahweh splits off from his creation: a breach central to that other patriarchal dualism expressed as a spirit / matter opposition. Genesis thus posits a hierarchical "chain of being," with the sky-god Yahweh at the top of the ladder, the angels a bit lower, then Adam, then Eve, then all other species, with nature (and the devil) at the bottom. For our purposes here, the most resonant moment may be Genesis 3:17, in which the angry God curses the very ground because of Adam and Eve's transgression.

A thousand years later, institutionalized Christianity (as of the third century A.D.) had amplified that curse into a view of earthly life itself as "corruption" – with both body and woman the signs of defilement that keep Man from a most unearthly heaven. Over the centuries, Western patriarchy has given us a series of deep splits or false oppositions that have been pitted against each other both in our psyches and in the external world: an absolutely good God vs. an absolutely evil Devil; light vs. dark; male vs. female; mind vs. body; spirit vs. matter; human vs. animal. But under patriarchy, these so-called "oppositions" have also been scripted to mean that one must triumph over the other. The absolutely good God must triumph over the absolutely evil Devil; light must triumph over dark; male is superior to female; mind is triumphant over body; spirit is better than matter; humans are superior to all other species.

But perhaps the most subtle, yet most damaging, split is the spirit / matter duality, reinforced by Yahweh's curse of the very ground. Even three thousand years after Genesis was first recorded, that curse still reverberates through Western patriarchy. As Jamake Highwater, author of *The Primal Mind*, has noted:

> For most primal peoples the earth is so marvellous that their connotation of it requires it to be spelled with a capital "E." How perplexing it is to discover two English synonyms for Earth – "soil" and "dirt" – used to describe uncleanliness, *soiled* and *dirty*. And how upsetting it is to discover that the word "dirty" in English is also used to depict obscenities![5]

Writing from a cultural perspective that considers the ground itself as sacred, Highwater reveals the extent to which even our dominant language reflects patriarchy's profound dis-ease, unease, about both embodiment and being grounded in the natural realm.

In Jungian terms, body and nature have been patriarchy's "shadow": rejected, feared, and despised as the inferior and loathsome "evil" side of the human condition. As a result, whatever patriarchy has perceived as "closer to nature" has also been perceived as "further from God" – an obvious prescription for exploitation. Not surprisingly, the patriarchal shadow has been projected onto women, people of colour, "primitive" societies, peasant peoples, non-human species, and the planet itself. Since, in terms of hierarchical dualism, "further from God" means "closer to the Devil," exploitation has over the centuries rarely troubled the patriarchal conscience.

Thus, it is no accident that the so-called Age of Enlightenment, which began in the sixteenth century, coincided with the onset of the slave trade, the plundering and decimation of the indigenous people of the New World, and the centuries of witch-burnings. A zeitgeist that posits light-male-mind-spirit on the side of God and dark-female-body-matter on the side of the Devil can easily perceive the "other" as not human, "mere animal" or "devil."

These historical phenomena were an intrinsic part of a Scientific Revolution that would take the Western patriarchal paradigm to its logical conclusion: the triumph of Mechanism over Vitalism in the Cartesian world-view.

Before the Age of Enlightenment, nature was perceived as "inferior" and "feminine," but nevertheless alive. Under Descartes, Locke, and others involved in the Scientific Revolution, the entire cosmos would henceforth be perceived as a mechanistic "clockworks" set in motion by an aloof, transcendant, and finally absent deity. All animal species were perceived as unfeeling "machines," and matter itself became mere "dead matter" to be manipulated by the superior white male mind. This denial of life itself to the natural realm (including the body) was patriarchal split-consciousness taken to its ultimate, but it coincided with other (unspoken) losses, including the loss of meaning and feeling, and certainly the wilful loss of millions of people perceived as being less than human.

As Carolyn Merchant has written in her extraordinary book, *The Death of Nature*:

> The removal of animistic, organic assumptions about the cosmos constituted the death of nature – the most far-reaching effect of the Scientific Revolution. Because nature was now viewed as a system of dead, inert particles moved by external, rather than inherent forces, the mechanical framework itself could legitimate the manipulation of nature. Moreover, as a conceptual framework, the mechanical order

had associated with it a framework of values based on power, fully compatible with the directions taken by commercial capitalism.[6]

The triumph of Mechanism over Vitalism, finally achieved by the end of the nineteenth century, found its ultimate expression in a twentieth century that has moved relentlessly toward planetary annihilation. It is as though patriarchy itself in all its forms, so long estranged from body and nature, is soaring off into that unearthly perfection of mind and spirit called "heaven." In the process, it is killing off 150,000 species per year in its continuing rape of the Earth, waging wars of oppression across the planet to feed its power drive, spending $2 million every minute on military weaponry, and eliminating diversity itself under the aegis of that modern monotheism called Technocracy.

Whatever else it may be, ecofeminism is nothing less than the transformed return of Vitalism (but devoid of patriarchal projections) as a conscious political and spiritual challenge to the prevailing Mechanistic zeitgeist. In its reweaving of the ripped web of life, ecofeminism asks us to rethink all hierarchical dualisms and thereby change everything. It may be fair to say that neither feminism nor environmentalism has, by itself, gone so deep.

Such a critique helps us to understand the phenomenal blossoming throughout the 1980s of Earth-centered spirituality in a wide diversity of forms and practices. But common to each of these forms and practices are three core concepts: 1) immanence – the concept that sacredness is inherent in all Creation; 2) interconnection – that all parts of the living cosmos are linked; and 3) compassion – the ability to see ourselves as answerable and accountable to those who are different from us, to value all other lives as we value our own.

But ultimately, ecofeminism challenges the very basis upon which all current economic systems have been built: the belief that sees "the other" as a resource to be exploited for profit. Whether that other is an oppressed class, race, sex, or the planet itself, all are linked by our shared oppression in a system that must rank Being itself for the gain of the few. As Judith Plant, editor of *Healing The Wounds,* writes in her introduction, "There is no respect for the 'other' in patriarchal society. The other, the object of patriarchal rationality, is considered only insofar as it can benefit the subject. So self-centered is this view that it is blind to the fact that its own life depends on the integrity and well-being of the whole."[7]

An alternative paradigm based on immanence, interconnection, and compassion thereby challenges every patriarchal institution on the planet. Such concepts provide an imperative towards action in the world: an activism that links the political and the spiritual. As Starhawk writes, "Instead of replacing political action, earth-based spirituality provides a repository of energy that can resurge in new cycles of political momentum."[8] Ecofeminism is the inheritor of feminist spirituality rooted in Earth-centred traditions.

The richness of ecofeminism is in the extent to which it makes explicit the interconnections of human systems of oppression and posits a vital alternative to the patriarchal paradigm based on hierarchy and dominance. Into the 1990s, ecofeminism will continue to speak the unspeakable in a society that wants us to remain ignorant of interrelationships, isolated from one another, and fragmented in our efforts towards social change.

(1990)

NOTES

1. Adrienne Rich, *On Lies, Secrets, and Silence* (New York: W.W. Norton and Company, 1979), p. 199.

2. Chinua Achebe, remark at the 54th International PEN World Congress, September 1989, Toronto, Canada.

3. Eduardo Galeano, *Memory Of Fire*, 3 volumes (New York: Pantheon Books, 1982, 1984, 1988).

4. Elizabeth Dodson Gray, *Green Paradise Lost* (Wellesley, Mass.: Roundtable Press, 1979), p. lx.

5. Jamake Highwater, *The Primal Mind: Vision and Reality in Indian America* (New York: Meridian, 1982), p. 5.

6. Carolyn Merchant, *The Death of Nature: Women, Ecology and the Scientific Revolution* (New York: Harper & Row, 1980), p. 193.

7. Judith Plant, "Toward A New World: An Introduction," in Judith Plant, ed., *Healing The Wounds: The Promise of Ecofeminism* (Toronto: Between The Lines, 1989), p. 2.

8. Starhawk, "Feminist, Earth-based Spirituality and Ecofeminism," in *ibid.*, p. 177.

❐ Flying Chernobyls: Plutonium Flights over the Canadian North

There will be no overflights over Canada with respect to carrying plutonium unless the Government of Canada finds it is safe, that it is in
order to do so, and gives its consent.... We will not say an anticipatory
no when we have never been asked to say yes or no. It would be ridiculous and contrary to our international obligations to do so.

> – John Crosbie (Minister of Transport),
> House of Commons, November 5, 1987

THE DEADLINE YEAR is 1992. That's the date that Japan's prototype
"fastbreeder" reactor is set to come on line, utilizing 1,400 kilograms
of plutonium for its nuclear core and consuming another 500 kilograms of plutonium every year thereafter. It's also the date that Britain's THORP nuclear reprocessing plant is scheduled to begin operation, transforming spent nuclear fuel of U.S. origin into plutonium
usable in mixed-oxide fuels for Japan's thirty-five light-water and
breeder reactors. And 1992 is the year that plutonium shipments to
Japan from Britain's and France's reprocessing plants are expected to
begin on a regular basis: three times per month. If the powers that be
have their way, 500 kilograms of powdered plutonium will be flown
over the Canadian North every month en route to Tokyo.

This is an astounding scenario for disaster. One-half kilogram of
released plutonium could cause forty-two billion cancers. But by the
year 2000, Japan wants to have stock-piled forty-five tons of the stuff:
presumably not for nuclear weapons (which its Constitution forbids),
but for its long-term nuclear-power program, for potential space
flights (rockets like the U.S. Challenger are now fuelled by plutonium), and for nuclear-powered satellites.

Unfortunately, the Mulroney government thinks we have an "international obligation" to provide the level playing field over which this high-flying international game of plutonium roulette will take place. Along with stealth cruise missiles and NATO jet fighters, Canada's northern skies will most likely next be filled with flying Chernobyls making their thrice-monthly run from Europe to Japan. Of course, it all started behind closed doors....

In 1982 the United States and Japan quietly began negotiating a new agreement that would give Japan thirty-year blanket approval to reprocess U.S. spent nuclear-fuel rods in order to obtain the plutonium for its own burgeoning nuclear industry. Having tied its electricity needs to the nuclear "option," Japan has been building nuclear-power plants at a rate that would make even Ontario Hydro jealous. Between 1981 and 1989, Japan built thirteen light-water reactors, bringing its current total to thirty-five, with long-range plans for many more, each dependent on plutonium for operation.

Since the United States does not itself reprocess spent nuclear fuel, and since Japan's reprocessing facilities remain minimal, the secret agreement worked out between the two countries dictated that spent U.S. fuel would be reprocessed in Europe, where Britain and France have been carving out a niche for themselves as important players in the whole nuclear-fuel cycle. The resulting plutonium would then be flown to Japan, while the United States would pocket $250 million annually for the use of its spent fuel.

The draft agreement between the United States and Japan was quietly signed (but not ratified) in January 1987. Since the deal hinged on transporting the plutonium on a flight-path over Canada, the Nuclear Control Institute – an independent U.S. lobby group that tries to monitor nuclear activity – kindly alerted Canadian newspapers. When the news story appeared in *The Globe and Mail* on the morning of March 23, 1987, it was startlingly clear that the Canadian government had never been consulted during the five years of bilateral talks leading up to the draft agreement, which stipulates that plutonium flights take place over "a polar route or another route that avoids civil disorder and natural disasters." The United States and Japan had decided between themselves that the Canadian North would fit the bill perfectly.

The day the news story broke, two opposition MPs – Douglas Frith (Sudbury) and Jim Fulton (Skeena) – raised the issue in the House of Commons, asking that the Mulroney government inform the United

States and Japan that their plans to use Canadian airspace for their "flying Chernobyls" (Fulton's phrase) would be categorically refused. Joe Clark and John Crosbie responded with bafflegab to avoid the issue, referring to Canada's "several options" in the matter, including what Crosbie called "an adequate legislative framework" in the Transportation of Dangerous Goods Act.

When questioned later by reporters, Crosbie explained: "Nuclear fuels have to be moved: dangerous goods have to be moved. That's why we have legislation on transportation of dangerous goods. As long as all proper and reasonable regulations are met and safety measures are taken, you can't, per se, say no."

Under the Transportation of Dangerous Goods Act, Canada will not allow any amount of "fissile" or potentially unstable radioactive material to be loaded in Canada or transported by Canadian carrier without prior government approval. But according to transport department lawyer Alan Pittrick, the Act does not apply to flights over Canada. When the issue heated up again the following day, Crosbie advised the opposition MPS to "relax." He stated, "If the time comes when we need to say 'no,' we will say 'no.' However, that time has not yet come."

That time never did come during the events leading up to the official ratification of the U.S.-Japan agreement in 1988. Although the issue was raised at least nine times in the House during 1987, and although every major newspaper in Canada editorially opposed the plans, the Mulroney government continued to insist that the whole matter was "hypothetical," thereby raising questions as to whether the continuing free-trade talks were lobotomizing the brainpan of an already servile and witless government.

To read Hansard is not for the weak-stomached, though it is a powerful lesson in representative "democracy." The 1987 parliamentary debates on plutonium flights were characterized by opposition MPS being called everything from "Pavlov's dogs" to "cashew nuts" and "Little Red Riding Hoods," while their concerns about the overflights were dismissed as "crying wolf" and "anticipatory hysteria." Obviously, John "The Mouth" Crosbie had gone into hypergear on the issue. Meanwhile, a different government refused to "relax."

The original flight plan in the draft agreement called for a Canadian overflight with a possible refuelling stop in Alaska before continuing on to Japan. The Governor of Alaska, Stephen Cowper, had been left just as much in the dark as Canada and only found out about the secret draft agreement in March 1987 when an environmentalist laid the Nuclear Control Institute's report-alert on his desk.

Cowper fired off a letter to U.S. Secretary of State George Shultz, demanding that Washington produce an environmental impact statement before asking Congress to ratify the agreement with Japan. In May the Alaska legislature was considering a resolution to prevent the use of state airports for plutonium flight refuelling stops.

Shultz's response to the Governor stated that the draft agreement was undergoing "rigorous interagency review," including issues such as "when and in what form any additional environmental review should be conducted." Shultz also told Cowper that the agreement would require "stringent physical security and safety requirements such as transfer exclusively by air (to minimize time spent in international transit), use of a cask certified to withstand a crash, armed guards, redundant communications, and detailed contingency plans." And he assured Cowper that the agreement would not necessarily constitute a decision to ship plutonium over Alaska.

The Governor was not convinced. By September 1987, Alaska's Attorney General had filed suit against the U.S. government, protesting the agreement. As MP Audrey McLaughlin (Yukon) stated at the time, "If Alaska can foresee the dangers of this proposal, why can't our federal government? Canada is being too polite for our own good. Hazards from transporting plutonium across our North can be prevented by saying NO and suggesting Japan build its own processing plants."

In response to Alaska's demands, the U.S. government conducted an environmental impact assessment (EIA), not an environmental impact statement (EIS), in late 1987. An EIS can take well over a year to complete, while an EIA is quicker, less detailed, and not comprehensive in scope. In this case, the assessment's conclusions saw no threat to the environment. But Alaska continued to fight back. Senator Frank Murkowski (Rep., Alaska) worked out an amendment to a budget bill specifying that casks containing plutonium be able to withstand a "worst-case" air accident. Further, the Murkowski Amendment recommended that a jumbo jet laden with sample containers actually be test-crashed to determine the safety of the casks.

Fine powdered plutonium particles do not dissolve in water, do not stick to soil, and cannot be absorbed by plants. If released into the environment by an airplane crash, plutonium could stay airborne for as long as sixty days, travelling hundreds or even thousands of miles from the crash site. This plutonium dust is deadly to any air-breathing being and it defies cleanup – as the plutonium disasters in Spain (1966) and Greenland (1968) indicate.

Former Liberal environment minister Charles Caccia told the House on August 13, 1987:

> Even one crash out of the over 700 flights anticipated could kill people as well as caribou, polar bears, and other Arctic wildlife through the slow death of cancer as a result of the toxic plutonium dust. Even residents of Yellowknife or cities further south, perhaps including Edmonton, could conceivably be threatened depending on wind and weather conditions, location of the crash site, and the extent of destruction to the casks carrying the plutonium. These risks are avoidable if we say no now.

To which the Mulroney government made the laughable assertion that Canadian safety standards are among the strictest in the world.

In the United States, the 1975 Scheuer Amendment recommends that a cask containing plutonium not rupture or release its contents in the "crash and explosion of a high-flying aircraft" – for which the U.S. Nuclear Regulatory Commission (NRC) has established a cask-impact speed of 288 miles per hour (129 metres per second) – the maximum legal air speed below 10,000 feet. The 1987 Murkowski Amendment further tightened that standard by stating that a cask must remain intact in a "worst-case" plane crash, which the NRC set at 630 mph.

Canada adheres to the standard of the International Atomic Energy Agency (IAEA), the international governing body whose plutonium transport standards are the same regardless of mode of shipment: by road, rail, sea, or air. Under IAEA, a container cask must survive an impact-speed of thirty miles per hour. The IAEA is proposing to upgrade this standard for air transport to an impact-speed of 190 miles per hour. Nevertheless, this is far lower than the U.S. NRC's standard.

According to Thomas Homer-Dixon, a Canadian in the MIT arms control and defence program, neither of these standards meets the reality of a worst-case scenario. Plutonium flights are likely to be travelling at 35,000 feet (not 10,000) and flying at a speed of at least 500 miles per hour – so they would hit the ground at a crash impact-speed of over 300 miles per hour. Nonetheless, the NRC's 288 miles-per-hour impact standard is preferable to the IAEA's standard:

30 miles per hour now and 190 miles per hour proposed. Perhaps not surprisingly, the discrepancy between U.S. and international cask safety standards has recently become the terrain of political wheeling and dealing. The race is on to develop a "safe" cask for air transport – or, in lieu of that, to lower the safety standards to facilitate the new plutonium economy underway.

In November 1987, the *Guardian* revealed that British Nuclear Fuels Ltd. (the brains behind the THORP plant) had been storing Japanese spent nuclear fuel for nearly a decade while Britain developed its reprocessing facilities. British Nuclear Fuels had also drawn up arrangements for plutonium flights to Japan without informing the British Parliament. Authorities further admittted to the *Guardian* that the company had begun tests on air transport casks at a military base in Wales in October 1987.

France has made similar storage, reprocessing, and flight arrangements with Japan behind closed doors. For years, fuel from Japan has been reprocessed and stored at the UP-2 plant of the French nuclear fuel company Cogema, located at Cap la Hague on the Channel coast. Cogema has produced as much as five tons of Japanese plutonium per year, waiting in storage for a "safe" transport cask. In all, British and French nuclear reprocessors have already signed contracts to provide Japan with forty-five tons of plutonium by the end of this century. According to a November 1987 U.S. Department of Defense report, by the late 1990s as many as three hundred shipments of plutonium annually will leave European processing plants for destinations in Japan and elsewhere in Europe.

France, Great Britain, West Germany, Belgium, Switzerland, and Japan (and some Eastern European countries as well) are all dependent on plutonium in the mixed-oxide fuels for their light-water or breeder reactors. According to research done in 1987 by physicists with the Federation of American Scientists, if these countries continue with current plans, by the end of the century more than three hundred thousand kilograms of plutonium (enough to build thirty thousand atomic bombs) will have been separated from spent nuclear fuel and placed on the commercial plutonium market. Simply in terms of Britain's THORP plant, set to start operations in 1992, European customers have already contracted for the reprocessing of at least seventeen hundred metric tonnes of spent fuel over the next decade. The plutonium economy is well under way.

Meanwhile, the U.S.-Japan draft agreement was officially signed on November 4, 1987, and sent to Congress for a ninety-day review. Although the Mulroney government continued to "relax," both the U.S. House of Representatives Foreign Affairs Committee and a special U.S. Senate panel rejected the draft agreement in terms of the Nuclear Non-Proliferation Act and sent it back to President Reagan for renegotiation.

Reagan was then faced with three choices: 1) agree to renegotiate the agreement, 2) exempt it from the non-proliferation act and send it back to Congress, betting on a majority support, or 3) insist on it becoming law and risk a fight with Congress. What happened was this.

Japanese Prime Minister Noboru Takeshita paid a visit to Reagan in January 1988. The president assured him that the agreement would proceed "despite congressional objections." True to form, on March 21, 1988, the U.S. Senate approved the agreement by a vote of 53 to 30, with approval apparently hinging on a change of flight-path to bypass Alaska. The U.S. State Department agreed that plutonium carriers would have to fly a zigzag route from Europe: flying non-stop up to the North Pole and then down the international dateline to Tokyo so that "the whole flight is above ocean." With regard to this Senate cave-in, the Nuclear Control Institute stated, "On March 21, the Senate succumbed to a nuclear industry and an Administration in thrall to Japanese economic reprisals."

Since neoconservative plans seemed to be falling into place quite smoothly, the British government admitted in Parliament that same month that Prestwick in Scotland had been chosen as the airport from which plutonium flights would leave. By April 1988, Tsutomu Ueki of Japan's Science and Technology Agency was telling *Globe and Mail* reporter Thomas Walkom that Ottawa would not be consulted on the final flight-path, "which will be decided in consultation with the u.s., France and Britain."

At least this got a rise out of the Mulroney government. On April 19, 1988, External Affairs spokesman Denys Tessier stated that Canada had warned Washington and Tokyo that permission will be required for any plutonium shipments that cross Canadian airspace. "If it's not safe, it will not fly," he said. But there's the rub: that word "safe."

By May 1988 the "U.S.-Japan Agreement on Peaceful Use of Nuclear Power" had been officially ratified by both Japan and the United

States. That summer a cask developed by the Battle Memorial Institute of Columbus, Ohio, was tested at the Sandia National Laboratory in New Mexico, but it failed to remain intact at an impact speed of 288 miles per hour, the NRC-recommended safety standard. So, by autumn, the U.S. State Department had rushed through a special-case "subsequent arrangement" that would allow Japan to transport plutonium from Europe by sea – a contingency not included in the official agreement. Japan made plans to build a special transport ship to be ready by 1992; nevertheless, jumbo jet transport remained the desired mode, since it is cheaper. To facilitate this goal, more manoeuvrings threatened to dismantle existing safety standards surrounding plutonium flights.

Several things have been happening at the same time. First, the IAEA has proposed to upgrade its international flight standards for cask safety from a 30-miles-per-hour impact speed (which no one will accept) to 190 miles per hour. This seems a transparent attempt to quickly be able to certify a cask as "safe" for doing business. In November 1989, a cask tested at the Sandia Laboratory again failed to withstand the U.S. NRC's impact standard of 288 miles per hour.

Second, the higher U.S. safety standards are not codified as law. Currently there is an effort to codify the NRC standard as mandatory, a move that would also help to reveal the lower IAEA standard as highly suspect. Third, as a result of this discrepancy (288 miles per hour vs. 190 miles per hour), the U.S. Department of Energy – which has its own deal with Japan to provide new breeder-fuel technology – has been lobbying for a reduction in the U.S. NRC cask standards to make them consistent with the weaker international IAEA proposal. This lobbying includes pressure to repeal the Murkowski Amendment, which governs foreign shipments of plutonium through *or adjacent to* U.S. airspace – apparently the only thing protecting Canada in terms of stricter regulations.

As the Nuclear Control Institute stated on January 31, 1990: "The bottom-line danger is that, by means of a series of regulatory adjustments, ways will be found to permit air shipments of plutonium from Europe to Japan to go forward through Canadian and U.S. airspace, utilizing shipping casks that could not survive a severe crash."

Because of these serious developments, the Institute wrote to the Honourable Benoit Bouchard, Canada's transport minister, at the end of January 1990, asking that Bouchard join with Alaska's Governor Cowper and Senator Murkowski in submitting comments in support of the codification of the NRC's stricter standards. Comment period closed on February 9, with nothing but silence from Canadian authorities. According to a spokesperson for the Ministry of Transport, Bouchard could not respond because it was up to the Atomic Energy Control Board to deal with nuclear safety standards and to External Affairs to make policy on the issue. Thanks, guys.

Given the overwhelming silence from the Mulroney government on the whole issue of plutonium flights, one must conclude that the administration will do anything necessary to facilitate the plutonium economy, even if it means endangering the Canadian North. A February 15, 1990, press release from Energy, Mines and Resources Canada proudly trumpets in its headline that Canada is "The Western World's Leading Uranium Producer" – in other words, Canada is at the start of the whole nuclear-fuel cycle, producing some 11,300 metric tonnes of pure uranium every year and exporting 85 per cent of that to the United States, Japan, and Europe.

On August 13, 1987, MP Bill Blaikie (Winnipeg-Birds Hill) queried the Mulroney government's "casual attitude" towards plutonium flights:

> Is it because we have compromised ourselves with respect to radioactive substances in the North by the Government's proposal for nuclear submarines for Canada's North? Is it because the Government has entered into an agreement, through AECL, with the United States and Japan vis-à-vis the research going on at Lac du Bonnet into the disposal of high level radioactive waste? Is that why we have this silence, this incredibly relaxed attitude toward a very serious problem? Or is it because of the general deference to all things nuclear to which the Conservatives have now become captive in the same way that the Liberals were before them? All these things give one cause to wonder just what is going on.

Unfortunately, what is going on is the relentless rise to supremacy of a globalized plutonium economy – an economy to which the Canadian government is indeed "captive." Since the overdeveloped world "needs" plutonium, and the entire nuclear-fuel cycle for its whole technological agenda, the trade-off for Canada will most likely be horribly two-fold: storage of U.S. nuclear wastes in the Canadian Shield, and more than seven hundred plutonium overflights – "flying Chernobyls" – during this decade.

(1990)

☐ Deconstructing Ecobabble: Notes On An Attempted Corporate Takeover

IF YOU CONSIDERED "biodegradable disposable diapers" a cop-out muddying the waters of the environmental movement, try to get your head around the new "Bio Safe chain-saw oil" made in Finland from canola oil. We are hip-deep in the Age of Oxymorons: those turns of phrase that try to marry contradictories. "O heavy lightness, serious vanity," quotes my dictionary to quaintly illustrate the oxymoronic phrase, but current examples would be these: "clean, safe nuclear power," "the managed forest," and that new corporate rallying cry, "sustainable development." Not surprisingly, much of this oxymoronic discourse is coming from the "progressive conservatives."

Ecobabble is the marketing and PR strategy of the 1990s. "For Us, Every Day is Earth Day," croons the multi-million-dollar ad campaign of the American Forest Council, which represents eighteen corporate loggers who clear-cut thousands of acres of trees daily. "We Share The Growing Concerns Of All Canadians With Our Environment," claims the new ad frm Alcan Aluminum, whose smelters in Jonquière, Quebec, pump out six hundred tons of deadly chemicals each year. "Our Commitment to the Environment," trumpets the headline for the latest McDonald's pitch. "You Care About B.C.'s Forests ... So Do We," gushes the B.C. Council of Forest Industries newspaper supplement. "Clean Air, Bright Future," promises the PR pamphlet put out by the Motor Vehicle Manufacturers' Association of Canada. Even Hydro-Quebec has gotten into the act. On the cover of its new glossy brochure hyping the $40 billion Stage II of the James Bay boondoggle, the bold print piously asserts, "La Grande Rivière: A Development in Accord With Its Environment."

Having degraded the ecosystem to a point possibly beyond recovery, the corporate powers-that-be are now heavily engaged in degrading environmental discourse itself – an attempted takeover evident in not just the "greenspeak" sloganeering, but in events like the Globe '90 business love-in held in Vancouver in March, the Des-Rosiers Automotive Conference ("The Automotive Industry and The Environment") held in Toronto in May, and the mammoth bizfest activities of Earth Day 1990 – reminding us that green is also the colour of money and the colour of bile.

Says Andre Carothers, editor of *Greenpeace* magazine, "In the trade, it's called 'repositioning,' which means taking the same old stuff and re-packaging it according to the latest taste." Adds Greenpeace's Peter Dykstra, "A major challenge for environmentalists and the press in the 1990s will be to cut through the growing forest of environmental doublespeak from politicians, polluters and others who see the advent of concern for the planet as nothing more than a nifty marketing tool."

But Paul Watson of Sea Shepherd warns, "We're in a situation right now where politicians and the system are co-opting the movement." As usual, that co-optation takes the form of defusing radical potential – a potential that scares the bejesus out of the powers-that-be. As Union Carbide's chairman Robert D. Kennedy has stated, "An aroused public can put us out of business."

It is well known that by 1989 the environmental crisis had become the top concern in every public opinion survey done on this continent. But less well known is a survey-finding guaranteed to make any corporate CEO foul his Guccis. Between 1986 and 1989, the percentage of North Americans who favoured environmental goals "regardless of their cost to the economy" made a stunning leap: from 40 per cent of the populace to 84 per cent – a doubling of that category called, in pollster jargon, "hard-core environmentalists."

When U.S. pollster Lou Harris announced this heretical trend in autumn of 1989, adding that "Health is more important to people than economic well-being," the fear and loathing in corporate boardrooms must have been palpable. Indeed, the DesRosiers Automotive Conference registration-form warned its participating auto and oil company executives: "Poll after poll is revealing that Canadians now rate the environment as their number one concern – ahead of taxes, trade policy, unemployment, national unity or language. And when respondents begin to think pollution, very soon they begin to think 'cars' and their role in the environmental equation."

But Lou Harris had really stunned the business-as-usual crowd by revealing that 84 per cent of respondents said they "would opt for a lower standard of living" if that meant clean air, water, and oil and a healthy planet. The spectre of a wide majority of citizenry choosing a lower standard of living is not something that brings joy to the power-breakfast. Voluntary simplicity combined with stringent regulation of polluters is a life-style scenario whose possible wide-scale adoption triggers the gag-reflex in boardrooms across the continent.

By mid-June of 1989, former Shell Canada PR manager Stephen Duncan was warning readers of the *Financial Post* about the frightening trend. Referring to the benefit concert organized by Ian Tyson to stop the Oldman Dam project in Alberta, Duncan wrote:

> Environmental groups grow increasingly more sophisticated in elevating localized issues to the national agenda. And they do it with stunning efficiency: Tyson carried off his star-studded concert for a reported $3,000. He simply called in some Brownie points with his friends. In the polarization that is occurring, debates about job creation and growth are seemingly holding less appeal....

Citing the withdrawal of Uniroyal Chemical's Alar spray and the shutdown of Sacramento's Rancho Seco nuclear plant – both the result of mobilized public pressure in the United States during a single two-week period – Duncan warned "there is a lesson here" for politicians and corporations, a lesson made patently obvious by the polling data four months later.

In other words, behind the veil of the new corporate Ecobabble there is tremendous fear. For the first time in centuries, the majority of North Americans say they are willing to choose a lower standard of living to protect the planet – a radical shift in consciousness towards an Earth First economy. As the DesRosiers Automotive Conference pamphlet warned its participating CEOS: "Environmentalism is not just another form of social activism. It transcends ideologies and national boundaries – never before has a movement been so sharply focused and global in scope. And that focus is being fixed sharply on the automotive industry!"

Well, it's not just cars, guys; it's the whole system and mind-set of "Earth-hating, land-raping scum-bags" – Sea Shepherd's Paul Watson has a way with words, doesn't he? – who run the world. More politely, deep ecologist Thomas Berry, author of *The Dream of the Earth*, notes, "The inner dynamism is rapidly passing out of the industrial-commercial-consumer economy." As Liberation activist Victor Lewis writes in *Creation* magazine, "The threat of ecocide [ecological suicide] is a pressing political and spiritual reality that transcends the ideological debate between 'capitalisms' and 'communisms.' If there is a human future, it will be a Green one."

But such a threat to business-as-usual is precisely the terrain of the corporate marketing and PR professions. By February 1990, *Fortune* magazine was advising its readers that "the new environmentalism" would be "global, more co-operative than confrontational – and with business at the centre." The only threat to this movement-takeover was cited by a PR spokesman who warned the *Fortune* reporter about "grass-roots groups" – those bioregional activists who cause such trouble. "The grass-roots groups are concerned about the value of their homes and the health of their children," complained the PR man. "That means they are relentless. In general, unlike the mainstream environmental groups, they are not interested in compromise." Nevertheless, *Fortune* predicted confidently, "Far fewer activists of the 1990s will be embittered, scruffy, antibusiness street fighters."

But by spring of 1990, the DesRosiers Automotive Conference organizers were not so sure. Citing "the broad basis of the new paradigm" – there are now more than 1,800 environmental activist groups across Canada alone – their pamphlet warned: "Too many businessmen, including many in the automotive sector, still shrug it off as a fringe element of diehard flower children, dogmatically opposed to business and economic growth. They do so at their peril. In the 1990s, ecoresponsibility will be the key element in building a positive corporate image and the increased market share and profits that will follow."

I guess that means it's time for my handy-dandy guide to deconstructing the tactics of Ecobabble. Deconstructing Ecobabble is more fun when it's played with some "diehard flower children," but any member of the "broad basis of the new paradigm" will do. Watch for any and all of these nifty ways to show "ecoresponsibility" in the 1990s from those who want "positive corporate image."

Quick Guide to Ecobabble Tactics

1   *Use a new symbol.* Preferably green, like the green flower-sort-of-thing chosen by the Irradiated Food Industry. Or buy

the federal government's new EcoLogo symbol (a maple leaf formed by three cute doves) for a mere $1,500-$5,000 (there's a sliding scale based on corporate sales volume) to stick on your new eco-gizmo, or the same old goop, as the case may be.

2 *Change the name.* Hooker Chemical did this back when Love Canal was giving them such a pain in the eco-gizmo. They became Occidental Chemical Corporation and "positive corporate image" improved. More recently, the City Fathers in Niagara Falls decided to follow suit: changing the name of Love Canal to Sunrise City. Already a hundred families are signed up to move in. Similarly, the Canadian Agricultural Chemicals Association has changed its name to The Canadian Crop Protection Institute. Now doesn't that make you feel better?

3 *Change the word.* Watch your language. If you're a forester, don't refer to old-growth forests as "cellulose cemeteries," "forest slums," or "tree ghettoes" as you do with your cronies, but call them "over-mature." If you're marketing a disposable product, refer to it with the new ecoresponsible term, "single-use."

4 *Add a word.* Words like "organic," "spring water," "non-chemical" currently don't have any clear legal definition or regulation and can be applied to any old goop. "Safe" is nice, "environment-friendly" isn't as punchy as Proctor & Gamble's "EnviroPak." "Photobiodegradable plastic" is impressive.

5 *Sound vaguely "left."* Like the new slogan of techno-giant Komatsu: "Work For The World, Care For The Community." It sounds so much like "Think Globally, Act Locally" that who would ever guess Komatsu makes those big earth-movers and tree-rippers? And it uses that neat Ecobabble word, "care"!

6 *Use a pretty nature picture.* Like the old-growth forests in the B.C. Council of Forest Industries' "Forests Forever" ads, or the pretty mountain-with-car photo in GM's Earth Day ad: "General Motors Marks 20 Years of Environmental Progress." This is a good example of bioengineered Ecobabble: splicing together Pretty Picture with Vaguely Left and that very important word, "Environmental."

7 *Use a scary picture.* Like Lockheed's new two-page spread entitled "Gilgamesh and Global Warming" where this big hulk is swinging an axe at a tree. Lockheed cares, you see,

even though it is one of the world's leading weapons suppliers, and even though the space technology it provides to NASA gobbles up more oil and gas than a whole herd of oil-spill-eating microbes.

8 *Get an eco-slogan.* Like "Naturally Resourceful" Domtar, or Nissan's "Get One For The Great Outdoors," or the "Heir to the Air" Saab; or, like Pan Am Airlines, call yourself "One Of America's Great Resources." Of course, the best is "Fur – A Renewable Resource."

9 *Display the planet.* Like the two-page spread from the Chemical Manufacturers' Association, representing 170 leading chemical companies. "Handle With Responsible Care," it says over the planet, a nifty way of telling all about the Responsible Care initiative being taken by the CMA member corporations.

10 *Disguise your wastes.* Like Viceroy Resources of Vancouver. The company wants to start a 900-acre gold mine in the Mojave Desert (an area soon to be a national park). Since such designations no longer hinder resource development, Viceroy wants to go ahead, but also to be ecoresponsible. So the company plans to dye its cyanide-laced mine-tailings brown so they look like the desert sand. The possibilities for disguising other wastes are only limited by your imagination!

Meanwhile, *Forbes* magazine is advertising its report to CEOs called "Protecting Our Environment: The Business Solution," written by Lee M. Thomas, former administrator of the U.S. Environmental Protection Agency. As the ad for the forthcoming report claims, "Everyone Is Talking About 'Protecting' Our Environment, But Who's Doing Something About It? Businesses Are."

This kind of PR green bilge had its origin in Canadian Loblaw's president Dave Nichol, who managed to get endorsements for his new line of one hundred "Green products" from Pollution Probe before the resulting furor led to the resignation of Probe's executive director Colin Isaacs.

Nichol told *Toronto Star* reporter Lynda Hurst during the height of the summer 1989 controversy:

Environmental groups have always sat on the sidelines carping and complaining. And under that scenario, nothing ever happened. Colin has been the first to break down the old role models of us being the bad guys and them being the wihte knights. His genius was in realizing the enormous power of the consumer to cause change by voting at the checkout. But someone had to produce the products, didn't they?

Nichol's questionable assertion that "nothing ever happened" as a result of environmental groups' "carping and complaining" was an attempt to depict Loblaw's as the new white knight of environmental action. Beyond the question of whether or not Loblaw's Green disposable diapers are really "biodegradable" (they're not), or whether its Green lawn fertilizer is really "toxic" (it is), is the larger question of what real change means.

Says Dan McDermott of Greenpeace, "I see business taking advantage of the environmental concern that is prevalent in our society. What they are usually arguing is for a product innovation that is just slightly less dangerous than before." Mike Rosell, co-founder of Earth First!, says, "I think it's naive to think companies will change unless they're forced to. We hope to take away the tremendous power that corporations have in our lives right now, and people will fill the gap – with local economies, self-reliance, and sustainable technologies."

But the February 1990 edition of *Fortune*, taking note of Loblaw's $60 million Green Line marketing success, advises its readers that "many environmentalists are moving from confrontation to the best kind of collaboration." The plank for that collaboration was provided by the Brundtland Report, which arrived like a *deus ex machina* to rescue the power-structure in the midst of the threatening polls. Its rallying cry, "sustainable development," provides the basis for most current Ecobabble, and the report itself has sown confusion among some environmentalists. For example, the *Canadian Green Consumer Guide* gushes enthusiastically over the Brundtland Report and interprets it to mean: "It's okay to develop, all right to have aspirations, respectable to grow, if our development is 'sustainable.' " The Brundtland Report needs a closer look.

Established by the UN General Assembly in 1983, the World Commission on Environment and Development, chaired by Norway's prime minister Gro Harlem Brundtland, was asked to formulate "a global agenda for change" to deal with the increasing environmental crisis. That agenda was released in the Commission's 1987 report, *Our Common Future*. It is not coincidental that within a year of the report's release, the corporate and political leaders of virtually all overdeveloped countries had become born-again environmentalists. The Brundtland Report provides an "environmental" platform that threatens no one and nothing but the planet itself.

In 1980, Gro Brundtland was a member of the Brandt Commission on North-South Issues established by Robert McNamara as president of the World Bank. This commission's report, *North-South: A Programme for Survival*, was supposedly an in-depth analysis of the international economy, leading to calls for increased aid to the Third World. The Brandt Report and its mostly uncritical reception prompted British leftist economist Teresa Hayter to write "an alternative view to the Brandt Report" entitled *The Creation of World Poverty* (Pluto, 1981).

The Brandt Report, wrote Hayter, "like most of the orthodox literature on development, notably omits to explain why the [Third World] poverty exists in the first place. If it attempted such an explanation, it might come to the embarrassing conclusion that the poverty is created precisely by the economic system which its proposals are supposed to protect." Filling in much of the recent history of the industrialized world's plundering of Third World countries, Hayter charged that the authors of the Brandt Commission report were "primarily concerned with the preservation of the existing world economic order."

A similar charge can be made of the Brundtland Report, *Our Common Future* (Oxford, 1987). The report is committed to "more rapid economic growth in both industrial and developing countries ... the international economy must speed up world growth while respecting the environmental constraints." In other words, as the report asserts, "sustainable development is *not a fixed state of harmony*, but rather a process of change in which the exploitation of resources, the direction of investments, the orientation of technological development, and institutional change are made consistent with future as well as present needs."

The report's concept of "progress" is essentially unchanged from 1950s boosterism. "Our report, *Our Common Future*, is not a prediction of ever increasing environmental decay, poverty, and hardship in an ever more polluted world among ever decreasing resources. We see instead the possibility for a new era of economic growth, one that must be based on policies that sustain and expand the environmental resource base."

This "expansion" is to be accomplished through the Commission's unquestioning belief in the technological fix – not just biotechnology, which is endorsed throughout the report, but all technologies, which are said to be nothing less than "the key link between humans and nature." With regard to limits to growth, the report states: "The concept of sustainable development does imply limits – not absolute limits but limitations imposed by the present state of technology and social organization on environmental resources.... But technology and social organization can both be managed and improved to make way for a new era of economic growth."

So intent is the Commission on not offending the aspirations of technocrats that it tacitly endorses the concept of nuclear reactors in orbit, provided they are "limited in size and properly shielded" to withstand reentry into the Earth's atmosphere. With regard to the use of petrochemicals in agriculture, the report advises that "where environmental consequences of residues are not yet a problem," those countries "can and should increase yields by greater use of chemical fertilizers and pesticides."

Thus, the prevailing hope of the Brundtland Report is the expanded role of multinational corporations – who have caused most of the pollution in the first place. Our Common Future emphatically asserts that the multinationals need to "play a larger role in development" and "have a special responsibility to smooth the path of industrialization in the nations in which they cooperate." To do this, the Commission warns that in the relationship between large corporations and small countries, "conflicts and suspicions must be reduced." No wonder the Brundtland Report has been readily embraced by the corporate sector. Obviously, the report serves its public-relations purpose for the United Nations – which promoted the whole multinationals-based economy in the first place.

Stephanie Cairns, international co-ordinator for Friends of the Earth, refers to the report as "having our message air-brushed" and warns of the effect of its "mutant strain of fluffy environmentalism" based on "opportunism and superficial understanding." "If we succumb to using the vocabulary of 'opportunity' and 'challenge,' " she says, "we lose the capacity to convey the critical urgency of our message. Only by painting things as they are – desperate – will we arouse the massive awakening and changes needed to brake our fall towards annihilation."

According to the April 1990 issue of the scientific journal Discover, the rate at which species are now going extinct is 400 species per day, 150,000 per year! Moreover, the dovetailing of the numerous environmental stresses indicates a looming crisis much bigger than any one problem considered on its own – a situation that Cairns accurately calls "desperate." No doubt to Loblaw's Dave Nichol and the other "sustainable developers," this is just another example of the usual "carping and complaining."

The Brundtland Report is a peculiarly "Canadian" document. Virtually one-third (298 out of 904) of the worldwide submissions made to the UN Commission came from the Canadian private and governmental sectors. As well, Brundtland Commission member Maurice Strong (chairman of Strovest Holdings Inc. in Vancouver) and Ex-Officio member Jim MacNeill (UN Secretary General of the Environment) are both Canadians. Not surprisingly, those Brundtland buzzwords, "sustainable development," provided the basis for the Globe '90 bizfest in Vancouver, where both Maurice Strong and Gro Brundtland were key-note speakers.

As Julia Langer of Friends of the Earth stated during the week-long megaproject, "If Globe '90 is the answer, then I'm not sure what the question is."

Globe '90 – featuring five hundred speakers, six hundred industrial exhibitors, and four thousand delegates from sixty-two countries – was billed as "The Most Important Trade Fair & Conference Of The Decade." With *Business Week* a major partner in the $6 million event (along with the B.C. government and the feds), the unsurprising focus was "the development of long-term market-oriented solutions to today's environmental challenges." As *Globe and Mail* business columnist Terence Corcoran enthused during the event, Globe '90 could provide "meaningful economic solutions of the hard-nosed, make-a-buck variety."

"Sustainable development is a good enough idea that it's worth getting on with," asserted Rex Armstead, president of the trade fair component. "Let's cut out the talk, let's start doing something about it. The trade fair represents the tools and the technology that's available to do the job." With their eyes glued to the projected $100 billion per year environmental-cleanup industry, the co-sponsors of Globe '90 included twenty federal ministries, every provincial government, and more than fifty industry associations – including most of those wonderful folks who brought us free trade.

The quality of the rhetoric at Globe '90 can be characterized as vintage gag-me-with-a-spoon style, typified by Toronto mayor Art Eggleton, whose ten-year reign has turned the city into the concrete (suc)cesspool of the North. "There are many decades of environmental neglect to overcome," he told the delegates. "I, for one, would be much prouder to have Toronto known as a 'healthy city' than as a 'world-class city.'" Tell it to the Olympics '96 committee, Art.

But the not-so-hidden subtext of the event was the need to prevent stringent government regulation of polluters by parading a "green" veneer of corporate competence. Such a $6 million charade (partially paid for with our tax dollars) was hardly necessary, since Lucien Bouchard, at the time federal environment minister, was readily reassuring the Globe '90 audience, "The marketplace will decide what's best for the environment, rather than regulations."

Meanwhile, outside B.C. Place, some seventeen environmental and Native groups picketed the business love-in. Catherine Stewart of Greenpeace called it "a showcase for the CEOs of some of the worst polluting corporations to wrap themselves in a cloak of environmentalism and say, 'We care and we have it under control,' and that's a lie."

"I find the whole concept of this conference distressing," stated Friends of the Earth's Julia Langer. "We have a government that's doing nothing for the environment and which doesn't fund anybody else to do anything, and they're spending all this money on this conference." Georges Erasmus, Chief of the Assembly of First Nations, was equally succinct: "Polluters are behind this conference. They made millions polluting the world and now they're trying to tell the world the pollution can be cleaned up and they're the people to do the job" – and make another huge profit in the process.

Inside Globe '90, the bizfest was turning bitchfest as participants unleashed a defensive volley of hostility.

Adam Zimmerman, chair of Noranda Forest Inc.: "Recognition of the palpable change in the Canadian corporate culture is very slow in coming. I have seen very little public praise or even recognition of the many corporations that are part of industry organizations that have established their own industry environmental code, as has the Canadian Pulp and Paper Association.... I personally have been in the trenches so long that I'm getting sick of the antagonism and the frequent statements of doom and gloom. I'm really very fed up with the ridiculous claims of some of the environmentalists which invariably and always receive far more attention than they could possibly deserve. But only because they amount to a kind of verbal flashing."

Earle Harbison, president of Monsanto Corporation: "There's only one judge of the value of a product and that's the marketplace."

Ian Smyth, president of the Canadian Petroleum Association: "Those environmentalists who know us also know we're generally recognized to be a leader in Canadian industry in environmental protection. Those who don't, carry traditional intellectual baggage and hit us over the head with it.... Finger-pointing, theatrical posturing and stereotyping may be useful attention-getters, but they serve no good purpose. Nobody at the table has a monopoly either of virtue, of information, or of good ideas."

Alan Robinson, executive director of the Packaging Association of Canada: "There's not one consumer package on the market that uses more packaging than its predecessor."

Christopher Hampson, executive director of Imperial Chemical Industries: "Companies will make the difference. Only companies have the resources to do the research and development, while government must create the incentives. The big question is to find out what is the right mix of carrot-and-stick between government and industry."

Julian Carroll, spokesperson for the packaging industry: "Packaging is an indispensable component if we want to maintain our standard of living.... The achievements of the packaging industry have been ignored. Packaging is not wasting our resources but helping to save them. It saves energy in food production, storage and transportation. It saves money in food preservation."

George Miller, president of the Mining Association of Canada: "We need a co-operative land-use approach. Prospectors need a lot of space to look for new mineral deposits, and no part of Canada can be totally set aside as having no significant mineralization."

Alfred Prowis, chair of Noranda Corporation: "Noranda was among the first in Canada to create an environmental policy and state that it would strive for sustainable development – meaning that it will not consume renewable resources faster than it can replace them."

Terence Corcoran, business columnist for The Globe and Mail: "The environmental issue has been too long overburdened with reverential do-gooders and zealots.... It is certain that if the world had to depend only on businesses, scientists, equipment makers, inventors, and salespeople who want to make money, hopes for a cleaner globe would rise exponentially."

Lucien Bouchard, federal environment minister: "The marketplace will decide what's best for the environment, rather than regulations."

The defensiveness is a transparent cover for the corporate alarm being felt as the utter irrelevance of their "solutions" becomes obvious. Hoping to prevent stringent regulation by putting in place a whole new layer of technologies – including the new oil-spill-eating microbes engineered in biotech labs – that serve to prolong polluting practices and will very likely compound the ecological disaster, the powers-that-be have made it clear that they can respond only by doing more of the same old thing.

As Dave Foreman, co-founder of Earth First!, observes, "The technological fix often creates twice as many problems as it solves. We need fewer 'solutions' and more humility. Our environmental problems originate in the hubris of imagining ourselves as the central nervous system or the brain of nature."

Such an attitude shift would entail dismantling polluting practices rather than finding ways to "control" them, and ending the North American consumerist binge rather than "greening" it. Says Julia Langer, "Overconsumption got us into this mess. Switching brands is not going to solve it." Greenpeace's Andre Carothers agrees: "The real answer to the crisis of ecological degradation is not consuming appropriately, it is consuming *less* – a pitch you will not see coming out of Madison Avenue." Or Bay Street, for that matter.

But ironically it is also not a pitch issuing from some of the mainstream environmental groups. As a British wag has stated with reference to all the new green consumer guides, "When the going gets tough, the greens go shopping." For example, the current VISA ad sports a picture of Randy Hayes, executive director of the Rainforest Action Network. The ad copy reads: "Join Randy as a cardholder, and we'll contribute $2 to time-tested groups working for peace, human rights and a cleaner environment. Plus five cents more every time you use your card." Similarly, the *Canadian Green Consumer Guide* advocates using "affinity credit cards" provided by the Bank of Montreal and Canada Trust in order to direct a percentage of each purchasing transaction to certain environmental groups.

The ironies of this are not lost on the corporate sector, which is confidently poised to co-opt those born to shop. As Thomas d'Aquino of the Business Council on National Issues stated during Globe '90, there is "an incredible amount" of co-operation building between business and the environmental movement. "There is some coming together," he observed. "In Canada in particular, I think the worst of the split is behind us." Noting that many CEOS now consider themselves "chief environmental officers," d'Aquino claimed that "Businessmen can advance the environmental agenda by recognizing that the economy is an integral part of the environment."

But as David Suzuki astutely observed in his *Toronto Star* column during the week of Globe '90:

> Global economics make no ecological sense. The GNP [gross national product, a measure of a country's goods and services] has become an indicator of a nation's wealth and its annual change a measure of a country's economic success. Growth in GNP is perceived as essential if we are to "progress." The Exxon Valdez spill injected $2 billion into the U.S. economy by creating thousands of jobs resulting from the accident and cleanup. The spill actually increased the GNP and thus, in economic terms, registered as a net benefit.

It is such absurdities of the multinationals-based, growth-obsessed economy that our corporate "chief environmental officers" would like us to ignore. Similarly, they would like us to be lulled into a stupor by their "green" manoeuvring. The "Clean Air, Bright Future" pamphlet put out by the Motor Vehicle Manufacturers' Association of Canada tells us, "Any matter put into the air can pollute. It can come from natural sources like volcanoes, swamps, forests, livestock.... Because our auto industry is closely linked to the American industry by the 1965 AutoPact, it only makes sense that the [emissions] standards and the timetable for meeting them be the same in the two countries. It makes economic sense – so we can keep the cost to you, the consumer down – and it makes environmental sense – because we share the air."

"For gutsy environmental far-sightedness," enthuses *Fortune*, "few companies can top Applied Energy Services." The private, Virginia-based power-plant management firm is financing a tree-planting program for every coal-fired power plant on its drawing boards. "We pride ourselves on being part of the solution, not part of the problem," says CEO Roger Sant.

As Ecobabble proliferates faster than an oil-spill-eating microbe, it becomes obvious that our mainstream leaders (elected and otherwise) are into heavy denial – a sure sign of addiction which, unchecked, will clearly waste the planet in our lifetime. Playing the role of badgering partner hoping to reform the addicted spouse – the usual game played in a co-addictive relationship – will get us nowhere fast. Indeed, putting energy into "reforming the system" helps keep that system in place in an unending cycle of moves and countermoves, of which Ecobabble is the latest manifestation.

As every poll shows, the majority of the North American populace say they are ready and willing to shift their priorities from the consumerist binge to a healthy planet – by consciously and conscientiously choosing a lower standard of living. Making clear the real implications of such a choice – as well as the steps for unplugging, and unplugging from, the mainstream insanity of business-as-usual – are significant goals for the 1990s.

(1990)

☐ Culture and Agriculture: The Ultimate Simulacrum

> Once everything will have been cleansed, once an end will have been put to all viral processes and to all social and bacilliary contamination, then only the virus of sadness will remain, in this universe of deadly cleanliness and sophistication.
>
> – Jean Baudrillard[1]

WE LIVE AND DIE by metaphors, by the vicissitudes of our mother tongue. Each language both reflects and constrains highly arbitrary cultural bounds of thinkable thought. Recognizing the conceptual constrictions imposed by a given language is possible only by comparison to the range of another. In simply the linguistic sense, we need each other, need the Babel of tongues, need the diversity of languages to maintain a rich and fertile variety of world-views – especially so that we may recognize the limitations of our own.

For example, in his profound book, *The Primal Mind*, Native writer Jamake Highwater laments that "two English synonyms for Earth – 'soil' and 'dirt' – are also used to describe 'uncleanliness,' as in *soiled* and *dirty* and that "the word 'dirty' in English is also used to depict obscenities!"[2] Writing from a cultural mind-set that perceives the ground itself as sacred, Highwater alerts us to a problematic attitude reflected in our common language usage.

Similarly, radical U.S. farmer Wes Jackson, founder of the Land Institute in Kansas, has ironically noted with regard to farmers' standard practice of drenching the soil with chemicals: "You know, they just treat it like dirt. Treat the soil like dirt."[3] Clearly, a society in which soil and dirt are considered "unclean" and the lowest form of matter is bound to be in environmental trouble. "He treated me like dirt," we say, or else "He treated me like shit." Two of the ingredients traditionally most necessary to good agricultural praxis – dirt and manure – have become, in our society, the epitome of debasement.

The words "culture" and "agriculture" both stem from the same Latin root: *colere*, meaning "to care for." In the case of the word "agriculture," that caring is directed towards the *ager*, meaning "field," while the word "culture" leaves the caring open-ended, implying an attitude towards living. In past centuries (and indeed, past millennia) that caring necessarily extended to the manure so central for fertilizing pastures, with even human excrement considered part of the whole cycle of agricultural practice. As Carolyn Merchant documents in her book, *The Death of Nature*, in parts of Europe during the sixteenth century, an entire industry developed around what was called "night soil":

> An extensive manure trade was pioneered by the city of Groningen, an area with rich peat layers covering sand. Human excrement, or night soil, was offered by the city to farmers attempting to cultivate the underlying sandy soils. Ships exporting peat to Holland returned with additional night soil. Sheep and pigeon dung were also exported to the tobacco district around Amersfoort.[4]

Until the mid-twentieth century, manure was also central to North American agriculture, and indeed, a component part of farmers' self-sufficiency. In his book, *Altered Harvest*, Jack Doyle describes the cycle of sustainability typical of most farmers before World War II:

> Much of what [the farmer] needed for farming was taken from his own land: grain was saved for seed, animal manure was spread for fertilizer, and crops were used for livestock feed. Mixing these home-grown ingredients with his own hard work, the whimsical elements of nature, and a bit of intuition, the farmer hoped for a good harvest.[5]

But these aspects of traditional farming were at odds with the gathering tenets of twentieth-century modernity, fuelled by the leading industrialists' desired goals of increased efficiency and mass production through scientific management schemes, Taylorism, time-motion studies, and the perfection of the assembly line. Having achieved these goals at the factory plant during the 1920s, the corporate sector, led by the Rockefeller Foundation, addressed their new goal: "the rationalization of agriculture through science."[6]

The usual explanation for the mid-twentieth-century "revolution" in North American farming praxis has been the desire for increased crop yields, considered the sign of increased efficiency. But we might look for other explanations, including corporate erosion of farmers' self-sufficiency and independence through the growth of what is called "the non-farm sector" – a new realm of business to supply what farmers once provided and recycled for themselves: seeds, feed, and fertilizer. Indeed, the transformation of the family farm into the factory farm of agribusiness can be told through the fate of each one of these elements, but here I will focus primarily on that last element, fertilizer – less delicately called shit. A central (but usually unacknowledged) part of the farming "revolution" was to treat shit "like dirt" and, ultimately, dirt "like shit" – an attitude that has had far-ranging consequences for the entire planet.

It is generally agreed that the first major step in the "rationalization of agriculture through science" was the introduction by the non-farm sector of hybrid seeds (especially corn) in the 1930s to replace the many open-pollinating varieties that had evolved through centuries on this continent. In his book, *First The Seed*, Jack Kloppenburg writes:

> The genetic variability of open-pollinated corn varieties posed a serious problem for the agricultural engineer. Plants bore different numbers of ears at different places on the stalk. They ripened at different rates and most varieties were susceptible to lodging [falling over]. Mechanical pickers missed many lodged plants, had difficulty stripping variably situated ears, and tended to shatter overripe cobs. Genetic variability is the enemy of mechanization.[7]

These "imperfections" in the way of full mechanization could be eliminated through the use of hybrids developed by corporate science. "Hybrid varieties resistant to lodging that ripened uniformly and carried their ears at a specified level greatly facilitated the adoption of mechanical pickers. The breeders shaped the plant to the machine."[8]

The introduction of hybrids had several important repercussions beyond the increase in crop yields – which was the key selling point in hyping them to farmers in the 1930s. First, the widespread adoption of hybrids meant that farmers now had to buy their seed for each planting rather than use their own, since hybrid grains do not yield good replantable seed. This was a significant step in the erosion of farmers' independence and the growth of the non-farm sector to supply commercial hybrids. Seed had become a commodity.

Second, the reliance on hybrids greatly reduced the diversity of plant varieties propagated on the continent. For example, four generations ago North American farmers grew more than 320 varieties of corn. By 1989 only six corn varieties accounted for 71 per cent of all corn grown.[9] This loss of diversity is now being recognized as increasing the vulnerability of crops to pests and disease.

Third, hybrids tailored to mechanical pickers encouraged the reliance on mechanization to replace human labourers hired seasonly for hand-picking. This, in turn, created a greater dependence on fossil fuels (oil and gas) to run the machines "necessary" for the newly rationalized farm. Thus, we can understand the Rockefeller Foundation's interest in transforming agriculture to the benefit of oil companies like Exxon, its backer. And fourth, the standardization of each plant to better facilitate machine pickers, as well as the loss of diversity in germplasm through the reliance on a few hybrid varieties, were part of the assembly-line mind-set overtaking agricultural praxis.

Nevertheless, the economic Depression of the 1930s tended to retard these "advances" for the time being. Few farmers could afford to adopt the goal of full mechanization being pitched by the non-farm sector. Indeed, many farmers could no doubt see the wisdom in maintaining their own self-sufficiency through providing their own seed (much of it cross-pollinated by themselves to meet their own standards), their own intuition and expertise, and their own communal labour for the harvest. As usual in this century, it would take a war to turn the reluctant tide.

Part of the massive fallout of World War II was the extraordinary expansion of the petrochemicals industry, which developed a wide range of oil-based products for the war effort and also greatly expanded the production of ammonia and nitrogen necessary for explosives.[10] Since both ingredients were also the basis for chemical fertilizer – a ton of oil makes a ton of ammonia, which is then converted into two or three tons of nitrogen fertilizer – the petrochemicals industry recognized that this expanded production capacity might generate a potentially profitable postwar spin-off.

At least one year before the war ended, the leading industrialists of the United States had already decided among themselves (and with the endorsement of the military chiefs) that it would be necessary for the health of capitalism to maintain a "permanent war economy," rather than demobilize production levels at war's end.[11] This decision behind closed doors was decisive in every way for the postwar world, but especially for agricultural praxis.

Before 1945, the amount of agrichemicals applied to North American crops was negligible.[12] But the war effort had generated a greatly expanded petrochemicals industry looking for new markets in the postwar future. Unwilling to demobilize its wartime production of ammonia and nitrogen, the industry found ready allies even during the war for the continued production in postwar years:

> The 1942 annual meeting of the American Society of Agronomy was held in conjunction with a conference addressing the anticipated problem of surplus fertilizer production. Increasing farmers' use of commercial plant nutrients appeared to be a profitable solution. ASA president Richard Bradfield told the assembled plant scientists that: "There seems little question but that after the war there will be available for use as fertilizer at least twice as much nitrogen as we have ever used at a price much less than we have ever paid."[13]

The "anticipated problem" could have been solved, of course, by simply cutting back on production of nitrogen, but that would not have been a "profitable solution" for the petrochemicals industry.

Thus, the non-farm sector was faced with a new problem: how to increase farmers' use of agrichemicals, and especially something farmers had never needed before – artificial shit. Part of the solution was to be found in changing the attitudes of farmers themselves towards their own practice. The traditional view of farming as a felicitous mix of home-grown and recycled ingredients, intuition, and expertise based on a "feel" for the land and the changing weather, was obviously at odds with both modernity and the growth of the non-farm sector. What was needed was to see farming as *science*. Kloppenburg writes:

> The noted corn breeder G.W. Sprague has observed that "the objective in plant breeding is to develop, identify and propagate new genotypes which will produce economic yield increases under some *specified management system*." From the 1940s, the specified management system for which hybrid corn was being bred presupposed mechanization and the application of agrichemicals.[14]

Changing farming into a corporate science-led praxis which would follow a "specified management system" necessarily entailed a certain amount of propaganda directed at farmers themselves.

In Canada, the wartime NFB partly served this purpose through a variety of films made for the rural circuits. Films like *Bacon for Britain* (1943), *Do Unto Animals* (1939), *Farm Front* (1943), *Farm Improvement Series* (1944), *Farmers' Forum* (1942), *Hands for the Harvest* (1943), and *New Plans for the Land* (1943) all tended to stress the new scientific methods being developed by the non-farm sector to achieve greater and more efficient yields. But underneath this message was another: traditional, individual, and regional variations in farming practice were unacceptable, outdated, outmoded, and an impediment to central authority's co-ordination.[15]

Both messages echoed wartime NFB founder John Grierson's highly positive attitudes towards scientific management, rapid technological innovation, a rising technocracy, and the expanding multinational corporations – especially the oil and petrochemicals industry with which he maintained important links from the 1930s through the postwar period. Since the petrochemicals industry was (and remains) central to the developing non-farm corporate sector, it is not surprising to learn that Grierson's attitude towards the family farm was less than favourable.

Filmmaker Julian Roffman, who worked at the wartime NFB and who also accompanied Grierson to New York in the immediate postwar period to help with Grierson's new venture, World Today Inc. (initially funded by the Rockefeller Foundation), states:

World Today had contracts for distribution of three series of theatrical shorts with United Artists. I was one of the director-producers working for the company. The series were *World Eye, World Ways, Worldwise.* Grierson received some funding from the National Farmers' Union to make a film on the plight of the family farm, which I was to direct. But Grierson wanted me to have the film glorify the big corporation farms, which were actually driving farmers off their land. He admired the efficiency of the big technology, the big distribution system of corporate farming, and wanted me to romanticize all that. I changed the direction. He was not happy about that.[16]

Roffman's film, *Seed for Tomorrow,* became a docu-drama focusing on one small farm family that was going under in the face of the corporate takeover of agriculture. He recalls showing the completed film (which featured Lee Hays as a farm union organizer) to Grierson: "I don't remember his vituperative commentary, but I do remember that I threw the film at his feet and said, 'We're finished!' I knew damn well I wouldn't get another assignment from Grierson. And I was rebel enough to protest what was happening to farmers at the time."[17] *Seed for Tomorrow* was not picked up by any of the three series for United Artists. When World Today Inc. folded in the late 1940s, the film went to the National Farmers' Union, which found distribution for it through Brandon Films.

But ironically, even those big corporation farms so admired by Grierson found that they could not entirely adhere to the directives issuing from the non-farm sector – especially that new "need" being pushed by the petrochemicals industry at war's end: increased use of chemical fertilizer. The hybrid seeds in use at the time "were not suited to the higher nutrient levels made possible by the availability of cheap fertilizer. The plants responded to fertilizer application by developing weak stalks, and lodging again became a problem."[18]

The answer, of course, was to redesign the hybrids so that they would withstand massive doses of artificial fertilizer. Once this was accomplished, the petrochemicals industry could finally "justify" its decision to not demobilize wartime production levels of ammonia and nitrogen. A "need" had been created. As Kloppenburg notes, "Whereas there were but 7 firms producing ammonia (the basis of much nitrogen fertilizer) in 1940, there were 65 firms by 1966."[19]

This change in practice was, in turn, a boon to other aspects of the non-farm sector. Heavy chemical fertilizer applications resulted in an increase in crop insects, disease, and weeds, which thrived in the changed conditions. Thus there was a need for new pesticides, fungicides, and herbicides to control these factors as well. Virtually the only thing left to commodify in that former triad of farmers' self-sufficiency – seed, feed, and fertilizer – was animal feed. Here, too, the postwar non-farm sector found the answer: antibiotics and growth hormone additives to make commercial feed a saleable commodity. As Jack Doyle writes in *Altered Harvest*:

> The manufactured ingredients of agriculture have contributed dramatically to increasing American farm productivity.... Yet what is now called the productive power of the American farmer is not really his power at all, but rather those who supply him. The power of productivity has moved off the farm, and in a sense to the city – to the university and the corporation – to the centers of high science.[20]

The postwar transformation of farming into agribusiness meant that by 1981 North American farmers were spending more than $18 billion per year on purchased feed, $9 billion for chemical fertilizer, $3 billion for pesticides, $4 billion for seed, and $9 billion for farm machinery.[21] Since at least $31 billion of this annual $43 billion outlay was going for elements that farmers had once freely provided for themselves through their own traditional recycling practices, we can perceive the highly lucrative dimensions of this shift in productive power to the non-farm sector.

While this shift was part of a larger postwar economic shift towards globalized markets, it was also part of a new mind-set fascinated by the wonders of high science itself. The 1950s were steeped in a romance with synthetics in every aspect of daily life: a romance based on "unlimited" oil, disposable plastics, and other oil-based consumer products that matched the "desires" of a culture already addicted to fossil fuels through the automobile. The postwar petrochemicals "revolution" in agriculture was an intrinsic part of this larger societal addiction.

But such developments invite us to look deeper into the cultural mind-set. That ultimate simulacrum of our times – artificial shit – is surely the sign of a culture obsessed with what Baudrillard calls "deadly cleanliness." Indeed, behind that watchword of the twentieth century – efficiency – we find the increasing removal of all signs of life through supposedly "clean" petrochemical and technological substitutes. It is in this sense that Arthur Kroker's otherwise insightful text, *The Postmodern Scene*, errs in its subtitle referring to "excremental culture."[22] Instead, we have arrived at what might be called a postexcremental culture – one so removed from earth and body that even shit has its simulacrum.

I asked someone highly informed about agribusiness practices to explain what happens to the real shit generated in the massive feedlots of modern farms. "I'm not sure," he answered, "I guess they throw it away." "But there's no 'away' to throw anything," I responded. "Where do they put it?" He paused for what felt like a long time. "Your guess is as good as mine," he said.

Not surprisingly, the postwar "revolution" in North American agriculture coincided with the rapidly rising star of a man who would make simulacra the centrepiece of his world-view. In *The Disney Version*, Richard Schickel writes: "The career of Walt Disney is ... much conditioned by the hatred of dirt and of the land that needs cleansing and taming and ordering and even paving over before it can be said to be in genuinely useful working order."[23] Disneyland of the 1950s reflected not only Walt's obsession with cleanliness and order and his hatred of the land, it epitomized what William Irwin Thompson has called "that curious cultural mixture of Hollywood fantasies and Big Science" that has so typified this American Century.[24]

As Thompson notes, "The content of Disneyland was the turn-of-the-century small town, but the invisible structure was computerization."[25] This mix of the comforting, nostalgic artifact to encase the futuristic, robotic infrastructure was perhaps a recognition of the subtle ambiguity in 1950s society towards the rapid changes under-way, especially with regard to urbanization and the changing relationship to land and nature. What Disneyland provided were technological signs of "nature" without the dirt, "animals" without the shit – the very triumph of that Biblical injunction to subdue the earth and have dominion over all other species. Robotic simulacra, more perfect in every way and fully obedient to the computer program, reflect that obsession of both Disney and patriarchy itself: control. But such an obsession also has its price. As Umberto Eco notes, "Love of nature is a constant of the most industrialized nation in the world, like a remorse."[26]

The genius of Disneyland, however, was that it subtly transformed that remorse into something else. Eco writes:

> When there is a fake – hippopotamus, dinosaur, sea serpent – it is not so much because it wouldn't be possible to have the real equivalent but because the public is meant to admire the perfection of the fake and its obedience to the [computer] program. In this sense Disneyland not only produces illusion, but – in confessing it – stimulates the desire for it; a real crocodile can be found in the zoo, and as a rule it is dozing or hiding, but Disneyland tells us that faked nature corresponds much more to our daydream demands.[27]

If Disneyland was thus an early advertisement for biotechnology, with its goal of implanting biochips to monitor and control living species, it was also a spectacular advertisement for the end of nature. As Eco notes:

> When, in the space of twenty-four hours, you go (as I did deliberately) from the fake New Orleans of Disneyland to the real one, and from the wild river of Adventureland to a trip on the Mississippi, where the

captain of the paddle-wheel steamer says it is possible to see alligators
on the banks of the river, and then you don't see any, you risk feeling
homesick for Disneyland, where the wild animals don't have to be
coaxed. Disneyland tells us that technology can give us more reality
than nature can.[28]

More importantly, Disneyland and its later clone, Disney World,
which is 150 times bigger than its predecessor, tell us that technological simulacra are superior to their biological counterparts. In this
sense, the real Disney message is far more disturbing than its cultural
commentators have usually noted. Aside from the "happy participation in fantasies of progress,"[29] Disneyland and Disney World reflect
Walt Disney's greatest obsession – in Richard Shickel's words, "an
obsession with death."[30] That obsession is evident in every aspect of
the theme parks – indeed, it is their major theme – where the only living beings are the human guides and visitors who themselves "must
agree to behave like robots."[31] As signs of the times, Disneyland and
Disney World reveal a society more fascinated by what is "lifelike"
than by what is alive.

Over the past forty years, agribusiness has similarly followed this
cultural penchant for the lifelike: providing crops and foods that are
hyperreal in their appearances as "perfect" specimen, but which are
so steeped in the chemistry of high science that they are more
embalmed than alive. Indeed, in 1971 a non-farm-sector spokesman
for agribusiness explained the priorities: "As we solve *the more pressing needs*, such as giving our growers [seed] varieties which will be
healthy, mature evenly, machine pick, and merchandise properly, we
are going to go back to refine these varieties and incorporate in them
the colour, tenderness, flavour, and quality factors to which the consuming public is entitled."[32] Most of us have stopped waiting.

But the desired goal of "cleansing" the planet has still not been
reached, even though some twenty-four billion tons of topsoil
(treated like dirt) are lost every year.[33] So Shell Oil has now developed
the perfect seed for our times: a seed coated in more than seven layers
of herbicides, pesticides, fertilizers, growth stimulants, and other
pharmaceuticals that is intended to be drilled into bedrock to grow
without soil at all.[34]

Clearly, dirt and shit have become the "noise" in that managed
and purified information system called agribusiness. But as Erik
Davis reminds us, "In information theory, noise is not just random

static, but also signals that interrupt other signals. Noise is negative: entropy, degradation, disruption, violence, no information. Noise breaks down worlds, gouges out the smooth surface of simulation, disturbs the system."[35] It is in this sense that alternative farming practices, based on dirt and shit, actually are radical challenges to that "positive" (and positivist) agribusiness praxis, and they convey a very different "signal" about living matter, embodiment, and the dark, loamy underside of life. Otherwise, as the Disneyfication of culture and agriculture proceeds unabated, only Baudrillard's "virus of sadness" will remain, for a time, to remind us of what has been lost.

(1990)

NOTES

1. Jean Baudrillard, *The Ecstasy of Communication* (New York: Semiotext(e), 1988), p. 38.

2. Jamake Highwater, *The Primal Mind: Vision and Reality in Indian America* (New York: Meridian, 1981), p. 5.

3. Quoted in Evan Eisenberg, "Back To Eden," *The Atlantic* (November, 1989), p. 74.

4. Carolyn Merchant, *The Death of Nature: Women, Ecology and the Scientific Revolution* (New York: Harper & Row, 1980), p. 53.

5. Jack Doyle, *Altered Harvest: Agriculture, Genetics, and the Fate of the World's Food Supply* (New York: Penguin, 1985), p. 116.

6. Jack Ralph Kloppenburg Jr., *First The Seed: The Political Economy of Plant Biotechnology, 1492-2000* (New York: Cambridge University Press, 1988), p. 74.

7. *Ibid.*, p. 117.

8. *Ibid.*

9. John David Mann, Anna Bond, and David Yarrow, "Seeds Of Hope," *Solstice* (Sept/Oct, 1989), p. 11.

10. Kloppenburg, p. 118.

11. Joyce Nelson, *The Perfect Machine: TV in the Nuclear Age* (Toronto: Between The Lines, 1987), p. 36.

12. Kloppenburg, p. 118.

13. *Ibid.*

14. *Ibid.*, p. 117.

15. Joyce Nelson, *The Colonized Eye: Rethinking the Grierson Legend* (Toronto: Between The Lines, 1988), p. 135.

16. Letter to the author by Julian Roffman, March 7, 1989, and telephone interview by the author, January 15, 1990.

17. *Ibid.* Roffman adds that Grierson later offered him a chance to direct with the Group Three Unit in England.

18. Kloppenburg, p. 118.

19. *Ibid.*

20. Doyle, p. 117.

21. *Ibid.*

22. Arthur Kroker, *The Postmodern Scene: Notes On Excremental Culture* (Montreal: New World, 1986).

23. Richard Schickel, *The Disney Version: The Life, Time, Art and Commerce of Walt Disney* (New York: Simon & Shuster, 1985), p. 53.

24. William Irwin Thompson, "Gaia and the Politics of Life: A Program for the Nineties?" in William Irwin Thompson, ed., *GAIA: A Way of Knowing* (Great Barrington, Mass.: Lindisfarne Press, 1987), p. 176.

25. *Ibid.*, p. 175.

26. Umberto Eco, *Travels In Hyper Reality* (New York: Harcourt Brace Jovanovich, 1986), p. 52.

27. *Ibid.*, p. 44.

28. *Ibid.*

29. Thompson, p. 175.

30. Schickel, p. 145.

31. Eco, p. 48.

32. Quoted in Kloppenburg, p. 127.

33. Dick Russell, "The Critical Decade," *E: The Environmental Magazine* (Jan/Feb, 1990), p. 32.

34. Chris Scott, Speaker at the "Remembering Tomorrow" Conference, Toronto, November 11, 1989. Scott is an Ontario writer and organic farmer highly critical of contemporary agribusiness.

35. Erik Davis, "The Dark Mind of Gnosis," *Gnosis* (Winter, 1990), p. 40.

☐ The Saga of Space Dorks: Lost Boys in Orbit

ⁱ

IN NOVEMBER 1989 I attended a small Toronto conference organized by members of Science For Peace to bring together people from a wide variety of disciplines. The purpose was to discuss The Crisis We Are In during this last gasp of the fading millennium – a crisis encompassing ecological, social, spiritual, and political dimensions. The hope was that out of the alchemy of our combined insights, some sort of synergistic approach to solutions might arise.

During this weekend event, two eminent white male scientists rose to address the gathering as keynote speakers. Not coincidentally, each made reference to the Moon Landing of 1969. Until that moment, I had forgotten that in certain circles 1989 had been earmarked as the twentieth anniversary of the Apollo Mission (or The Boot On The Moon, as I call it), rather than any number of other events in that extraordinary year of 1969. *Chacun à son gout.*

In any case, the first scientist informed us that the moon rocks have turned out to be "no different from any other rocks" you might find in an alley in Moose Jaw, but, he said, the $28 billion spent on the project was "justified" because "for the first time human beings were able to look at the Earth and see it as a beautiful jewel shining in the firmament." The second scientist also waxed poetic about the Apollo Mission, calling it "a turning point in the history of humanity." "For the first time in human history," he exclaimed, "we were able to see that the Earth is whole, an intricate ecosystem, that is our beautiful home."

By this point, my blood pressure was rising fast, and I was having serious doubts about the alchemy that might arise in our gathering. I wanted to interrupt both eminent speakers and say, "Hey, guys, it's white suburbanites who were the last to know!" Ancient non-patriarchal and Native cultures have known for millennia that the Earth is a living and intricate ecosystem, and they have certainly considered it "our beautiful home." For such pagan heresy they were killed off in droves, especially in the centuries following the Cartesian revolution in science.

While I was trying to decide which was more galling – the unconscious racism expressed in the rhetoric about "the first time in human history," or the attempt to "justify" that $28 billion price tag for (in the words of the early 1970s rap song) putting "Whitey on the moon" – an Ontario organic farmer-writer named Chris Scott stood up and reminded the eminent scientists about a member of their fraternity, Giordano Bruno, who had been burned at the stake in 1600 for coming to the same ecological insights 350 years before The Boot On The Moon.

But of course the real payoff of the Apollo Mission was ideological and psychological – summarized by that other object brought back by the astronauts, which, unlike the moon rocks, has not been demystified by analysis and time. That object is the photograph of planet Earth that now graces the covers of "environmental" editions of many mainstream magazines, which has become the potent symbol used in every form of corporate / governmental ecobabble, and which is the numinous logo for the new Earth Flag ("Because Every Day Is Earth Day"), available in "full-size or child-size," screen-printed on blue polyester with brass grommets, and retailing for a mere $39 U.S.

The $28 billion photograph is also displayed on the editorial page of *Scientific American*'s 1990 Special Issue called "Exploring Space" – an edition sponsored entirely by Lockheed (one of the world's premier weapons suppliers), with fourteen pages of Lockheed ads. Under the Apollo photo of Earth, editor Jonathan Piel reiterates the rhetoric about "a vision unseen and unseeable before the space age" – don't these guys read anything but science? – and calls the photograph "a symbol of the millennial human achievement in exploring space. The human eye, drawn close to the planets and their many moons, has now seen the earth in new perspective. It is a perspective that also enables us to glimpse cosmic beginnings and ends." (It's those "cosmic ends" that have me worried, especially with Lockheed and all the other military-industrial Space Dorks running the world. These guys get billions of dollars of government handouts and unlimited planetary resources to fuel their ambitions.)

So, anyway, as a mandala for our time, that $28 billion photograph of the blue-green planet is getting a lot of mileage these days. Before we examine the meaning of this photograph, however, we must delve into the murky realm of psychology: specifically, the psychology of the space program and, even more specifically, the psychology of what the Jungians call the *puer aeternus* archetype, what men's group leader and U.S. poet Robert Bly calls "the flying boy," and what Peter Pan apologists might refer to as the psychology of the Lost Boys.

The Latin *puer aeternus* means "eternal boy," and, as an archetypal pattern of behaviour and attitude, the *puer* has been studied extensively. The literature ranges from the wonderfully readable work of Jungian analyst Marie Louise von Franz (*Puer Aeternus*), to the less accessible prose of Jungian James Hillman (editor of *The Puer Papers*), to the pop psychology of Dr. Dan Kiley (*The Peter Pan Syndrome* and *The Wendy Dilemma*), the more personal approach of John Lee (*The Flying Boy*), and the increasingly popular (and very important) work of men's group leader Robert Bly, who focuses on various aspects of this psychological pattern.

The *puer* (pronounced "pooh-air") archetype is a rich one and difficult to briefly summarize, but the above experts would very likely agree on this: a person who is possessed by, and thus living out, this archetype has profound difficulties being a grounded adult living in the mundane, daily reality of the world. The *puer* is the dreamer, the romantic, the restless wanderer, the high-flying dare-devil in every field (well, usually they don't go into accounting) who refuses to be "tied down" by conventional ways. Bly contrasts "the flying boy" with what he calls "the plodder" and says that most North American males fit into either of these two categories, but that currently most boys and men are "flying boys."

The positive and negative qualities of the *puer* are expressed in such literary classics as *The Little Prince* by Antoine de Saint-Exupéry (analyzed by von Franz) and *Peter Pan* by J.M. Barrie (which Kiley's work addresses). A more recent example of the *puer* can be found in the movie made from Isak Dinesen's book, *Out Of Africa*, where the Robert Redford character is a classic *puer*: actually a flyer-pilot and reluctant to commit himself to anything except the "never-never land" of his adventurous exploits.

Always appealing for his youthful exuberance, the *puer* is nevertheless likely to die young, usually by becoming ungrounded – whether from the "high" of drugs (like Jim Morrison, Jimi Hendrix,

John Belushi, etc.) or by actually flying and crashing (like Saint-Exupéry himself and the Redford character) or some other tragedy that replicates the fate of the son of Icarus: that mythic *puer* who ignored the advice of his father and flew too close to the sun, thereby melting his acquired wings and crashing down to his death. It is "coming down" that is the hard part for a *puer*.

These examples remind us that there is a female equivalent called the *puella aeterna*, an equally rich archetype (explored in Linda Schierse Leonard's *The Wounded Woman*), but here I'll focus on the *puer*, since not that many women become Space Dorks. We do, however, imitate the negative Icarus-pattern in the form of addictions whose high-flights and crash-landings can kill as surely as they killed those lovely *puellas*, Janis Joplin, Karen Carpenter, Marilyn Monroe, etc.

Perhaps the essence of the archetype is expressed in Saint-Exupéry's *Wind, Sand and Stars*, where, on the one hand, "He who would travel happily must travel light" and, on the other, "We all yearn to escape from prison." Thus, the *puer* is usually unburdened by the conventional baggage (in every sense) and can thereby reach heights of vision, insight, or ecstasy denied to "the plodders." Not surprisingly, good artists are usually working from the "eternal youth" side of themselves, which knows how to "travel light." But at the same time there is the danger of perceiving the mundane world, daily life, earthy groundedness, and even the body itself as a "prison" from which one yearns to escape.

The necessity for being grounded in the body as the balance for high-flying is precisely what troubles the typical *puer*. Reconciling the highs and lows, flight and ground, "the sacred and the profane," is the challenge in this archetypal pattern. As Robert Bly says (commenting on his own career as a "flying boy" poet), "Changing the diapers brought me down" to earth. For the *puer*, the impulse is to "stay up" all the time, like the Lost Boys led by Peter Pan who don't know how to take care of daily routine (like eating and sleeping) until "the Wendy" arrives to play surrogate mother.

Turn-of-the-century author J.M. Barrie thus provides a clue to the neurotic form of the archetype as it functions in a patriarchal culture: women are stereotypically supposed to supply the earthy grounding (like "the Wendy" does) for the high-flying *puer* who, as the bumper sticker says, "would rather be hang-gliding." Where Robert Bly's (and others') men's group work is so important is that it is helping men to ground themselves and each other, rather than to rely on women to try to do this for them – since it rarely works.

The perennial popularity of Peter Pan throughout this century (the stage play has just finished another successful run in Toronto) indicates the centrality of "the flying boy" in our cultural zeitgeist. But I would argue that the *puer* is caught in those false dichotomies that characterize Western patriarchy: mind vs. body, spirit vs. matter, sacred vs. profane – with the first term in each "opposition" scripted in our society to triumph over the other. Although the Jungians don't say this, I will: the extreme expression of the *puer* archetype is the Space Dork – the technophilic "flying boy" (completely at home in B.C. novelist William Gibson's cyberspace) whose dream is to soar off and colonize space.

As the predominant archetype of Western patriarchy, the neurotic *puer* advanced into Techno-think around the turn of this century – which began with both *Peter Pan* and the success of the Wright Brothers, went on to deify flyers like Billy Bishop, Charles Lindberg, Amelia Earhart, and will likely end with a permanent lunar base for even further Dorky exploits. On July 20, 1989, President Bush (an aging "plodder" who wishes he were a *puer*) voiced his support for such a project in his speech commemorating the twentieth anniversary of The Boot On The Moon. Soon afterwards, the Canadian feds expressed their Space Dork complicity by giving massive financial injections to the aerospace industry. By March 1990, *Scientific American* was providing details of the plans to mine the moon and set up observatories there, for which the April 24th Shuttle "Discovery" blast-off was the next necessary step.

But the ultimate living Space Dork is probably Marvin Minsky, founding father of artificial intelligence (AI) at the Massachusetts Institute of Technology. Minsky has influenced many Space Dorks, instilling the belief that not only is planet Earth passé, but also that the ultimate human goal is to "download" the human brain into a computerized robot that will "live" forever and make wonderful journeys into the farthest reaches of outer space. "I think it would be a great thing to do," says Minsky. "I think people will get fed up with bodies after a while."

Thus, the problem with Space Dork patriarchy is that it has completely "concretized" its high-flying *puer* impulse: pouring trillions of dollars into a space program that is a tragically literal-minded expression of the archetype by which it is possessed. By contrast, we need only consider the fate of the Earth during the same historical period: treated as a sewer, a toxic dump, mere "resources" for the great patriarchal goal of, in *Scientific American*'s words, "embarking on more ambitious and challenging manned missions, such as those to Mars." But as Robert Bly's work suggests, the really challenging mission for our Space Dorks would be to do something simple and mundane, something respectful of embodied daily life – like changing the diapers.

Which gets us back to that planetary mandala, that ubiquitous Earth-Flag logo, that $28 billion photograph said to signify "a turning point in the history of humanity." Taken from the astronautical perspective miles from Earth, it shows us where we're at as a culture: spaced-out, in orbit, ungrounded, virtually disembodied, lost, and flying like that *puer* Peter Pan, who has a horror of "growing up." Paradoxically, "growing up" can only be done by "growing down" – reconnecting to the planet, to the body, to the space-time of the divine human animal: respectful of limits and of those not-to-be-discounted but lesser flights of the embodied soul.

The photograph of planet Earth illustrates the choice we're all being asked to make in our time. We can continue to soar off into "never-never land" – which is where the Space Dorks of every First World country want to go, though they call it Mars or Venus – a goal that is wasting the planet daily, or we can return to Earth where we started and get to know it for the first time: a pretty blue-green planet (now much the worse for wear) trying to make it through the latest round of Space Dork millennium fever.

(1990)

☐ Top Guns: The Budget, the BCNI, and Bush's New World Order

> The measure of a country's commitment to defend itself, its values, and its way of life – and to participate in collective efforts to defend others while promoting international stability – is a very real measure of its status and maturity as a nation. If Canada is to achieve full maturity, it will inevitably have to assume a greater responsibility for national and collective security.
>
> – Business Council on National Issues task force, 1987

THE DEPARTMENT OF National Defence (DND) has been getting a lot of press these days, what with Vice-Admiral Charles Thomas's resignation in protest of navy funding, DND Minister Marcel Masse's 6 per cent cut ($900 million) to the overall 1991-92 military budget of $12.8-billion, bickering between the DND and External Affairs over the fate of those seven thousand Canadian troops in Europe, and newly released (but three years old) internal DND documents claiming the Canadian Forces are inadequate for responding to major domestic crises like "environmental disasters" or "a breakdown in public order."

The whole controversy has been useful for a variety of reasons, which include the resultant surfacing of some previously hidden players. For example, did we know before May 18, 1991 (the date of the $900 million cut) that Canada has two hundred primary defence contractors and that they are represented by a lobbying organization called the Canadian Defence Preparedness Association? The organization's general manager, Jim Bond, made front-page news with his claim that the cuts would have a "disastrous effect" on Canada's weapons manufacturers and would likely be "a knockout blow" to smaller companies so engaged.

As I write, associate defence minister Mary Collins is promising that Canada's new defence policy will be announced "soon." It's been four years since the last government white paper on defence was issued: former defence minister Perrin Beatty's 1987 long-range $200 billion shopping list for new CF-18 fighter jets, frigates, minesweepers, helicopters, tanks, and those ten nuclear-powered submarines later scuttled by massive popular opposition.

Since 1987 a few things have changed on the international scene that tend to pull the rug out from under military spending-as-usual. Now that the Cold War can no longer be used to "justify" the world's leaders pouring $2-million-per-minute into weaponry, the real reason is there for all to see. As John Ralston Saul wrote during the Gulf War, high-tech weapons are "the most important capital good produced in the West and the most important single sector in international trade."

Joe Clark's External Affairs report of March 1991, detailing the "insane" international arms bazaar, revealed that in 1990, Canada exported some $158.8 million in military goods to fifty-four nations, including sales of $10 million to Saudi Arabia, $11.9 million to South Korea and $4.4 million to Pakistan. Interestingly, Clark's report failed to include Canadian military sales to the United States, which may well be Canada's biggest military trading partner. Now that the United States has moved into the top position in arms sales, accounting for 40 per cent of the global market, Canada's military trading links with its neighbour may pose somewhat of a problem to the Mulroney and Clark call for "a program of action" on the whole arms-trade issue.

Thus the current controversy surrounding the future role of Canada's military and defence commitments is merely the tip of an iceberg that, beneath the surface, is actually about economic trade. This means that behind the Mulroney government's promised white paper on defence, we must assume the significant advisory role of the Business Council on National Issues, that "senior voice of business in Canada," which, since the late 1970s, has functioned effectively as a virtual shadow cabinet.

Judging by two BCNI policy papers delivered behind-closed-doors, the priorities of the organization have to do with a highly militarized future for Canada – a future that, according to the BCNI zeitgeist, would signal Canada's "maturity" and "status" as a nation. Perhaps not surprisingly, finance minister Michael Wilson's budget of February 26 paralleled BCNI advice on almost every particular; and then, as the new trade minister, Wilson introduced legislation that would ease the sale of Canadian-made armaments to foreign countries through an amendment to the Criminal Code.

In this sense, Wilson's remark to *The Globe and Mail* on March 2 is significant: "What we, as a government, have agreed to do is to set some disciplines that are not just disciplines that a minister of finance talks about once a year but are disciplines that we will work towards as principal parts of a long-term vision that we have on the economy." That "long-term vision" on the economy is, I would argue, one that posits the centrality of increased weapons production for Canada's economic future – and at the expense of both alternative economic initiatives and Canada's social policies in general. For this, we must thank the BCNI and its "social realism."

In its advisory paper entitled "Social Policy Reform and the National Agenda," delivered in Ottawa in December 1986, the BCNI recommended: "Although many of Canada's social programs have by and large worked quite well in the past, new demographic, economic and fiscal challenges suggest that the time has come to consider seriously how they might be made more effective.... Major reforms are required in several principal areas of social policy."

The key areas targeted by the BCNI for major reforms are: family benefits, unemployment insurance benefits, old-age pensions, health-care spending, and university funding. The BCNI advised that the federal government make budgetary cuts in every category, use greater selectivity for benefit recipients, and place constraints on transfer payments to the provinces in order to "heighten the provinces' concern to find more efficient methods to deliver health care." In terms of post-secondary education, such constraints on transfer payments would have the useful effect, according to the BCNI, of both raising tuition fees to a more realistic level and enhancing "the corporate-university interface."

In its call for cuts and major reforms to Canada's social policy and programs, the BCNI document argues that the Council is acting from a sense of "social realism" regarding the annual $55 billion spent by the feds in those areas. But six months later – in June 1987 – another policy draft indicated exactly what kind of realism the BCNI intends.

The next advisory paper, "National Security and International Responsibility: A Reassessment of Canadian Defence Policy," was drawn up by a BCNI task force on foreign policy and defence – whose members included the CEOs of such defence-related conglomerates as ITT Canada, Control Data Canada, Honeywell, the SNC Group, and CAE Industries. The task force's advisors were George Bell, president of the Canadian Institute of Strategic Studies, John Halstead, former Canadian ambassador to NATO, and C.R. Nixon, former deputy minister of the DND.

This 1987 task force recommended "significant, real and sustained increases in defence spending," with "annual increases of 4-6% to be maintained until the end of the 1990s." As well, it advised increased Canadian involvement in "the military dimensions of space activities," including the possible establishment of "a national military space program." But most crucial, the BCNI specifically advised that "future increases in defence spending *be financed by reallocating resources from existing government programs and activities* and not by adding to the federal deficit."

Obviously, this is exactly what Wilson's February 1991 budget was designed to do: cutting drastically into virtually every other area of federal spending while enhancing the budgets of three key beneficiaries, all of them in that category euphemistically known as domestic security. Widely considered to be the most austere and right-wing budget in the history of Canada, Wilson's "deficit-reducing package" exploded in the face of Canada's social programs, health-care policy, environmental goals, cultural aspirations, and potential for justice in a society where one out of every four people lives below the poverty level.

At the same time, the Department of National Defence gets a generous 6.9 per cent budgetary increase, raising its blood transfusion to $12.4 million for the new fiscal year, not including the special $600 million bonuses allocated to it to help pay for Canadian adventures in the Gulf. While Masse's $900 million cut rolls back most of this year's increase, we have yet to hear the fate of that other aspect of Wilsonian largesse to the DND: legislation that would grant it annual budgetary increases of 5 per cent over the next five years, while placing a capital spending freeze and a 3 per cent ceiling on almost every other federal department for the same period.

Wilson's budget also gives the Canadian Space Agency a whopping 166 per cent increase, raising its funding to $298.4 million, with the biggest part of that annual transfusion going to finance the Space Station Freedom project. Here, too, Wilson dutifully followed BCNI priorities recommended by its defence task force: that "Canada, in its own national interest, ensure that it is an effective participant in appropriate space programs and defence systems for continental aerospace defence." Within days of the announced budget, Spar Aerospace of Toronto, Canada's premier space company, received a $195 million contract from Ottawa, and its CEO, John MacNaughton, told reporters that his firm "may be in line for up to $700 million of remaining federal money slated for the space station."

As well, Wilson's budget granted a 12.6 per cent annual increase to the Canadian Security and Intelligence Service (CSIS), raising its financing to $213.9 million to cover another year of domestic surveillance. Apparently that, too, is a sign of a "mature" nation, though the BCNI did not mention CSIS in its policy document. There are some things this government doesn't have to be told. On the very day of this financial bonanza, Solicitor General Pierre Cadieux rejected virtually all 117 recommendations from an all-party Commons committee to make CSIS subject to greater controls.

There is a larger pattern in this federal spending that, as Wilson told us, does reveal a "long-term vision" on the economy. And here, things start to get somewhat Machiavellian, with intricacies that are necessarily entangled in the free-trade deal – another feature of our future brought to us by the BCNI.

In that same June 1987 policy draft on defence spending, the BCNI task force recommended: "In order to ensure a national capacity to produce or acquire the necessary equipment needed to sustain Canada's armed forces in time of war, Canada [must] move toward greater cooperation with the United States in the area of defence production. In this respect, the Business Council supports the development of a North America Defence Industrial Base." The desire for a North American defence industrial base – or, in layman's terms, industry geared towards manufacturing weapons – neatly coincides with the terms of the free-trade deal as hammered out by the BCNI itself in its able manoeuvrings behind-closed-doors.

One of the horrible ironies of the free-trade agreement is that Canada's ostensible objective for entering into it in the first place was to eliminate the ability of U.S. corporations to challenge Canadian government policies as "unfair subsidies" to trade. The agreement completely failed to achieve this objective, and as a result Canadian policies are being dismantled at every level – just as the BCNI advised in its call for social realism. But one area where free trade's effects tie directly into the BCNI's desire for a North American defence industrial base is in the area of regional development programs.

In the free-trade deal, Canadian regional development programs are considered unfair subsidies to trade and thus federal subsidies to the poorer regions of the country can and are being challenged. But the free-trade deal makes one exception: if any government subsidy for regional development is "sensitive to the defence of the country," it is permissible.

Thus, as thousands of jobs are lost in other manufacturing sectors thanks to free trade, building military weaponry is the one area in which our provincial and federal governments can subsidize and intervene as much as they want. What this means is that there will very likely be an increased focus on military industries in the economies of the poorer sections of Canada. By 1989, defence-related industries in Quebec were expanding, while textile companies were relocating in low-wage/low-tax havens in southern U.S. border states, Mexico, and the Third World. Obviously, this feature of free trade is a useful mechanism for developing that North American defence industrial base desired by the BCNI and a wonderful opportunity for moving towards "greater cooperation with the United States in the area of defence production."

Accordingly, the Mulroney government has established a little-known federal program called the Defence Industry Productivity Program, through which significant financial funding is given to Canadian aerospace and defence industries across the country. It is through this program that the European buyers of de Havilland (France's Aerospatiale and Italy's Alenia) are expecting and expected to receive $500 million in federal support as a "Canadian" company.

Similarly, Computing Devices Company – a high-tech firm based in Ottawa with subsidiaries in the West – has received a $2 billion contract to develop a new mobile field-radio system, and the Montreal engineering firm Lavalin – the company for which Marcel Masse served as vice-president before his 1984 election – appears to have the favoured bid for a $450 million contract to build twelve mine-sweepers.

With Canadian and branch-plant industries rapidly fleeing to offshore and other locations, it is likely that rising unemployment in Canada will be met by increased defence production co-ordinated with the needs of the United States. Thus trade minister Wilson's legislation to amend the Criminal Code on arms sales could be worth as much as $800 million to General Motors of Canada in its expected sale of armoured vehicles to Saudi Arabia. In this sense, the Tory "long-term vision" on the economy is directly interrelated with Bush's new world order.

George Bush's vision of a new world order suitably came to him, according to his aids, while he was playing golf last summer. With the end of the Cold War, the two superpowers could now act in concert to quell and control disturbances arising from smaller nations and tribal peoples around the globe. (Most of the more than 120 shooting wars taking place in 1990 before the Gulf War were resistance wars taking place in the southern hemisphere.) As a NATO spokesperson put it, "We had one Soviet bear to worry about before, now we have lots of smaller bears."

Virtually all of these conflicts have much the same pattern as the one that occurred at Oka in the summer of 1990: a state government uses military force against the tribal peoples contained within its boundaries to obtain land or access to natural resources. Shifting from an East-West Cold War to a highly concerted and militarized North-South resource grab is the real meaning of Bush's new world order – in service, of course, to the expanding multinationals, whose voracious appetite for resources is unending.

In this sense the Gulf War was a test case to see what, if anything, the Soviet or any other government would do. Because most governments have now been sucked into the globalized economy and its agenda for "progress," we know the answer. That agenda includes the now revitalized space industry which, during the Reagan and Mulroney years, was given massive budgetary transfusions, including the latest boost from Wilson's 1991 budget. As the BCNI sagely recommended: "If Canada is not involved in any of the military dimensions of space activities, there is a great danger that it will become increasingly irrelevant to its own defence and that its research and development and industrial sectors will not be able to participate in the wide range of high technology activities associated with space developments."

It is highly doubtful that those are the priorities of most Canadians, but the "long-term vision" of the BCNI, the Tory government, the free-trade deal, and Bush's new world order all point towards a highly militarized economy in which Canada provides both the natural resources and the "defence industrial base" for increased weapons production. Thanks to the BCNI's advice, the Canadian economy is rapidly being dismantled and reassembled along new lines suitable to Bush's new world order. As unemployment increases in the coming years, building weapons will seem to be the only game in town: weapons useful for the next mini-series wars planned for during adventures in the Gulf.

At the height of the war, as Canadian and U.S. defence contractors watched their stock-market values soar, a Wall Street analyst expressed a common worry at the time. Byron Callan, a stock analyst at Prudential-Bache Securities, told Associated Press that if Iraq were to be thoroughly defeated, "Saudi Arabia would lose its primary impetus for plans to double its armed forces. In addition, the long-term military threat to Israel might be reduced." Such an outcome would have been a disaster for business – which helps explain the momentary tiff between Stormin' Norman Schwartzkopf and George Bush over the president's refusal to let the general bomb Iraq to oblivion. No doubt, a quick briefing on economics helped Norman see the light.

After all, during the war, the White House had secretly approved a $1 billion sale of F-16 combat jets and anti-tank missiles to Egypt, as well as $1 billion in aid to Syria, which used the money to buy $1 billion worth of Scud-C ballistic missiles from North Korea. Thus, Bush's May 29 "major initiative" to halt the spiralling arms race in the Middle East seems somewhat after the fact. Similarly, Bush's claim that his plan would work to reduce the area's stockpiles of conventional arms "while supporting the legitimate need of every state to defend itself" is the same forked-tongue rhetoric used by Canada's External Affairs department. In defence of trade minister Wilson's arms-sale legislation, External Affairs spokesperson Catherine Nagy has argued that the sale of GM Canada's armoured vehicles to Saudi Arabia is "not an offensive military threat" and, after all, "countries have a right to self-defence."

More clearly, the North American economy is fully dependent on this sector of international trade. As Bush told the workers at a Patriot-missile factory, the war was "a triumph for American technology" in the face of economic threats from Japan and the new European Community. As the Gulf War illustrated, there are lots of new weapons to be built: everything from the A6E Intruder, the F-17A Stealth, the F-14 Tomcat, the F-15 Eagle, and the F-4G Wild Weasel to the E-3 AWACS Sentry, the AH-1W Sea Cobra, the CH-47 Chinook, the

Tomahawk Cruise Missile, the Patriot Missile, and, of course, more CF-18s. The allure of such high-tech efficiency seems not to have been lost on associate defence minister Mary Collins, who subtly signalled the likely orientation of Canada's next defence policy: "We'll be looking for efficiencies, so that we have more money to spend on equipment. There's no sense having airmen or sailors if they don't have equipment to use."

If at certain levels the Gulf War was a giant advertisement for high-tech military prowess with its leaner-and-meaner "surgical" strike-force capabilities and glamour, at other levels it was an effective smoke screen for the Top Guns whose long-term vision of the economy is a disaster to Canada and its peoples. There was thus a highly ironic dimension to the hoopla given to the Canadian troops returning from the Gulf. As our social programs, health-care policy, old-age pensions, unemployment benefits, regional development programs, and post-secondary education funding are redirected into a very different vision of Canada's future – a future directly tied to a militarized high-tech economy – that same 70 per cent of the Canadian population that supported the Gulf are about to be stuck with an economic restructuring that will make its collective head spin. But here too the BCNI was prescient in its 1987 policy draft: recommending that the Canadian government "encourage greater public understanding of security issues and support for Canada's defence program."

As we become fully integrated into that North American defence industrial base in the coming years, building weapons for the new world order, the only solace will be that, in BCNI terms, we will have finally achieved full maturity as a nation.

(1991)